Motivational Interviewing
for Effective Classroom Management

The Guilford Practical Intervention in the Schools Series

Kenneth W. Merrell, Founding Editor
T. Chris Riley-Tillman, Series Editor

www.guilford.com/practical

This series presents the most reader-friendly resources available in key areas of evidence-based practice in school settings. Practitioners will find trustworthy guides on effective behavioral, mental health, and academic interventions, and assessment and measurement approaches. Covering all aspects of planning, implementing, and evaluating high-quality services for students, books in the series are carefully crafted for everyday utility. Features include ready-to-use reproducibles, lay-flat binding to facilitate photocopying, appealing visual elements, and an oversized format. Recent titles have companion Web pages where purchasers can download and print the reproducible materials.

Recent Volumes

RTI Team Building: Effective Collaboration and Data-Based Decision Making
Kelly Broxterman and Angela J. Whalen

RTI Applications, Volume 2: Assessment, Analysis, and Decision Making
T. Chris Riley-Tillman, Matthew K. Burns, and Kimberly Gibbons

Daily Behavior Report Cards: An Evidence-Based System of Assessment and Intervention
Robert J. Volpe and Gregory A. Fabiano

Assessing Intelligence in Children and Adolescents: A Practical Guide
John H. Kranzler and Randy G. Floyd

The RTI Approach to Evaluating Learning Disabilities
Joseph F. Kovaleski, Amanda M. VanDerHeyden, and Edward S. Shapiro

Resilient Classrooms, Second Edition: Creating Healthy Environments for Learning
Beth Doll, Katherine Brehm, and Steven Zucker

The ABCs of Curriculum-Based Evaluation: A Practical Guide to Effective Decision Making
John L. Hosp, Michelle K. Hosp, Kenneth W. Howell, and Randy Allison

Curriculum-Based Assessment for Instructional Design:
Using Data to Individualize Instruction
Matthew K. Burns and David C. Parker

Dropout Prevention
C. Lee Goss and Kristina J. Andren

Stress Management for Teachers: A Proactive Guide
Keith C. Herman and Wendy M. Reinke

Interventions for Reading Problems, Second Edition:
Designing and Evaluating Effective Strategies
Edward J. Daly III, Sabina Neugebauer, Sandra Chafouleas, and Christopher H. Skinner

Classwide Positive Behavior Interventions and Supports:
A Guide to Proactive Classroom Management
Brandi Simonsen and Diane Myers

Motivational Interviewing for Effective Classroom Management

The Classroom Check-Up

WENDY M. REINKE
KEITH C. HERMAN
RANDY SPRICK

THE GUILFORD PRESS
New York   London

© 2011 The Guilford Press
A Division of Guilford Publications, Inc.
370 Seventh Avenue, Suite 1200, New York, NY 10001
www.guilford.com

Printed in the United States of America

This book is printed on acid-free paper.

Last digit is print number: 9   8   7   6   5   4   3   2

The authors have checked with sources believed to be reliable in their efforts to provide
information that is complete and generally in accord with the standards of practice that are
accepted at the time of publication. However, in view of the possibility of human error or changes
in behavioral, mental health, or medical sciences, neither the authors, nor the editor and publisher,
nor any other party who has been involved in the preparation or publication of this work warrants
that the information contained herein is in every respect accurate or complete, and they are not
responsible for any errors or omissions or the results obtained from the use of such information.
Readers are encouraged to confirm the information contained in this book with other sources.

Library of Congress Cataloging-in-Publication Data

Reinke, Wendy M.
    Motivational interviewing for effective classroom management : the classroom check-up / Wendy
M. Reinke, Keith C. Herman, Randy Sprick.
        p. cm. — (The Guilford practical intervention in the schools series)
    Includes bibliographical references and index.
    ISBN 978-1-60918-258-8 (pbk. : alk. paper)
    1. Classroom management.   I. Herman, Keith C.   II. Sprick, Randall S.   III. Title.
    LB3013.R43 2011
    371.102′4—dc22
                                                                                    2011014645

To Kennedy China Reinke Herman
and all the teachers who will influence your life

About the Authors

Wendy M. Reinke, PhD, is Assistant Professor in School Psychology at the University of Missouri and Co-Director of the Missouri Prevention Center. She developed the Classroom Check-Up, an assessment-based classwide teacher consultation model. Her research focuses on the prevention of disruptive behavior problems in children and on increasing school-based implementation of evidence-based practices. Dr. Reinke presents nationally, has published numerous peer-reviewed articles, and is coauthor of the book *Coaching Classroom Management: Strategies and Tools for Administrators and Coaches, Second Edition.*

Keith C. Herman, PhD, is Associate Professor in Counseling Psychology at the University of Missouri and Co-Director of the Missouri Prevention Center. He is a member of the Motivational Interviewing Network of Trainers (MINT), an international group of motivational interviewing (MI) experts. Dr. Herman presents nationally and has published over 50 peer-reviewed articles and chapters. Much of his work focuses on applying MI in working with teachers and families to promote effective environments for children.

Randy Sprick, PhD, is Director of Teaching Strategies, a company that provides inservice programs throughout the country. Each year he conducts workshops and classes for over 20,000 teachers and administrators. He has been a classroom teacher of students with emotional and behavioral problems and has worked as a teacher trainer and supervisor of teachers at both the elementary and secondary levels. In addition, Dr. Sprick has written numerous articles and developed audio and video inservice programs addressing topics such as classroom management, schoolwide discipline policies, playground discipline, and bus behavior. He is the author of several widely used books, including *CHAMPs: A Proactive and Positive Approach to Classroom Management, Second Edition.*

Acknowledgments

The ideas for this book were initially formulated during Wendy Reinke's graduate training at the University of Oregon. Her mentors at the time—including Tom Dishion, Teri Lewis-Palmer, Ken Merrell, George Sugai, and Randy Sprick—all profoundly influenced her thinking and contributed to the development of the Classroom Check-Up (CCU). Jim Knight and his Instructional Coaching Group deserve special recognition as well for early piloting and adaptation of the CCU for instructional coaches. We also would like to acknowledge the Center for Prevention and Early Intervention at Johns Hopkins School of Public Health for ongoing support in the development, adaptation, and evaluation of the CCU. We are grateful to Nick Ialongo, Director, and Catherine Bradshaw, Co-Director, for their ongoing support and encouragement. In addition, Jenn Pitchford has been an outstanding CCU coach from the Center, and she has provided helpful insights into the model. We are grateful to all the teachers who allowed us to pilot elements of the CCU over the years, and especially the teachers and students who have participated in the CCU studies. Thank you to the highly skilled consultants who shared their insights and wisdom. We would also like to thank Heather Klemp and Lindsay Borden for reading and editing sections of the book. Finally, we would like to acknowledge our parents and families, especially Wendy and Keith's daughter, Kennedy, who was supremely patient as her parents took turns working late into the night to finish this book.

Contents

CHAPTER 1

Introduction to
the Classroom Check-Up

Have you ever been frustrated by the unwillingness or inability of the person with whom you are consulting to implement an intervention? Have you ever tried to persuade a teacher to change his or her classroom behaviors? Have you ever found yourself working harder to solve problems as a consultant than the people with whom you are consulting?

These are all common experiences for classroom consultants. Although many, if not most, of the teachers in a given school are fully motivated to implement new practices, some are not. In fact, when we examine teacher motivation to change more closely, it parallels what we know about human motivation to change any behavior. That

> **For classroom consultants, frustrations about helping others change can be amplified by the fact that much is known about effective classroom management practices.**

is, interest in and willingness to adopt new behaviors fluctuate over time. Some days, or some times during a day, a teacher may be more or less receptive to consultation feedback and more or less likely to try new strategies.

For classroom consultants,[1] frustrations about helping others change can be amplified by the fact that much is known about effective classroom management practices. Consultants may find themselves thinking, "If only struggling teachers would listen to me, I have so many tools that could help them." If only there were a bridge to help consultants connect struggling teachers with effective practices. The Classroom Check-Up (CCU) was developed, in part, to serve as that bridge, as a framework and set of tools that could maximize a consultant's likelihood of helping teachers develop better classroom management practices.

---

[1] We do not distinguish between the terms *consultation* and *coaching*. Although we use the terms *consultant* and *consultation* throughout, this book is also meant for individuals who refer to themselves as *coaches*.

ORIGINS OF THE CCU

When the first author, Dr. Wendy Reinke, was a graduate student at the University of Oregon, she had the good fortune of taking coursework from several brilliant school behavior consultants, including Dr. Randy Sprick. Randy taught her all of the critical skills needed to be an effective teacher consultant. In many of her school practicum courses, though, she saw the real-world struggles of attempts to help support teachers in their adoption of new and better classroom management practices. As Dr. George Sugai, another mentor, once insightfully told her, "We know how to change student behavior. The hard part is getting adults to change." At the same time, Wendy was working in Dr. Tom Dishion's Child and Family Clinic, where he was training students to deliver the Family Check-Up (FCU), a brief motivational intervention for promoting change in families. It was apparent to Wendy that a similar model could be developed for working with teachers to help resolve the challenge that George had described and that she had experienced in classrooms. As fate would have it, her husband, Dr. Keith Herman, a counseling psychologist and the second author of this book, had expertise in motivational interviewing, the clinical method that guides the FCU. Wendy developed the CCU as part of her dissertation and refined it over the years, inspired by these amazing mentors and assisted by her husband.

WHAT IS THE CCU?

The CCU is a consultation model for working with teachers to increase their use of effective teaching practices with a focus on classroom management. The CCU works to change practices at the classroom level, rather than targeting changes in individual students. A key assumption is that improvements on the classroom level will produce benefits for individual students. Moreover, students who would benefit from additional supports can be more readily identified if effective classwide practices are in place. Although the CCU can help identify students who need additional supports, the interventions developed as a part of the CCU are focused on changing the classroom context. Therefore, the CCU is not intended as a model for developing individualized student support plans. See Crone and Horner (2003) for a model designed to help build individual student behavior plans.

> A key assumption is that improvements on the classroom level will produce benefits for individual students.

WHY DOES THE CCU TARGET EFFECTIVE CLASSROOM MANAGEMENT?

Classroom discipline problems are a major concern for teachers, school administrators, and parents (Rose & Gallop, 2002). Studies across elementary and secondary classrooms (Anderson, Evertson, & Brophy, 1979; Evertson, Anderson, Anderson, & Brophy, 1980) have indicated that this concern is legitimate. The increasing numbers of students with challenging behaviors entering school, and the inclusion of students receiving special education services in general education classrooms present new complexities for teachers working to provide instruction and manage classroom behaviors among diverse learners. Disruptive behavior in the classroom takes time away from instruction, hinders student academic and social growth, and contributes to student and teacher stress, making effective behavior management vital to student learning and emotional health.

Supporting teachers in their efforts to provide effective behavior management in classrooms is important yet often neglected. Recently, we conducted a survey of over 200 teachers, asking them what they found to be their greatest challenge. By far, the greatest challenge reported was difficulties in managing behavior in the classroom (Reinke, Stormont, Herman, Puri, & Goel, 2011). When asked about areas in which they felt they needed additional training, teachers in this study reported that the number one area for which they needed training and support was in managing challenging classroom behaviors. In fact, many teachers did not feel that the supports that they had received in this area were adequate. For instance, one teacher who completed the survey commented, "My [classroom management] training has been on-the-job trial and error."

The information gathered by our survey is not new. Research and surveys over the years have pointed to this same challenge for teachers. For instance, a nationwide survey of teachers conducted in 2006 across all grade levels also found that teachers feel a strong need for additional training and support in classroom behavior management (Coalition for Psychology in Schools and Education, 2006). Although these teaching challenges are well documented, the problems persist, and as a result, managing classroom behavior continues to be an ongoing issue faced by many teachers.

We have also known for some time that ineffective classroom behavior management is associated with negative outcomes for students and teachers alike. For instance, research has shown that students in classrooms in which behavior is

> **Classroom discipline problems are a major concern for teachers, school administrators, and parents.**

poorly managed receive less academic instruction (Weinstein, 2007) and are more likely to have negative long-term academic, behavioral, and social outcomes than students in well-managed classrooms. More specifically, students from classrooms with more disruptive behavior are (1) more likely to display challenging classroom behaviors in the future, (2) more likely to be identified for special education services, and (3) more prone to develop emotional problems, including depression and conduct disorder (Ialongo, Poduska, Werthamer, & Kellam, 2001; Kellam, Ling, Merisca, Brown, & Ialongo, 1998; National Research Council, 2002). However, many teachers simply are not adequately prepared to manage behavior problems in the classroom; some even enter the workforce without having taken a single course on behavior management (Barrett & Davis, 1995; Evertson & Weinstein, 2006; Houston & Williamson, 1992). Thus, it is not surprising that teachers identify classroom behavior management as one of their primary concerns (Maag, 2001; Reinke et al., 2011). In fact, nearly half of new teachers leaves the profession within 5 years, many citing student misbehavior as a primary reason (Ingersoll, 2002).

Although there are many books on the topic of classroom behavior management, most do not focus on supporting teachers in their implementation of these practices. Typically, the books are written for teachers in an effort to provide them with strategies to work out on their own. However, it can be difficult for teachers to transfer this information effectively into practice. This book offers a unique and innovative approach toward increasing the use of effective behavior management in the classroom by utilizing motivational interviewing, an empirically driven theory of behavior change, within a classroom-level consultation model. We believe that the integration of motivational interviewing (MI) with the CCU, a teacher consultation model operating at the classroom level (vs. individual student level), can create meaningful and lasting change for students and teachers.

WHAT IS THE PURPOSE OF THIS BOOK?

This book is designed to provide practice guidelines for working with teachers and other school personnel to improve classroom behavior management. The material in this book is helpful for school psychologists, special education and behavioral consultants, administrators, counselors, and other school professionals working to assist teachers in using effective classroom behavior management. The goal is to provide a useful model for consultation that leads to increased use of effective behavior management practices in classrooms.

Chapters 1 and 2 discuss the contexts and challenges faced by teachers as a result of the disruptive and difficult classroom behaviors exhibited by students. Additionally, the importance of utilizing effective classroom management strategies and the critical factors identified by research as associated with effective classroom management are described.

Chapters 3 and 4 provide an overview of MI and specific motivational strategies for working with teachers. MI is an innovative, well-established approach for enhancing readiness to change a variety of behaviors. We provide a summary of the MI model and then focus most of this section on applications with teachers. Some specific motivational enhancement strategies include giving personalized feedback to teachers on classroom behaviors; encouraging personal responsibility for decision making while offering direct advice, if solicited; developing a menu of options for interventions; and supporting teacher self-efficacy by identifying existing strengths and times when teachers have successfully changed classroom behaviors in the past. Additionally, the qualities and practices of effective consultation are discussed.

Chapters 5 and 6 introduce the CCU, a consultation model that utilizes these effective consultation practices and motivational strategies to increase the likelihood that effective behavior management strategies at the classroom level will be implemented and maintained. These chapters describe all aspects of the CCU process and provide clear direction for its application in teacher consultation.

Chapters 7 and 8 present specific classroom management interventions across varying grade levels that can be mapped directly onto the CCU consultation process and individually tailored to meet the needs of the specific classroom and teacher. This final portion of the book is devoted to presenting the mechanics of what are needed to provide effective consultation across different contexts and how the CCU framework can be used to increase other effective classroom practices.

We have structured the book so that the chapters align with the actual consultation process. The early chapters provide the necessary background information to prepare consultants to deliver the CCU. Prior to using the CCU, consultants need to be familiar with research on effective classroom management (Chapter 2) and consultation skills (Chapters 3 and 4). Chapters 5 through 7 then describe the stepwise procedures for completing the CCU assessment, feedback, and planning process. After completing the CCU, consultants need to be prepared to help teachers select and implement interventions to improve their classroom practices. Thus, Chapter 8 describes a wide range of interventions upon which consultants can draw in helping to support teachers in changing any practices that were identified as needing improvement during the CCU process.

As such, this book is intended to produce five primary outcomes:

1. Describe the research base in effective classroom management practices and the need for classwide consultation to support teachers toward utilizing these strategies.
2. Provide an effective consultation model for supporting teacher use of effective classroom management practices.
3. Define specific procedures for implementing the CCU consultation model.
4. Increase consultation skills in the areas of MI, providing objective feedback, and tailoring interventions to the specific needs of the classroom by utilizing data.

> **This book is designed to provide practice guidelines for working with teachers and other school personnel to improve classroom behavior management.**

5. Discuss how the CCU model can be used to facilitate a range of effective practices in the classroom.

FOR WHOM IS THIS BOOK WRITTEN?

This book aims to prepare educational personnel (school psychologists, counselors, special educators, behavior specialists, teachers, and others) who consult with individuals within schools to improve behavior management at the classroom level using an effective, useful, and innovative model of classwide behavior consultation. The book also has value for administrators and management teams that have the task of designing effective behavior support systems and resources.

Readers may ask, "I am a teacher looking to improve my use of effective classroom management, but on my own. Can I still benefit from reading this book?"

The answer is a resounding "Yes!" You will find that the material in this book can be helpful in assessing which areas of classroom management you may want to improve, and gaining the ideas to help you do so. You can learn to self-monitor how well you are implementing new classroom strategies and to determine if they are working. Additionally, the information on effective consultation, including the use of MI, is helpful for anyone working with others, including those working with families.

CHAPTER 2

Effective Classroom Behavior Management
What Is It and Why Is It Important?

Classrooms that are effectively managed are characterized by low levels of conflict and disruptive behavior, smooth transitions from one activity to another, respectful communication and problem solving, a strong interest in and focus on task, and a supportiveness and responsiveness to students' needs (Pianta, 2003). Effective classroom management is proactive; it is focused on preventing behavior problems rather than on solely responding to disruptive behavior. However, effective classroom management is not simply about gaining compliance from students. Rather, it is about working proactively with students to prevent disruptive behavior, intervening in misconduct when necessary, and providing engaging and meaningful academic activities throughout the day with the goal of maximizing student participation in these activities (Brophy, 1983). In other words, classrooms that are effectively managed allow students to flourish by providing stimulating and engaging academic activities in a safe, positive, and supportive environment. Sounds easy, right? The fact is, managing a classroom of 20 or more students who have varying levels of academic and social skills is a complex undertaking. Effective classroom management is multifaceted, requiring the use of organizational, instructional, and behavioral strategies. No wonder it is so demanding!

Given these challenges, it is important to focus attention on supporting teachers in the use of effective classroom management. Considerable research has demonstrated that effective classroom management can reduce disruptive behavior (Hawkins, Catalano, Kosterman, Abbott, & Hill, 1999; Kellam et al., 1998; Walker, Colvin, & Ramsey, 1995) and enhance social and academic achievement (Brophy, 1996; Coladarci, & Gage, 1984). Well-trained teachers can help children who are aggressive, disruptive, and uncooperative to develop the appropriate social behavior that is a prerequisite for their success in school (Walker et al., 1995). In classic research on effective classroom management, Brophy and Evertson (1976) found that effective management techniques were associated with increased student learning. More recently, using a cross-sectional and a longitudinal design, Kunter, Baumert, and Köller (2007) found that effective behavior management strategies also promoted student interest in learning.

In contrast, ineffective classroom behavior management practices interfere with instruction, child development, and academic achievement. Managing students' disruptive classroom behavior can be a consuming task that reduces the amount of time teachers spend on instruction (Reider, 2005; Weinstein, 2007). In poorly managed classrooms, children have no structure or support for consistent behavioral expectations and, as a result, they are off task more and engage in higher rates of disruptive behaviors (Jones & Jones, 2004). Negative teacher–student interactions are also more likely to occur in poorly managed classrooms (Conroy, Sutherland, Haydon, Stormont, & Hardon, 2009), and ineffective classroom environments contribute to children's risk of developing behavior problems (Webster-Stratton, Reid, & Hammond, 2004). In addition, poor classroom management has been linked to negative long-term academic, behavioral, and social outcomes for students (Kellam et al., 1998; National Research Council, 2002; Reinke & Herman, 2002).

Luckily, over the years research has identified a number of critical categories to address regarding effective classroom management (see Gable, Hester, Rock, & Hughs, 2009; Simonsen, Fairbanks, Briesch, Myers, & Sugai, 2008). When effective classroom management strategies are implemented well and with consistency, they prevent disruptive behavior and support academic achievement. The overarching intent of classroom management is to create safe and effective classrooms.

> **Classrooms that are effectively managed allow students to flourish by providing stimulating and engaging academic activities in a safe, positive, and supportive environment.**

When consulting with teachers to increase their use of effective classroom management, it is vital that you are aware of strategies that are supported by research. This chapter provides an overview of the critical categories to address to achieve effectively managed classroom environments, and it describes the empirical knowledge base that links each category to positive student outcomes. We have grouped these critical features of effective classroom management into the following categories: (1) classroom structure; (2) teacher–student relationships; (3) instructional management; (4) responding to appropriate behavior; and (5) responding to inappropriate behavior. The following section provides definitions and descriptions of the strategies associated with each category. Although we have compartmentalized these critical classroom management components into discrete categories, in reality effective classroom managers use a combination of all of the practices to achieve optimal results. Each category contains preventive strategies, strategies to increase appropriate behavior, or strategies to decrease inappropriate behavior. These three types of strategies can be a helpful way of thinking about the critical components of

> **Ineffective classroom behavior management practices interfere with instruction, child development, and academic achievement.**

effective classroom management because all classrooms need a dose of each to function at an optimal level.

CLASSROOM STRUCTURE

The term *classroom structure* refers to the amount of teacher-directed activity that occurs, the extent to which expectation and routines are explicitly defined and taught, and the actual physical layout of the classroom. In general, classrooms with higher levels of structure have been shown to promote appropriate academic and social behavior among students, including increased attention, friendlier peer interactions, and less aggression (Huston-Stein, Freidrich-Cofer, & Susman, 1977). Classrooms with a balance between adult-directed activities and student autonomy are likely to create optimal outcomes. Teachers are able to find this balance by carefully managing classroom routines, maintaining vigilant supervision, and systematically manipulating antecedents (i.e., events that occur immediately before a behavior) and consequences (i.e., events that occur directly following a behavior) (Good & Brophy, 2003) to achieve optimal behavior in students. Such classrooms promote student self-control of behavior, a skill that is demonstrated when student behavior is appropriate for learning regardless of the presence of an authority in the room (see Doll, Zucker, & Brehm, 2004).

Physical Layout

Crowded and cluttered classrooms can set the stage for problem behaviors (McGill, Teer, Rye, & Hughes, 2003). Therefore, reducing crowding in the classroom is a preventive strategy associated with effective classroom management. Although teachers rarely have control over the size of their classroom or the number of students in their class, they do have control over the physical layout of the classroom. Weinstein (1977) demonstrated that by altering the classroom layout (e.g., changing location of materials, use of shelving) students distributed themselves more evenly across locations and demonstrated an increase in appropriate and engaged behaviors.

> **Crowded and cluttered classrooms can set the stage for problem behaviors.**

The ideal classroom setup allows a fluid traffic pattern in which the students and teacher can move about the classroom without bumping into one another or other objects, and without distracting others at work (see Trussell, 2008). The physical arrangement of the classroom is set up to maximize teacher–student interactions while minimizing distractions. The teacher should be able to speak directly and with a reasonable amount of privacy to any student in order to praise or correct and to answer questions or provide instruction. If the teacher has to speak over or past several other students, the interactions are no longer personal and can have more of an element of theater. The physical arrangement of furniture should also allow the teacher to move easily throughout the classroom to provide active monitoring. Desks are arranged to optimize the most common types of instructional tasks.

Classroom materials and equipment are neatly organized to prevent clutter and facilitate easy access—items such as pencil sharpeners, wastebaskets, and other necessary materials are readily accessible without students having to squeeze into corners or move objects. Classrooms are free of objects that obscure students' view of instruction, and teachers can visually scan and actively monitor student work and behavior with ease. This rather simple design strategy can create safer, more efficient classrooms that lead to improved outcomes for students.

Classroom Expectations, Rules, and Behavioral Routines

Classroom environments in which expectations are unclear or unknown are prime settings for problem behavior. As you might expect, if students are unclear of the expectations, misconduct is more likely to occur. Furthermore, in a setting where the expectations for behavior are unclear or inconsistent, students can unwittingly exhibit misconduct, which is then met with a punitive response from adults. This in turn can lead to a cycle of negative interactions between the teacher and students, making further misbehavior more likely (Mayer, 1995; Reinke & Herman, 2002).

To promote a classroom environment with consistent and clear expectations, a first step is to develop and clearly convey classroom rules. These are explicit statements that define behavioral expectations and that help to establish a predictable teaching and learning environment (Grossman, 2004). Rules can be thought of as the foundation of effective classroom management. They encourage students to accept responsibility for their own behavior. However, classrooms are no longer filled with long lists of rules indicating each and every misbehavior that should not occur. Rather, there is general agreement that the number of rules should be kept to a minimum. Most classrooms can function well with three to five rules. Effective rules are (1) age-appropriate (in terms of both language and expectations); (2) specific and observable; (3) stated positively, indicating what students *should* be doing rather than what they *should not* be doing (e.g., "Keep hands, feet, and objects to yourself"; "Listen when others are talking"); (4) easy to understand; and (5) enforceable (Burden, 2006; Grossman, 2004; Scheuermann & Hall, 2008; Sprick, 2006). Once developed, the classroom rules should be posted in a location visible to all students and anyone entering the classroom. Classroom rules need to be taught explicitly to the students and revisited frequently over time. Teachers must consistently follow through by providing positive consequences for students who adhere to classroom rules and imposing appropriate consequences for students who violate them. When correcting rule violations, the teacher can point to the posted rules. This gestural component serves as an additional reminder that the teacher is following through on the preestablished procedures. Classroom rules that bring no consequences have little or no positive impact on student behavior (Madsen, Becker, & Thomas, 1968). Moreover, inconsistent enforcement of rules can lead to increased teacher–student conflict.

A study by Witt, VanDerHeyden, and Gilbertson (2004) highlights the importance of establishing clear classroom rules. They found that several factors influenced whether students complied with teacher requests in the classrooms. These factors included student training on the rules and the consequences of not following them, teacher monitoring, immediate and consistent teacher response to children who violate a rule, and frequent teacher acknowledgment of rule compliance. Furthermore, teachers with classrooms in which students were more successful and less disruptive were known to teach classroom rules and expectations to their students at the beginning of the school year (Emmer, Evertson, & Anderson, 1980; Evertson & Emmer, 1980). As a measure of how clear and how well students understand the classroom rules, students should be able to verbally explain what it looks like to be following the rules, what happens if they follow each rule, and what happens if they violate each rule in the classroom.

> **Classroom rules need to be explicitly taught to the students and revisited frequently over time.**

Rules versus Expectations

Until recently, the goal of classroom rules was more likely to elicit student compliance than to build students' behavioral skills. However, with the shift to fewer, more specific, and positively stated rules, this has changed. Today, teachers are encouraged to emphasize classroom *expectations* and to use rules only as supporting guidelines in teaching students how to best meet these expectations (Gable et al., 2009). Expectations are globally stated standards of conduct, comprised of positive characteristics that lead to success across many settings (e.g., "Be respectful," "Be safe," "Be responsible"). Expectations are helpful in defining appropriate classroom behavior while building cohesion among students (Henley, 2006). Classroom rules support students' efforts to meet the classroom expectations by specifically defining what they can do to meet an expectation. For instance, being respectful (expectation) is demonstrated by listening to, and your eyes on, the speaker (classroom rule). In this way, the classroom rules teach students skills that will lead to success in the classroom, and likely in other settings as well. To use an example from the adult world of driving, rules would be equivalent to stop signs and speed limits, whereas expectations would be equivalent to "Drive safely, drive courteously, and drive defensively."

Establishing Consistent Behavioral Routines

Whereas rules and expectations provide the foundation for effective classroom management, well-defined classroom routines and procedures are the infrastructure. Routines simplify situations by making transitions predictable. Well-defined routines and procedures support students in mastering the steps it takes to complete a task, minimize confusion, and decrease disorganization (Peterson, 1992). Not only are predictable and well-structured classrooms more efficient, but they also reduce stress for both students and teachers (Conners, 1983). Effective classrooms have well-established routines that align with the rules and expectations. The routines are explicitly taught and reinforced in the same manner as the classroom rules. Some of the most common classroom routines include procedures for transitioning from one activity to another, student use of the restroom, entering and leaving the classroom, handing in assignments, passing out materials, and sharpening pencils, among others. Taken together, classroom rules, expectations, and behavioral routines allow teachers to operate a predictable environment that aids in the prevention of disruptions caused by student confusion or misunderstanding. To extend the driving metaphor, routines and procedures are like the routines involved in driving to work: collecting your keys from your storage dish (if you have such a routine); the steps you take to start your car, fasten your seatbelt, and put the car into gear; and the specific route you take to work.

> **Effective classrooms have well-established routines that align with the rules and expectations.**

Precorrections

Another research-based classroom practice that leads to positive outcomes for students is the use of precorrective statements. A precorrection is a statement that provides a specific description of the behavioral expectation for the upcoming task—often a new activity or transition—in which the teacher has noticed that students often struggle to complete without some problem behavior (Colvin, Sugai, & Patching, 1993; De Pry & Sugai, 2002). Precorrection strategies are typically more effective in classrooms in which the rules, expectations, and behavioral routines have been taught and reinforced. Precorrections are preventive, rather than punitive, because they occur before students display problem behaviors. They describe and teach the students how to effectively master their next task. For instance, if the teacher finds that students often have difficulty in leaving the classroom to go to another class, despite having taught, modeled, and reinforced the appropriate way to exit the classroom, the teacher can anticipate the challenge and prevent it by providing a precorrective statement (e.g., "Students, when the bell rings, please gather your materials and wait quietly at your seats until I dismiss you"). To use an individual example, if a teacher knows that a student will be upset when seeing a marked-up assignment returned that has portions that need to be redone, before giving the student the marked-up assignment, the teacher might say: "Armondo, I am about to give you your assignment, and there are portions that need to be redone. Redoing this will not take that much work, and I know that you will be able to handle this responsibly. In addition, I want to help you with the portions that need to be fixed, okay?" Research indicates that when adults increase their use of precorrective prompts for appropriate behavior, especially when used in combination with active supervision and praise, problematic classroom behavior decreases (Colvin et al., 1993; Stormont, Covington, & Lewis, 2006). Using simple strategies such as precorrections can improve classroom climate by reducing the need for reprimands and increasing time for academic instruction and learning opportunities.

Active Supervision

Active supervision, another feature of effective classroom structure, has been shown to positively impact student behavior. For instance, De Pry and Sugai (2002) found that the introduction of active supervision produced a classroom-wide decrease in minor behavioral incidents. Another study found that active supervision increased students' participation in classroom activities (Schuldheisz & van der Mars, 2001). The teacher who frequently scans and constantly moves about the classroom, providing positive feedback for on task student behavior, is aware of who is on-task, who needs assistance, and can provide prompts that divert challenging or disruptive behavior before they become unmanageable. Thus, active supervision is another preventive strategy. The active presence of the teacher also serves as a continual reminder for students to follow the rules, in the same way that we are more likely to adhere to speed limits and other rules if there is a police officer visible where we are driving.

EFFECTIVE TEACHER–STUDENT RELATIONSHIPS

Classrooms in which students feel supported, respected, and valued are characterized by effective teacher–student relationships. These relationships are most effective when they are warm, engaged, and responsive, and when teachers clearly communicate high demands and high expectations and provide the class with structure and clear limits (Pianta, 1999). Building relationships with students is foundational to effective classroom management because students who feel respected and who respect their teacher will place greater value on feedback (positive or negative) provided by the teacher and are more likely to comply when asked to do something. Students who do not value the relationship with a teacher will not find praise or positive feedback reinforcing and will be less likely to comply with directives, even resorting to acting out/misbehavior in the classroom setting. Thus, building relationships with students is vital to the success of all other strategies to actually take root in the classroom setting. To use a metaphor, teacher–student relationships are the water and nutrients that keep classroom management strategies healthy and viable.

Effective teacher–student relationships are associated with increased academic engagement and student satisfaction with school (Chaskin & Rauner, 1995). Poor relationships engender school disengagement; students who drop out of school consistently report that their main reason was because no one really cared about them (Phelan, Yu, & Davidson, 1994; Stevenson & Ellsworth, 1993). Some ways in which teachers can work to support effective relationships with their students is by utilizing the strategies outlined in this chapter for creating effective classrooms, including (1) creating a classroom structure that is consistent, with clear expectations and ongoing reinforcement for appropriate behavior; (2) having more positive than negative interactions with students; (3) providing engaging and meaningful instruction; and (4) providing respectful corrections and constructive feedback. Other areas on which teachers can focus their attention when building effective relationships with students include taking a conscious interest in each student, providing noncontingent interactions, and holding appropriately high expectations that they share with their students.

Noncontingent Interactions

A *noncontingent interaction* is one in which a teacher spends positive time with students without making that time dependent on students' behavior. Examples of noncontingent interactions include asking a student about his or her weekend, greeting students as they enter the door with "Hello, welcome to class," and telling a student in the hallway as you pass, "It's great to see you today." In other words, the interaction is simply a way for a teacher to show an interest in the student and demonstrate that he or she is important and valued. In fact, a recent study evaluating the impact of greeting middle school students at the door as they entered the classroom found that this simple intervention increased student on-task behavior significantly (Allday & Pakurar, 2007). Noncontingent interactions are a vital component of the teacher's effort to build a positive relationship with each student.

INSTRUCTIONAL MANAGEMENT

There is a direct link between how instruction is delivered in a classroom and the behavior of students. By definition, students who are engaged in instruction (e.g., listening to the teacher, writing, answering a question) are not displaying disruptive or off-task behaviors (e.g., getting out of seat, talking when inappropriate). When students are engaged in academic instruction, they demonstrate higher levels of achievement (Greenwood, Terry, Marquis, & Walker, 1994). Therefore, finding ways to improve engagement in instruction can prevent problem behaviors in the classroom and increase academic achievement. Research indicates that providing instruction that is rigorous, relevant, and delivered at a pace appropriate to the content is likely to keep students engaged in learning and decrease disruptive behavior. Furthermore, developmentally appropriate academic opportunities (i.e., those that are not too easy or too difficult) provide students with mastery experiences that can increase their academic efficacy (Bandura, 1977; Doll et al., 2004).

> **Providing instruction that is rigorous, relevant, and delivered at a pace appropriate to the content is likely to keep students engaged in learning and decrease disruptive behavior.**

Opportunities to Respond

One way to increase engagement is by providing students with opportunities to respond to academic questions at a pace that maximizes learning and engagement. An *opportunity to respond* (OTR) is a teacher behavior that solicits a student response. Examples include asking a question (e.g., "What is the capital of Missouri?") or providing a prompt or directive (e.g., "Write down the capital of Missouri on your white board."). The use of brisk pacing during teacher-led instruction has been shown to decrease problem behavior and increase academic achievement. For instance, increasing the rate at which students were asked to academically respond resulted in improved academic performance in reading (Carnine, 1976; Skinner, Smith, & McLean, 1994) and math (Skinner, Belfiore, Mace, Williams-Wilson, & Johns, 1997). Additionally, positive effects have been noted for academic engagement and decreased disruptive behavior (Carnine, 1976; Sutherland, Alder, & Gunter, 2003). Several strategies increase the rate of OTRs, including direct instruction strategies such as choral responding (i.e., students answering in unison), response cards (i.e., students write their answers on erasable boards and then hold them up), and presenting questions that require every student to participate, such as "Everyone stand up if you think states rights was a major contributor to the Civil War; stay seated if you think it was only a minor factor. Be prepared to explain your answer." In addition, well-designed computer-assisted instruction can create frequent OTRs. See Simonsen et al. (2008) for a review of the strategies mentioned here.

RESPONDING TO APPROPRIATE CLASSROOM BEHAVIORS

Effective classrooms provide ample amounts of reinforcement to students exhibiting expected behaviors. The rule holds that if you want to see a behavior occur more often, you should give it attention. A host of research points to simple strategies that have been shown to increase appropriate academic and social behavior in students. For instance, the use of contingent behavior-specific praise has been shown to reduce disruptive behavior (Reinke, Lewis-Palmer, & Merrell, 2008), increase correct academic responses (Sutherland & Wehby, 2001), and increase academic performance (Good, Eller, Spangler, & Stone, 1981). Furthermore, teachers can use a continuum of strategies that focuses on identifying and recognizing appropriate behavior, including simple strategies such as contingent behavior-specific praise, and more complex strategies such as classwide group contingencies (Simonsen et al., 2008). The following sections provide a brief summary of evidence-based strategies for increasing appropriate behavior.

Contingent Behavior-Specific Praise

Teachers who deliver a high amount of praise typically experience lower off-task or disruptive behaviors from their students (Espin & Yell, 1994). Praise has been shown to increase appropriate behavior in disruptive students (Reinke, Lewis-Palmer, & Martin, 2007) and academic engagement of students in general (Hall, Lund, & Jackson, 1968). Decreasing disruptive behaviors and increasing academic engagement allow more time for instruction. Additionally, praise has been shown to increase the intrinsic motivation and sense of competence of students (Brophy, 1983; Cameron & Pierce, 1994).

Teacher praise is most effective when it is behavior-specific (Brophy, 1983). Behavior-specific praise explicitly identifies the behavior for which a student is being praised (e.g., "Kennedy, thank you for putting away your crayons"). Sutherland, Wehby, and Copeland (2000) found that when behavior-specific praise was increased in a classroom setting, on-task behavior increased from 49 to 86%. Using contingent behavior-specific praise in conjunction with other effective classroom management strategies can bolster the impact further. For instance, using praise in connection with established classroom rules increases classroom-appropriate behavior (Becker, Madsen, Arnold, & Thomas, 1967). Also, providing students with contingent praise and OTRs has been identified as an effective teaching practice. If teachers provide more OTRs, they have more opportunities to praise correct academic responses (Sutherland, Wehby, & Yoder, 2002).

Interestingly, in some cases, teacher classroom praise can become counterproductive if a student does not wish to please the teacher (Feldman, 2003)—a scenario that directly connects back to the quality of teacher–student relationships. If the teacher does not

> **Teacher praise is most effective when it is behavior-specific.**

have a supportive relationship with a student, praise will not be reinforcing. With secondary students, it is important that the specific praise not embarrass them in front of peers. This embarrassment factor can be reduced by delivering the praise in a slightly business-like fashion and as privately as possible. In addition, secondary teachers need to make sure that they provide lots of praise to many different students so that no student risks being teased as a "suck-up" or "teacher's pet." Providing frequent behavior-specific praise is also a vital ingredient in building positive relationships with students.

Group Contingencies and Token Economies

The use of group contingencies in the classroom involves setting a common expectation for a group of students and then providing a common positive outcome when the students engage in the expected behavior. In token economies students earn tokens (e.g., points, stickers, chips) when they produce the expected behavior; the tokens can then be redeemed for a reinforcing experience of some kind (e.g., desired item, preferred activity). Group contingencies and token economies are both supported by research and are often used in combination. For instance, a teacher may inform the class that he or she will allot points (tokens) to the class as a whole for students who are working quietly at their desks during reading. If the class is able to earn 15 points, all students will earn 5 minutes of extra recess (i.e., the reinforcer). When used in classroom settings, both strategies have been shown to increase student attention (Jones & Kazdin, 1975), decrease talk-outs and out-of-seat behavior (Barrish, Saunders, & Wolf, 1969), decrease transition time (Yarborough, Skinner, Lee, & Lemmons, 2004), and increase student achievement (Nevin, Johnson, & Johnson, 1982). Further, when group contingencies and token economies are combined with other effective classroom strategies, classroom behavior can be further improved.

Behavioral Contracts

Behavioral contracts are written documents that specify the relationship between student behavior and the associated consequence; the contract defines the expected behavior and the outcome associated with engaging, or not engaging, in it. Use of behavioral contracts has been shown to increase student productivity and assignment completion (Kelley & Stokes,

1984; White-Blackburn, Semb, & Semb, 1977), improve grades (Williams & Anandam, 1973) as well as student self-control (Drabman, Spitalnik, & O'Leary, 1973).

Effective classroom management requires that teachers utilize a continuum of strategies to reinforce appropriate classroom behavior. When used in combination with other strategies, behavior contracts increase the likelihood of positive outcomes. Further, the use of reinforcement to acknowledge appropriate student behavior makes students feel valued and respected, builds meaningful relationships, and creates an effective learning environment.

RESPONDING TO INAPPROPRIATE BEHAVIOR

Similar to responding to appropriate behavior, effective classroom managers use a continuum of strategies for responding to inappropriate behavior. As noted earlier, effective classroom managers consistently respond to rule violations and misconduct. Inconsistently applying consequences to inappropriate behavior can lead to student confusion and increase teacher–student conflict. The purpose of responding to inappropriate behavior is to decrease the unwanted behavior while providing an opportunity for the student to learn the expected behavior. If a student does not know why he or she is receiving a consequence or what the appropriate behavior is, then the consequence will not be effective. Effective classrooms have high levels of structure and ample reinforcement for appropriate behavior, allowing for the use of consequences in response to inappropriate behavior to remain at a minimum. The following sections provide a brief review of effective strategies for responding to inappropriate classroom behaviors, including planned ignoring, explicit reprimands, differential reinforcement, response cost, and time out.

Planned Ignoring

While there are many ways to deal with inappropriate classroom behavior, the use of planned ignoring is a tool that effective classroom managers use for behavior that has been maintained by adult attention. Planned ignoring occurs when the teacher systematically withholds attention or ignores a student when he or she exhibits the undesired behavior. For example, in a classroom where a rule states that students must raise their hand before answering, the teacher ignores the call-out when a student calls out the answer, and instead selects a student who is raising his or her hand. The underlying assumption is that by withholding attention, the student will cease to engage in the disruptive behavior that brings him or her no reinforcement. Of course, many behaviors cannot be ignored, such as dangerous or highly disruptive behaviors, and these should be handled immediately. Additionally, the effectiveness of planned ignoring depends upon the extent to which the undesired behavior has been reinforced previously by teacher attention. Research suggests that the use of planned ignoring in combination with other effective classroom management strategies (e.g., establishing rules and praising appropriate behavior) is associated with increases in appropriate academic (Hall et al., 1968) and social behavior (Madsen et al., 1968).

Explicit Reprimands

An *explicit reprimand* is a brief, contingent, and specific statement that is given when an inappropriate behavior occurs. The purpose of an explicit reprimand is to inform the student of an error that he or she can correct. This type of reprimand informs the student of the inappropriate behavior and tells him or her what to do in the future in a brief concise manner (e.g., "China, you are too loud—please use a quiet voice"). When teachers revert to making harsh or critical comments, students

> **Experts advise that teachers work to maintain a ratio of positive to negative interaction of at least 3:1 or 4:1.**

may actually increase disruptive behaviors in their classrooms (Van Acker, Grant, & Henry, 1996). The use of explicit reprimands following an undesired behavior, on the other hand, decreases such behavior (McAllister, Stachowiak, Baer, & Conderman, 1969). Researchers suggest that private, quiet, and discrete reprimands are more effective than loud ones delivered in front of an entire class (O'Leary & Becker, 1968). Reprimands should also be brief and used infrequently (Abramowitz, O'Leary, & Futtersak, 1988). Experts advise teachers to maintain a ratio of positive to negative interaction of at least 3:1 or 4:1 (Kalis, Vannest, & Paker, 2007; Shores, Gunter, & Jack, 1993).

Differential Reinforcement

Teachers can use differential reinforcement in the classroom to increase an appropriate behavior while simultaneously decreasing unwanted behaviors. This can be done by providing contingent positive reinforcement to a behavior that is incompatible with the undesired behavior. For instance, in a classroom in which students talk out frequently, the teacher provides reinforcement during times the students are quiet and on task. Teachers can also reinforce low rates of an undesired behavior in an effort to increase appropriate behavior. For example, if students come to class late each day, the teacher might set up a system to reinforce the students when only five come to class late, lowering the acceptable number of undesired behaviors until the behavior no longer occurs. The use of differential reinforcement has been shown to increase overall appropriate behavior and decrease inappropriate behavior (Didden, de Moor, & Bruyns, 1997; Zwald & Gresham, 1982).

Response Cost and Time Out

Response cost and *time out* are negative consequence strategies that when used sparingly (i.e., only for a limited number of specific misbehaviors) and appropriately (i.e., consistently, calmly, respectfully, and immediately), have been shown to decrease inappropriate behavior (Forman, 1980; Barton, Brulle, & Reppe, 1987). *Response cost* is a type of token economy in which a token (e.g., point, chip) is removed whenever an undesired behavior occurs. The effectiveness of response cost is related to how reinforcing the student finds the token and his or her perceived value of the reinforcers for which the token can be exchanged. *Time out* is a procedure employed to remove a student from a reinforcing environment (e.g., watching a movie with classmates) to a less reinforcing environment (e.g., a low-traffic corner of the room), contingent upon inappropriate behavior (e.g., hitting another student). As with all of the strategies mentioned in this chapter, response cost and time out are more likely to be effective when used in conjunction with preventive and positive strategies (e.g., classroom rules, reinforcement of appropriate behavior).

SUMMARY

Effective classrooms require careful planning and consideration. Teachers struggling with managing student behavior can begin the process with the help of a supportive and knowledgeable consultant. Being knowledgeable about the research described in this chapter is an important first step for consultants to take in being able to provide this support. In addition, assessing the current practices and procedures used in the classroom is vital to determining which can be strengthened and/or added to establish an effectively managed classroom. Chapters 5–7 outline step-by-step procedures for conducting the CCU, an assessment-based teacher consultation model. The CCU begins with the formation of the consultant–teacher relationship, in which the two identify areas of strength and areas in need of improvement, and leads to a collaborative action plan for implementing effective evidence-based classroom management practices. Chapter 8 then describes specific interventions (based on the extensive research literature reviewed in this chapter) that can be used to improve practices that were identified during the CCU as areas of concern.

CHAPTER 3

Ingredients of Effective Consultation

Given all that is now known about the benefits of effective classroom management, it is not surprising that there is great interest in supporting teachers in acquiring and maintaining these skills. Teachers get very little training in classroom management during their preservice education, and many report that they do not feel confident in their abilities to effectively manage classrooms (Evertson & Weinstein, 2006; Jones & Jones, 2004). Providing ongoing training and supervision to teachers during their inservice years becomes essential.

As we all know, helping teachers become more effective classroom managers is not as simple as telling them to do so. Giving them a book or day-long training is not enough either. Most teachers need ongoing consultation and supervision to develop and sustain their skills. The question becomes, what are the essential skills and qualities required for a consultant to be successful in supporting teacher skill development?

Before describing the structure and details of the CCU model (Chapters 5–7), it is important to consider the interpersonal skills and attitudes that set the foundation for any effective consultation relationship. Without this foundation, it won't matter how knowledgeable a consultant is or what model he or she is using. Instead, the consultant will be continually frustrated by his or her inability to get teachers to change their classroom practices.

In this chapter we describe the essential qualities of effective consultants. As you reflect on your own consultation experiences, it is likely that you will see yourself as possessing many or most of these qualities. If so, that's great! As you read, though, take time to consider which of these attributes come most naturally to you and which are areas you will need to spend more time developing. Often times, we find ourselves wanting to rush past these interpersonal qualities to get to the specific strategies of a given model. As research in clinical psychology, counseling, and education has repeatedly shown, models only work in the context of effective relationships.

EVOLVING PERSPECTIVES ON CONSULTATION

Indirect service delivery methods came into vogue as part of community mental health and community psychology movements in the 1950s and 1960s. School psychology, in particular, embraced indirect service delivery models as a primary tool for facilitating effective functioning in school environments. It made perfect sense for school-based clinicians, given their large caseloads and limited resources, to work with key adults in children's lives (i.e., teachers and parents) to provide more effective environments, rather than to work with each child individually.

Despite longstanding interest in consultation models, the prevailing models (until recently) have largely relied on traditional psychotherapeutic and instructional methods for facilitating change. That is, most consultation models prior to the mid-1990s used didactic instruction to teach skills and support development despite the known limitations of these methods (Watson & Robinson, 1996). Even behavior consultation, a preferred model and activity among school psychologists, suffered from this overemphasis on didactic instruction.

> **Targeting the classroom system is more efficient and efficacious because it is likely to reduce current student behavioral and academic difficulties as well as prevent future student problems.**

Direct Behavior Consultation

Watson and Robinson introduced direct behavior consultation in the mid-1990s as a more explicit model of behavior consultation where emphasis was placed on direct instruction, modeling, practice, and rehearsal. Other models have since placed greater emphasis on similar methods known to promote skill development. Still, even these newer models have not always attended to the broader aspects of consultation relationships (including the huge literature on the power of collaborative relationships, alone, to promote change). Furthermore, they had narrow perspectives on the role of motivation and were focused on consultation around individual cases (students) rather than broader teacher skill development.

For instance, although direct behavior consultation was attentive to teacher motivation, the emphasis was on skill development, or what might be labeled self-efficacy, as the primary barrier to teacher motivation. Watson and Robinson (1996) wrote that while traditional models have blamed consultation failures on teachers for being resistant, "It is probably more accurate to say that the consultee did not have the skills to perform the tasks at the various stages of the consultation process" (p. 275). As we will see with MI, low skills or efficacy beliefs are indeed one aspect of motivation to change, but there are other facets that can be equally critical. Further, a major limitation of most behavior consultation models is their focus on individual students rather than on changing the classroom system (Sheridan, Welch, & Orme, 1996). This has been true despite recent calls to target and intervene in systems (e.g., classrooms, schools) rather than at the individual student level (Strein, Hoagwood, & Cohn, 2003). Targeting the classroom system by providing consultation to increase effective classroom management practices delivered to all students is more efficient and efficacious because it is likely to reduce current student behavioral and academic difficulties as well as prevent future student problems.

Instructional Coaching

Complementing the behavior consultation models, a parallel literature has emerged during the past decade about effective instructional coaching practices. This literature was sparked by state and federal investments in instructional coaches to support high-quality classroom instruction. These coaching models typically target teacher behavior and thus overcome the barrier of focusing on one student at a time. Dr. Jim Knight at the University of Kansas has been a leader in this movement and has created a partnership approach to instructional coaching. In his model, an instructional coach supports the teacher in identifying appropriate teaching for diverse learners, models practices in the classroom, observes the teacher, and engages in supportive, dialogical conversations with the teacher about what he or she observes. The advantage of these coaching strategies is that they have been developed in the field, often using highly skilled teachers as coaches, and thus have a high level of credibility with teachers. A limitation of these methods is that very little research has evaluated which strategies work best in which settings.

Consultation Research

Researchers have entered into the coaching/consultation discussion in recent years, motivated by the need to address a very practical goal: getting teachers and other school personnel to implement evidence-based practices with high fidelity. Ringeisen, Henderson, and Hoagwood (2003) pointed to the considerable progress made over the last decade in terms of the development of evidence-based preventive and treatment interventions for school-age children. At the same time, they noted the need for more research on the factors associated with the considerable variation found in the implementation of these interventions in schools settings (Domitrovich & Greenberg, 2000; McCormick, Steckler, & McLeroy, 1994).

Seeking to fill this gap, Han and Weiss (2005) offered a model of the factors influencing implementation of interventions in school settings, drawing on extant theory and empirical findings. They defined implementation fidelity and sustainability as (1) the quantity of the intervention delivered, (2) the quality of the implementation with respect to the standards set by the program developers, and (3) the use of the core principles of the intervention in dealing with behaviors not addressed in the training and consultation phase. Han and Weiss conceived of the implementation process as a "self-sustaining feedback loop," with the training/consultation protocol playing the central role. Effective training consultation protocols that are attentive to quantity, quality, and principles foster high teacher-perceived efficacy to implement interventions and to attribute improvements in student behavior to the intervention. This, in turn, increases teacher motivation to implement the intervention with high levels of fidelity, further improving student behavior as well as the teacher's "experience of success" in implementing the intervention. In short, effective consultation occurs when consultants prepare and support teachers to implement practices that create meaningful and noticeable changes in their classrooms.

Han and Weiss's emphasis on the training/consultation protocol in establishing and sustaining implementation fidelity is consistent with extant theory and empirical findings. For instance, although most educators are familiar with classroom management practices, many struggle to implement effective practices in their own classroom. Although teachers may attend workshops on behavior management, these are often delivered in a didactic manner and use a one-shot, train-and-hope approach that is insufficient for changing actual classroom behaviors (see Fixen, Naoom, Blasé, Friedman, & Wallace, 2005).

The renewed interest in consultation and implementation among researchers, educators, and clinicians prompted a synthesis of the literature on implementation of school-based interventions and the most comprehensive review of the coaching/consultation literature to date by Dr. Dean Fixen and colleagues (2005). They reached three primary conclusions: (1) professional development training on its own is not effective in supporting implementation of school-based interventions in classroom settings; (2) implementation is most effective when practitioners receive coordinated training, consultation, and frequent performance assessments; and (3) organizations need to provide the infrastructure necessary for timely training, skillful supervision and consultation, and regular process and outcome evaluations. The key limitations of the consultation movement identified in the report were that very few empirical studies have evaluated the relative contributions of training and consultation. They concluded that more research is needed to better understand the interaction between training, consultation, and the selection of interventions, and how these interactions impact implementation.

PERSPECTIVES FROM THE FIELD: EXPERT CONSULTANTS

I find if I listen before I talk, I can learn a lot about a teacher's basic beliefs and values.
—NATIONAL CLASSROOM CONSULTANT in the field for over 20 years

We decided to supplement these growing theoretical and research descriptions of effective consultation with perspectives from expert consultants. We think that there is much to learn from professionals who are known for their skills in teacher consultation. We sampled a range of consultants, some having established reputations for decades as expert consultants and others relatively new to the field but already standing out as being very skilled in working with teachers. We also intentionally sampled consultants with different training backgrounds, ranging from general education to special education, school psychology, and counseling. We asked all of them to respond to two questions about consultation:

1. What do you think the most important skill/quality is to being an effective consultant when working with teachers (around behavior management)?
2. What is the greatest or most frequent challenge you have encountered in working as a consultant?

As can be seen in the summary comments in Table 3.1, the experts had many consistent comments about the elements of effective consultation. They all mentioned the importance of establishing effective and collaborative relationships. They also implied a hierarchy of consultation skills, with successful relationship partnering being a prerequisite for other skills such as direct instruction or giving advice.

> As I work with consultants across the country, and I ask them to reveal their greatest challenge, the overwhelming response is, "How do I get someone to change who seemingly doesn't want to?"
> —NATIONAL CONSULTANT AND TRAINER

We divided the primary barriers identified by these consultation experts into two domains: (1) lack of motivation and (2) lack of skill. They identified many factors that inter-

TABLE 3.1. Summary of Expert Comments

Most important skill/quality	Greatest or most frequent challenge
Building a relationship	Lack of interest/motivation
• Appropriate self-disclosure • Empathy • Active listening • Being respectful • Being genuine, caring, understanding, flexible, and consistent • Instilling hope • Being optimistic and positive • Being enthusiastic • Having patience and humility	• Variations in commitment to improvement from day to day. • Teachers not really wanting to make a change; more focused on getting a child out of their class. • *Philosophical opposition* to many effective practices. • *Unrealistic expectations:* Not having an understanding that change takes time and that although a lot of evidence-based practices aren't flashy and glamorous, they *do* work. • *Variability of implementation:* Teachers convinced that they are already using a practice, when in fact, they are not. • *People often take behavior so personally,* instead of viewing it simply as data. • *Personal problems/stress:* In severe cases, teachers who are depressed or in need of therapy/mental health services; most frequently, teachers who feel overwhelmed and/or overly stressed. • *Choice/historical bad practices:* Each person we work with is a professional; we must allow for choice. • *Lack of administrator support*
Collaboration	
• Creating a shared vision • Meeting teachers where they are (e.g., skill level) and having realistic expectations in setting goals • Being considerate of stress levels and other obligations	
Skills and knowledge	
• Having creative and practical ideas • Providing ongoing support • Providing problem solving • Being good classroom managers • Communicating knowledge clearly • Fostering vision • Observing, collecting data, providing feedback	
Student-focused	Lack of skills
• Able to balance needs of all players: win–win	• Lack necessary skills to effectively manage their classroom. • Extremely harsh/negative/punitive.

fered with teacher interest and motivation in adopting new practices and skills. These included philosophical opposition to evidence-based practices, personal challenges faced by teachers (either because of excessive and competing demands for their time or because of personal problems and stress experienced outside the classroom), unrealistic expectations (about how easy or fast change will occur), taking student behavior problems personally, and lack of administrator support.

> People often take behavior so personally, instead of viewing it simply as data. I try to help teachers see how antecedent strategies can greatly impact behavior. When they finally "get" this, they are able to step away from taking behavior personally or feeling helpless (or angry).
> —CONSULTANT for over 20 years

On the other hand, even when teachers are motivated, these experts noted that some lacked core skills that needed to be established before the consultation relationship could be successful. For instance, one barrier was that teachers sometimes think they are doing the skill, despite evidence to the contrary.

THE ROAD TO EFFECTIVE CONSULTATION

We attempted to integrate all of the perspectives described above into a framework for understanding the core skills and qualities of effective consultation. We conceptualize the consultation relationship as a journey along a road (see Figure 3.1). The prerequisite for a successful journey is a solid, collaborative partnership between consultant and teacher. At the beginning, the key consultant qualities all focus on relationship building. Without these qualities, your trip will be short. As you travel further in your relationship, these qualities are still essential because they allow you to expand your areas of focus and conversation. Further into your journey, you will have more opportunities to give constructive feedback and even direct advice. If you begin with (unrequested) advice without the other elements of consultation, it is highly unlikely that teachers will consistently follow through on your suggestions. The entire journey need not take long with all teachers; as you will see with the CCU, you can move through many of these elements in a few visits. Yet, with some teachers, you will find yourself at the beginning of a long and enduring collaborative relationship.

As a consultant you probably already have many of the skills and attributes described below. As you read the section, you might identify a few skills at which you are already good and that you want to solidify or extend. Alternately, you might identify one or two skills that you do less well as areas for growth. You may find it helpful to reread this chapter after reading the next one on MI, and see if you can use some of the MI-style self-reflection to help build your own motivation to improve these areas. This may serve as a useful exercise to gain further insight into the behavior change process we ask of teachers.

> **You may find it helpful to reread this chapter after reading the next one on MI, and see if you can use some of the MI-style self-reflection to help build your own motivation to improve these areas. This may serve as a useful exercise to gain further insight into the behavior change process we ask of teachers.**

FIGURE 3.1. The consultation road map.

Beginning the Journey: Building a Relationship

> Effective consultants must be understanding, flexible, genuine, caring, and consistent. They must understand the time constraints, stress, and challenges that teachers face in today's schools and be flexible in accommodating these challenges. They also have to be genuine. You can't just go through the motions. You need to really have a caring attitude and give 101% to the job and the relationship. You have to continuously check in with teachers and follow up on goals, offer feedback, and give support.
>
> —TEACHER CONSULTANT in a large urban district

• **Effective consultants use good social communication skills to build successful relationships.** Effective consultation is grounded in a solid collaborative relationship. Consultants create these relationships through social communication skills that engender trust. Effective consultants set the stage for such relationships to occur by first examining their own attitudes and biases, withholding judgments and conveying acceptance and understanding. No one wants to embark on an important journey with someone who is overly critical and evaluative.

Likewise, effective consultants are perceived by others as sincere. In other words, they truly care about what happens to the teachers and students with whom they work. They are empathic and communicate their concern and caring to the teachers with whom they consult. They validate the experiences of teachers with their empathy, but do so in a way that is empowering and not undermining.

Effective consultants are good listeners. They listen before they talk and before they recommend or advise. The style of their conversations is dialogical; that is, they seek to reach shared understandings and draw insights out of the teachers with whom they consult rather than communicating in a didactic manner. Furthermore, effective consultants are good at making social interactions fun, relaxed, and engaging. They are good at putting people at ease. They check in with teachers informally outside of more formal consultation times. They use well-timed and appropriate humor, engage in small talk, and offer to help and assist in small ways as needed.

Effective consultants are affirming in their consultation relationships. This means that they focus on strengths and resources as much as, if not more than, limitations and problems. They are humble and keep the focus on the teacher and classroom needs rather than on themselves. They use language to build self-efficacy by assigning successes to the teacher and not to themselves.

- **Effective consultants are respectful professionals.** A respectful professional maintains boundaries and recognizes the limits of his or her role, which is primarily to position others to create more effective environments for children. Thus, effective consultants honor individual autonomy and decision making. They trust that when provided with a nurturing, supportive, and reflective context, teachers will make the best decisions for themselves and naturally move toward positive changes in their classroom. Skilled consultants also respect and value individual differences. They are culturally competent and sensitive.

> Consultants communicate respect for the teacher's situation while helping
> him/her to see that they might be able to make the situation better.
> —National Consultant and Trainer

Respectful professionals are reliable. They do what they say they are going to do, when they say they are going to do it. They follow through on commitments. They show up to scheduled meetings on time and prepared. Effective consultants show their professionalism by ensuring the confidentiality of shared information except when the law mandates reporting.

Sustaining the Journey: Credibility, Facilitation, and Problem Solving

> Consultant credibility rests on a foundation of personal and professional qualities.
> Consultants need the personal qualities that establish trust. They need professional
> expertise in order to demonstrate their value to teachers and principals.
> —Teacher Consultant and State Leader

- **Effective consultation is guided by good theory.** Of course, we want our consultation experiences to be more than a relationship. The purpose of consultation, after all, is to connect teachers with a knowledge and skill base to which they might not have access otherwise. Thus, the effective consultant must have expertise in this desired information or skill set and be perceived as a credible disseminator of it.

Effective consultants have a defined knowledge base—in this case, knowledge about effective behavior management practices and how to help teachers and other school personnel use these practices. Equally important, they are able to communicate this knowledge base in language that others can understand and won't dismiss. Being guided by good theory helps consultants clearly define the problem, conceptualize potential causes, and select appropriate options for interventions. As one of our expert consultants eloquently noted, "One of the most important things is that you have to know what the heck you are doing!"

It is imperative that a consultant have a solid understanding of how behavior is learned and how it can be changed. Thus, consultants working with teachers to support effective classroom management will need to have an understanding of the basic principles of behavior modification. Having knowledge of behavioral principles and the practical applications of these principals is a key component to effective consultation.

Table 3.2 and Figure 3.2 provide a brief review of these principals, and Chapter 8 provides practical applications. (If you have a strong understanding of behavior analysis, you might simply skim the table as a brief review. If you are new to behavioral theory, you may want to review the table as well as review some of the additional resources outlined in Chapter 8.)

- **Effective consultants are credible.** In addition to having a guiding theory, effective consultants demonstrate additional qualities that enable them to build credibility and trust and continue the collaborative journey with teachers. For instance, consultants who share past experiences in managing a classroom or examples of strategies used by teachers with whom they have worked in the past, communicate credibility as well as build a personal connection. Additionally, effective consultants share their knowledge of relevant research, when appropriate, to support and guide the development of intervention ideas. Some additional qualities that go hand in hand with building effective relationships and credibility include being a good problem solver, collecting and sharing objective data without passing judgment, being flexible, and conveying confidence.

> Rarely does anything in the world of educational consulting go as planned, because we are dealing with human beings. In order to continue fighting the good fight every day, consultants have to believe that even the smallest step is wholly worthwhile. Consultants must balance a sense of urgency with a sense of acceptance on a continuous basis.
> —NATIONAL CONSULTANT AND TRAINER

- **Effective consultants are confident.** Effective consultants believe that the consultation and problem-solving process works to produce positive change. Effective consultants convey their confidence to others through body language, tone of voice, and eye contact. They also know when to access additional resources and how to help others access relevant resources as needed. In other words, they are comfortable in their interactions and aware of the extent of their knowledge base and expertise. Setting appropriately high expectations and believing that others can meet their own goals when supported also conveys confidence.

- **Effective consultants are good problem solvers.** Effective problem solvers are solution-focused, and they engage in a sequential problem-solving process that involves clearly defining the target behaviors, specifying goals, monitoring progress toward those goals by

TABLE 3.2. Basic Principles of Behavior Modification

In order to support teachers in managing classroom behavior effectively, consultants need a solid understanding of how behavior is learned and how it is changed.

Behavior is learned. Learning occurs as a result of the consequences of our behavior. In other words, our behavior is influenced by the events and conditions we experience. When our behavior is followed by a pleasant consequence, that behavior tends to be repeated and learned. When our behavior is followed by an unpleasant consequence, that behavior tends not to be repeated and thus not learned.

A *reinforcer* is a consequence that increases the likelihood of a behavior in the future. For instance, *positive reinforcement* occurs when a behavior is followed by a consequence that increases the behavior's rate of occurrence. Many behaviors are learned as a result of positive reinforcement. For instance, teachers who praise their students for organizing their materials at their desk may teach the students to be neat and organized; a teacher who gives attention to a student who calls out an answer may be teaching the student to continue calling out.

Negative reinforcement occurs when a behavior increases following an aversive or unpleasant consequence. Individuals learn that certain behaviors terminate the unpleasant consequence and therefore are more likely to demonstrate the behavior in the future. For instance, if a student who is asked to stop a fun activity begins to cry and the teacher relents, allowing the student to continue with the activity, the teacher learns that by not making the student comply, the aversive consequence (student crying) ceases.

Punishment describes the relationship between a behavior that is followed by a consequence that decreases the likelihood of that behavior occurring in the future. A *punisher* is something that decreases behavior.

Extinction occurs when a previously reinforcing behavior is no longer reinforced and therefore decreases until it no longer occurs.

Any behavior that occurs repeatedly is serving some function for the individual exhibiting the behavior. In striving to support teachers to help students, it is essential to understand and communicate that *every* behavior serves a purpose. Students who consistently complete work assignments, come to class on time, and behave responsibly do so because they find good grades, positive parent and teacher attention, and a sense of pride and accomplishment reinforcing. Similarly, a student who repeatedly disrupts class and argues with teachers is getting some benefit from this behavior. Although the teacher provides reprimands and the student's parents are frequently called, the student likely finds the immediate consequence of attention from teachers and school staff to be reinforcing. Finding other ways for the student to appropriately gain attention from adults could help to meet this need and decrease the student's argumentative and disruptive behavior.

Altering the classroom environment can change student behavior. Behavior is affected by events that happen immediately before a behavior (antecedents) and events that happen following a behavior (consequences). By changing the variables affecting behavior, we can increase or decrease behaviors in the classroom. This means that we can change student (and adult) behavior by manipulating these variables.

Consider the following example. The classroom teacher passes out an independent work assignment (antecedent). Rather than working on this assignment, students talk to one another about topics unrelated to the assignment (behavior) or inappropriately walk around the classroom (behavior) as the teacher sits in the back of the room grading papers (consequence = the misbehavior is ignored). We can alter either the antecedent or the consequence to change student behavior. For instance, let's say that the teacher provides a precorrection (antecedent manipulation), telling students that during independent work time, they are expected to work alone at their desks and if they have a question, to raise their hand. Another option is to change the consequence. Rather than grading at his or her desk, the teacher walks about the classroom providing praise to students working on the assignment and answering questions for those who need clarification on the assignment. In this example, changing the antecedent and/or the consequence will likely result in increased student engagement in the task. Figure 3.2 demonstrates the variables that affect behavior and how we can manipulate these variables to increase or decrease a behavior.

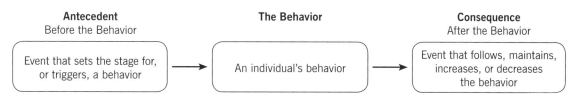

Below is a list of interventions that target each of the variables that impact behavior. Chapter 8 contains examples and suggestions for supporting implementation of these strategies in a classroom setting.

Antecedent Strategies	Teaching Behaviors	Consequence Strategies
Arrange physical layout of classroom to promote positive interactions and prevent disruptive behavior.	Actively teach students expected classroom behaviors.	Use behavior-specific praise.
Post positively stated classroom rules.	Teach classroom rules.	Use token economy systems to reward expected behavior.
Post daily schedule.	Teach behavioral routines.	Use group contingencies to reward expected behavior.
Use an attention signal.	Teach students to attend when a preset signal occurs.	Ignore inappropriate behavior.
Use active supervision.		Use explicit reprimands for inappropriate behavior.
Use precorrection.		Use differential reinforcement procedures to increase appropriate behavior.
Utilize effective instructional practices.		Use response–cost procedures for inappropriate behavior.
Actively engage students by providing ample opportunities to respond.		Use time out for inappropriate behavior.
Provide noncontingent attention to build positive teacher–student relationships.		

FIGURE 3.2. Variables that affect behavior.

collecting relevant data, and revising the plan, as needed, in response to the collected data. Rather than categorizing teachers as good or bad or as resistant or nonresistant, consultants look for the positives and the resources in each classroom. Other critical qualities of effective problem solvers are that they are patient, persistent, and believe that the set goals will be achieved. They proactively assess the plan and expect that it will need to be revised over time. They don't give up.

> **Rather than categorizing teachers as good or bad or as resistant or nonresistant, consultants look for the positives and the resources in each classroom.**

• **Effective consultants collect objective data.** Collecting data is a critical ingredient to effective consultation. Data can be used to provide feedback to teachers on what is going well in addition to what is in need of attention. Therefore, collecting data that teachers trust and feel are accurate is vital. One way to increase the likelihood that data are perceived by teachers as meaningful and useful is to make sure that they (i.e., the data) are objective. In other words, the data that you collect are observable, sensitive to change, and important. Additionally, the data will be most useful if they are shared with the teacher in a respectful manner that avoids implications of the teacher being at fault for student problem behavior. Just as we don't communicate that problem behavior is internal to children, teachers are not personally responsible for difficult classroom behaviors. Data simply provide information that can be used to improve the classroom environment. Lastly, although objective data are great, they may not always reflect the full picture. Checking in with the teacher about the data may provide additional insights. Simply asking the teacher, after conducting a classroom observation, about how typical the day has been or asking what he or she felt went well versus what did not go well during the observation is helpful toward collaborating on a plan for change.

- **Effective consultants are flexible.** Although their theory guides them in choosing which aspects to emphasize in each consultation case, consultants don't come with a formal plan for how to address problems. They recognize that effective plans are created in collaboration with the teachers who will be most directly involved in implementing the plan. In other words, their theory provides the parameters for the interaction and problem-solving discussion, but ultimately the plan is developed through conversation, brainstorming, and discussion with the key players.

- **Effective consultants provide structure to meetings.** Being flexible within a structure can be a challenging balancing act. However, establishing parameters to how time will be used during a meeting is critical to a consultant's success. Effective consultants make the purpose of meetings clear by reviewing the objectives and expected outcomes up front. Having an agenda does not mean that the consultant arrives with every idea detailed in full or a formal plan for intervening; rather, the agenda identifies steps that can be taken toward collaborative planning with the end result being an action plan. Additionally, consultants try to minimize surprises by communicating openly about the purpose of meetings, how data will be collected and when, and how progress toward the collaborative goals will be measured.

Detour Ahead: Collaborative Planning and Overcoming Roadblocks

> If we fully employ collaboration, we have to allow for choice. If the allowance of choice is not balanced by the pressure to change from someone who holds that person accountable, then good luck. Because even the most dedicated professional has very valid reasons to resist change in education today. We've approached change so poorly for years, we will be making up for it for many years to come.
> —NATIONAL CONSULTANT AND TRAINER

When teachers come to perceive consultants as trustworthy and credible, they are then more willing to engage in collaborative planning. The skill set here focuses on how to facilitate skill development and overcome barriers to change. These include giving constructive feedback and navigating difficult conversations.

- **Effective consultants provide constructive feedback about skill development.** Consultants provide high rates of positive feedback along with comments and suggestions about what might be improved. They ask permission from teachers to provide feedback about targeted behavior change. For feedback to be constructive, it needs to be specific, solution-focused, and directed toward an agreed-upon behavior that can be changed. Telling a teacher, "There are too many students in your classroom," is not constructive because that is probably not an aspect of the classroom that a teacher directly controls. Saying, "You need to work on your relationships with students," is problematic

> **Constructive feedback is specific, solution-focused, and directed toward an agreed-upon behavior that can be changed.**

because it is vague and does not give the teacher enough information to move toward a more positive behavior. Instead, consider the following feedback: "I counted ten times when you provided students with behavior-specific praise and five occasions when you checked in with students about their day. Teachers find that by increasing those types of interactions, they nearly always see a decline in disruptive behaviors." This type of statement is very concrete and gives the teacher a road map to improving his or her skills.

- **Effective consultants are able and willing to model target skills.** Consultants not only need to be knowledgeable about effective classroom management practices, they also need to be competent in showing teachers how to perform these practices. Modeling is a critical tool with which consultants help teachers learn new skills. Rather than simply telling a teacher to increase his or her rate of behavior-specific praise, a competent consultant needs to be able to demonstrate examples of behavior-specific praise and to model this skill in a classroom setting. Having teachers observe you as you model, collecting data on *your* use of praise and other key variables, is particularly useful because they stay engaged and focused on the skills being modeled.

- **Effective consultants have immediacy skills.** Inevitably, challenges or roadblocks will arise on the journey. Skilled consultants manage these challenges while still moving forward. To have immediacy skills means that one is able to monitor the immediate, present interactions and comment on these processes as needed. Understanding that change can be uncomfortable and that ambivalence about changing is normal supports this process. Effective consultants are aware of resistance or discomfort when it arises. Rather than urging people to change or countering resistant statements with reasons for why change is needed, they get out of the way; as discussed in the next chapter, they roll with resistance. They reposition themselves so that they let others tell them why they believe change is important.

- **Effective consultants are willing to have difficult conversations when needed.** Consultants need to be willing to talk about the "elephant in the room." On occasion, there are circumstances that are difficult to broach, for one reason or another. However, if the issue is ignored, little progress will occur. Being able to address challenging issues by discussing them in a respectful manner has been labeled *collegial confrontation*. Discussions of this type may include sentence stems such as "I'm confused" or "This is hard to talk about, but." Additionally, presenting data can be helpful when bringing up a difficult topic. As an example, suppose you are working with a teacher who reported having a very well-behaved classroom, but upon actual observation of the classroom, you note that the teacher uses harsh and punitive means and little or no positive practices to manage student behavior. While it may be difficult to discuss this issue with the teacher, it is absolutely necessary. You might use the CCU feedback form, placing the use of praise and reprimands in the red (i.e., need for attention), and then have a discussion with the teacher about the data, perhaps asking him or her to think about why it would be important to increase the use of positive reinforcement in the classroom and how that might benefit students. Of course, on occasion you may have to bring in research and past experiences to support the discussion, but moving forward as if the issue does not exist is unhelpful, if not detrimental, to the teacher's growth.

> **Consultants need to be willing to talk about the "elephant in the room." Being able to address challenging issues by discussing them in a respectful manner has been labeled *collegial confrontation*.**

   • **Effective consultants offer solicited advice.** After establishing a trusting and collaborative relationship and credibility, effective consultants give advice when requested to do so. Advice from a credible authority can actually encourage people to make important changes in their lives. Keep in mind, however, that for advice to be impactful, all the other elements of effective consultation need to be in place. It is also generally a good idea to ask permission before giving advice. For instance, you might say, "I have some ideas about what might work to make a difference in your classroom. Would you like me to tell you about some of these?"

MASTER CONSULTANTS

> **Effective consultants know where to focus their attention.**

Beyond the core skills and qualities depicted in the road map, we believe that there are two fundamental abilities that the best consultants master over time to ensure the success of the collaborative planning stage: (1) knowing where to intervene and (2) anticipating problems. We describe these below.

Knowing Where to Intervene

A clear vision of what needs to be accomplished is paramount. I've seen many endeavors fail because of lack of vision. In other words, the teacher, the administrator, the consultant may clearly see that change is needed in regards to classroom management, but they have not fully defined how that change will look. In education, I've seen too many people, including consultants, focus on the behaviors of an ineffective teacher that need to stop, but not fully define what replacement behaviors would look like.

—NATIONAL CONSULTANT AND TRAINER

Effective consultants know where to focus their attention. As a consultant, it is helpful to be aware of the multiple domains involved in the consultation process (see Figure 3.3). The first domain to consider involves classroom practices and where to focus attention with regard to the changes needed. Direction comes from the use of objective data to inform you regarding the needs of the classroom, in conjunction with a good theory that can align the data with effective strategies. Once the relevant targets for intervention are identified (e.g., define and teach expectations, increase use of behavior-specific praise), the second and third domains emerge as a focus of your attention: the teacher's capacity and willingness to implement the practices that can improve his or her classroom management. Those domains are important because they can impact whether the strategies actually get implemented. In our model, we conceptualize two primary domains as integral to effective implementation of classroom practices: teacher knowledge and skills and teacher motivation.

Even the best-laid plans will fail if consultants are not tuned into the "music" behind the conversation. Thus, effective consultants are perceptive and reflective. They listen for cues from teachers that signal what might go wrong with the best-intentioned plans. During conversations with the teacher, effective consultants listen with a third ear to determine: "Is this plan really going to work?"; "Will this teacher actually implement it?"; "Am I missing something important?" They ask questions to gain additional information from the teacher: "Is this something that is important to you?"; "How confident are you that you will be able to do this in your classroom?"; "What might get in the way of this happening?"

> **Even the best-laid plans will fail if consultants are not tuned into the "music" behind the conversation.**

Teacher Knowledge and Skill

A potential area for interference with intervention implementation is a teacher's lack of necessary skills or knowledge required to use a new strategy. In this case, you may want to play a more active role in implementation by engaging in active practice with the teacher through

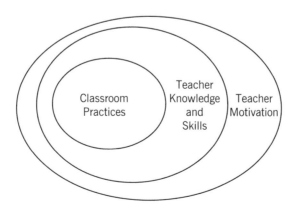

FIGURE 3.3. Domains of consideration in classwide consultation.

FIGURE 3.4. The relationships among motivation, knowledge, and self-efficacy.

role playing, modeling the new strategy in the classroom while the teacher observes, or having the teacher observe another teacher in the school who successfully uses the targeted strategy. Other effective strategies to support teachers in developing a new skill include providing them with a step-by-step guide, identifying useful resources, helping prepare materials, being close by and available when the teacher implements a new strategy for the first time, giving positive and constructive feedback following teacher implementation, and brainstorming ideas to adjust the strategy if necessary. Additional strategies include collecting data and providing ongoing performance feedback to support the teacher in honing his or her new skill.

Matching a teacher's skill level with the intervention is key to successful implementation. We have worked with very enthusiastic and motivated teachers who have wanted to implement eight new practices all simultaneously. While some teachers may be very capable of implementing multiple intervention practices at one time, this may not be reasonable or feasible for others. Knowing when to capitalize on enthusiasm while supporting the development of realistic goals is an important skill set for the consultant. Identifying one new strategy and supporting teachers toward success with this one strategy builds confidence and self-efficacy. Teachers who feel more efficacious will be more motivated to try new skills in the future (see Figure 3.4).

> **Knowing when to capitalize on enthusiasm while supporting the development of realistic goals is an important skill set for the consultant.**

> By the time teachers ask for assistance, they are so frustrated with a particular student that they really don't want help, they just want the student out of their room. In fact, if this is a strongly held position, the teachers may have no incentive to implement an intervention, because if it is successful, it disproves how severe the student/situation is.
> —National Trainer and Teacher Consultant for over 40 years

Teacher Motivation

Effective consultants need to be in tune with motivation issues. Motivation is a key contributor to the effective implementation of a new practice, and unless a teacher is ready and willing to attempt the intervention, it won't matter what skills he or she has; the intervention will be ineffective. On the other hand, if a teacher is ready and willing to try an intervention, then the focus can shift toward helping him or her do it. In fact, if a teacher is motivated to get started, you may actually undermine that motivation by spending too much time talking about it. However, if a teacher doesn't think that it is important to introduce new practices into his or her classroom, the consultant needs to spend time building motivation and determining what that teacher believes is important enough to try.

The CCU model employs a number of strategies to support teachers in their efforts to make important changes in their classroom, including providing them with personalized feedback and developing a menu of options (see Chapter 7). For instance, the use of feedback specific to a classroom that includes both student and teacher information is presented to allow for a discussion about any discrepancy between what the teacher would like for his or her classroom and what is actually happening. For example, a teacher may feel that having a positive and supportive classroom is important, but the data collected might point out that much more attention is given to misbehavior and that the teacher is using more punitive strategies than proactive ones to manage student behavior. When presented with

> **Providing options increases buy-in because the teacher is the one making the choice rather than you, as the consultant, telling him or her what to do.**

this feedback, the teacher may be more willing to try new proactive strategies in an effort to better align his or her classroom vision with actual practice. Another effective strategy for increasing motivation to implement new management practices is to develop a menu of strategy options that can be used by the teacher in the classroom. Providing options increases buy-in because the teacher is the one making the choice rather than you, as the consultant, telling him or her what to do. Additionally, MI strategies can be useful when consulting with a teacher who is less ready or willing to introduce new classroom management strategies. The key point is that, as a consultant, you need to recognize when to give attention to motivational factors and when to move forward. Spending time on building a plan that the teacher finds important and is willing to try is essential for effecting change.

WHEN PERSONAL ISSUES INTERFERE WITH PROFESSIONAL PRODUCTIVITY

It has become increasingly common to encounter teachers for whom stress, depression, or other personal issues interfere with their classroom performance. Personal issues or on-the-job stress may inhibit a teacher's readiness to implement new practices. The teacher may feel overburdened by the current classroom situation and be at a point where he or she is simply trying to get through the day. Some attention will need to be given to this topic if it is an issue that may interfere with a teacher's willingness to implement new strategies in his or her classroom. First, simply validating the feeling of the teacher is a good start (e.g., "Teaching is becoming more stressful, and you have fewer resources to do everything you are asked to do"). Further, providing emotional support by listening, validating concerns, and highlighting the teacher's successes can be useful. Empathizing with the teacher while communicating that change can happen when he or she is ready to make it happen may encourage dialogue about even the smallest of steps toward increasing effective management practices.

Being aware of the multiple domains requiring attention during the consultation process will allow you to support the teacher in changing not only current but also future classroom practices. As teachers become more knowledgeable about and successfully implement effective classroom practices, they become motivated to continue the practices as well as to attempt new practices. In turn, each year students enter the classroom of a teacher who values, understands, and utilizes effective classroom management practices.

Anticipating Problems

How many times have you looked back on a situation and thought, "How did I not think about that?" Over time, as you gain experience consulting with teachers, you learn to anticipate potential problems by maintaining a mental list of all the barriers and mishaps that interfere with effective implementation of an intervention in the classroom. Your ability to effectively anticipate these barriers depends not only on your understanding of behavioral theory, but also on what is actually feasible in classrooms with limited resources, across teachers with varying levels of skill. As you move forward with a plan, make it a priority to consistently ask yourself (and the teacher), "What can go wrong or get in the way of this being successful?" Assessing these issues prior to having a teacher implement new strategies in the classroom can help avoid potential roadblocks to success.

> **Over time, you learn to anticipate potential problems by maintaining a mental list of all the barriers and mishaps that interfere with effective implementation of an intervention in the classroom.**

SUMMARY

In this chapter we describe the important qualities of effective consultants, derived from existing research on the topic and from conversations with expert consultants. We conceptualize effective consultation as a journey, with collaborative relationship-building skills serving as the prerequisite for embarking. Only further along the journey, after establishing a collaborative relationship, are the more nuanced skills of effective consultants (immediacy skills, modeling, advice giving) even relevant. Attending to this road map also serves as the starting point for learning to do motivational interviewing and to use the CCU. As the next chapter clarifies, most of the skills needed to do effective motivational interviewing align with the attributes of effective consultants.

CHAPTER 4

Motivational Interviewing Applied to Teacher Consultation

> The most challenging part of consulting with teachers is getting them to do what I want them to do.
> —Classroom Consultant

How much control do you have over whether a teacher follows your recommendations? The answer to this question depends on what we mean by *control*. You actually have virtually no *direct* control over what others choose to do. Ultimately, what people decide to do is up to them. On the other hand, you can have a great deal of *influence* over the decisions that people make. The choices we all make are the result of an internal decision-making process that is shaped, at least in part, by our interactions with others. The purpose of this chapter is to describe how you can capitalize on these social leverage points and maximize the influence you have in your consultation relationships.

HOW DO PEOPLE CHANGE?

Historical View

For many years, researchers, consultants, and clinicians lamented the lack of application of behavior change technologies. In the social and educational sciences, we now have a vast literature about how to help people change their behaviors and learn new skills—if only they wanted to change. For some reason, probably because it was easier, the motivation of our clients/consultees has not been a primary focus of our clinical or consultant interventions and research, until recently. Tradition told us that people had to want to change before we could help them. Consider the conventional view of alcoholism, that people had to "hit rock bottom" before they could recover. Nobody knew what rock bottom would be for a given person (for one it might be a DUI, for another it might take losing his or her home and family); when people started their recovery, *that* was taken as evidence that they had hit their bottom. The impact of this perspective is that it leaves the consultant on the sidelines waiting for the moment when the consultee is ready to change. In this view, we have minimal influence over whether someone decides it is time to change. Our best hope is to help our consultees see the errors of their ways.

A typical response style that develops from this perspective of client motivation is to become directly persuasive, if not confrontational. Most treatment programs for alcoholics prior to the 1990s approached this motivation challenge by creating logical, informational, and at times adversarial interactions with their clients. The assumption seemed to be that providers could help their clients reach rock bottom more quickly by hammering them over the head with facts and information.

Although teacher consultation approaches are generally not as hostile as some of these past alcohol interventions may have been, they sometimes share a similar perspective on teacher motivation. Typically, teacher motivation is not directly considered as a key concern of consultant interventions. When low motivation impedes the consultation process, consultants often try to directly persuade educators to change by providing them with facts, information, and logical arguments.

Do factual or confrontational approaches to enhance motivation work? Before we review research about this question, first take a moment to reflect on your own experience with changing personal behaviors.

Reflections on Personal Experiences with Change

It helps to consider your own experiences with trying to change challenging behaviors or learn new skills to understand what may be most helpful in getting others to do the same. Most of us have tried to change personal habits, be it exercise/diet routines or other lifestyle changes, and know firsthand how difficult this can be. We also recognize that sometimes even when we know that a new habit or routine may be in our best interest (e.g., eating better, exercising more) it can be very difficult to change. In short, most of us know from personal experience that logic and factual information alone are not necessarily enough to get us to adopt new routines and behaviors.

We also know from our own experiences that having others tell us that we need to change and why is generally not particularly persuasive. Picture your spouse or a friend

> **Logic and factual information alone are not necessarily enough to get us to adopt new routines and behaviors.**

telling you that you really should exercise more because it will help you lose weight and extend your life. Rather than becoming more motivated to exercise, you might think, "I'm exercising as much as I can right now," and then come up with a list of reasons why you are not able to exercise more. It seems that the more people tell us why we need to adopt a new behavior, the more it inspires us to think about why we haven't.

Finally, take a moment to reflect on someone who had a great deal of influence on your life, someone who shaped the decisions you made in life, who inspired you to be the person you became. Often people reflect on a teacher or an important adult in their lives when they were younger. Now take a moment to describe some of the attributes of that person, his or her personality, or ways in which he or she acted that made him or her so influential.

We have conducted this type of exercise many times with large groups of clinicians and consultants and found that the characteristics that people remember, when reflecting on influential others, are fairly universal. Common attributes include being a good listener, supportive, encouraging, persistent, accepting, trusting, honest, and dependable. In addition to these relationship qualities, people often mention that people who inspired them were curious, asked good questions, and believed in their potential.

> **The interpersonal context that you create in your consultation relationships holds the key to whether or not teachers will be motivated to change.**

Now put these personal reflections and qualities together to answer the first question that began this chapter. How much control or influence do you have over teachers' behavior? You are most likely to influence the decisions that teachers make and the actions they take when you adopt the attitudes and behaviors of these influential others. The interpersonal context that you create in your consultation relationships holds the key to whether or not teachers will be motivated to change. The more that you try to educate and convince them why they need to change, the less likely they will. The more you establish a supportive, collaborative relationship marked by reflective listening, encouragement, and trust, the more likely you are to help them to consider and implement change.

What Does the Research Say?

It is comforting when research findings align with personal experiences. Such is the case with research on what motivates people to change. Many studies across consultation topics and clinical areas have shown that people are much more likely to change when the interpersonal climate described above is present.

Some evidence comes from studies that have directly manipulated the components of interest during the course of clinical consultation. In one clever and very compelling study, Patterson and Forgatch (1985) monitored the moment-to-moment interactions between consultants and families during parent consultation meetings. They were particularly interested in determining whether supportive versus direct persuasion statements made by the consultants elicited different responses from the families. They found that teaching (e.g., giving instructions or suggestions, providing rationales) and confrontation responses from the consultant produced immediate increases in family resistance; specifically, these direct persuasion tactics led to a three-fold increase in family-resistant comments within a few seconds. In contrast, supportive comments made by the consultant (e.g., paraphrasing, affirming, agreeing, empathizing) were followed by a decreased likelihood of family resistance statements. In a randomized study, Miller, Benefield, and Tonigan (1993) directly manipulated similar constructs. In one condition, therapists responded to client-resistant statements with direct persuasion (directive-confrontational); in another condition, therapists responded to these statements with empathy (client-centered). The direct persuasion condition produced more resistance from clients, and they had worse outcomes 1 year later. Thus, as our own experience also tells us, trying directly to persuade people to change often has the opposite effect.

Other evidence showing the benefits of a supportive collaborative response style comes from studies that have tested MI, an intervention that incorporates all of these elements. Hundreds of studies across many consultant and clinical topics have shown the benefits of this approach in producing change in others (see Miller & Rollnick, 2002). The rest of this chapter focuses on the key principles of MI as applied in an educational consultation context.

AN OVERVIEW OF MI

MI was developed by Drs. William Miller and Stephen Rollnick. In the 1980s, Miller and Rollnick were working on solving a primary conundrum of clinical work: how to motivate people to change. They collaborated on their first book in 1992. MI received extra attention when the findings from a large federally funded study, Project MATCH, showed that four sessions of MI produced changes in individuals with alcoholism that were comparable to much more time-intensive interventions. MI applications have now been extended to include virtually any area where motivation to change or compliance to a regimen is of interest (e.g., adherence to dietary, exercise, or medical or psychological treatment regimens). One study even showed that MI could be used to motivate an entire African community to adopt new, healthier water purification practices (Thevos, Fred, Kaona, Siajunza, & Quick, 2000).

MI and related approaches are grounded in social psychology research and client-centered counseling principles. The primary goal of MI is to help people resolve their ambivalence about changing desired behaviors. In MI, ambivalence about changing any behavior is seen as normal and adaptive. Change creates disequilibrium and can be uncomfortable and challenging. Rather than viewing teachers as either motivated or unmotivated, this perspective on ambivalence considers motivation to be much more dynamic. When teachers are ambivalent about change, you can think of the reasons for and against change as being roughly equal and balanced in their mind. They generally know the reasons why change might be good for them, and yet the reasons against change are just as compelling. At any given moment, the balance might shift in either direction, making someone more inclined toward or against changing. As a consultant using MI, the goal is to position yourself such that people are more likely to move towards positive practices as they resolve their ambivalence.

As you will see, MI is full of wonderful acronyms to help you remember all the big ideas and strategies of the approach. So that you do not get lost in the acronyms, we want to highlight two fundamental ideas of MI that you should always keep in mind. If you are attentive to these two ideas, you are very likely to be on track in learning and doing MI.

The Spirit of MI

First, effective MI is about establishing and maintaining collaborative relationships. Miller and Rollnick refer to this as the *spirit of MI*. More advanced MI strategies only work if they are delivered in the context of a helping relationship. In other words, resist the temptation to skip ahead to the specific techniques of MI. If you try to use these techniques without attending to the spirit of MI, you will undermine your own work. As it turns out, the more that we as consultants are invested in getting someone to change, the less likely he or she is to do it. Instead, the music behind all of our successful interactions has to be focused on trusting that our consultees will do what they need to do.

Essentially, when we refer to the spirit of MI, we are talking about the microskills of counseling and those qualities of significant others who inspired us. Miller was deeply influenced by the work and teachings of Carl Rogers, who developed client-centered counseling. Rogers summarized effective counseling skills as being composed of three parts: unconditional positive regard, congruence or genuineness, and empathy. If you are able to convey all of these attributes to your consultees, you are well on your way to creating the spirit of MI. We will have more to say about these microskills below, but as you go forward in learning MI skills, remember this: If your consultees come to believe that you genuinely accept and understand them, then you can trust that you have created the setting for them to move in positive directions.

Of course, MI is more than client-centered, nondirective counseling. You may have sensed that there is gentle push that comes with MI, a certain level of directedness and intentionality. What is that push and in what direction do we go in MI?

Change Talk

The answer is the second big idea that you should always keep in mind when you are doing MI. Listen for change talk, and it will be your guide. *Change talk* refers to language that conveys a person's desire, ability, reasons, need, or commitment to make a change. It can be a simple statement of concern about the status quo ("I'm really concerned about my class this year.") or about a personal goal ("I'd really like to become better at ignoring minor distractions."). When teachers list reasons why they want something to be different, this is a type of change talk ("It seems like I don't have any time for instruction this year with all of the students who are off task."). Change talk can also be statements about why the teacher believes he or she can make personal changes in his or her behavior ("I'm really an organized person, so keeping track of a student's behavior sheets won't be a problem for me."). Finally, change talk can come in the form of personal statements about one's intention to change ("I'm definitely going to increase my opportunities to respond in class tomorrow.").

> **Listen for change talk—language that conveys a person's desire, ability, reasons, need, or commitment to make a change.**

More examples of change talk are given below:

- *Desire:* "I wish...." "Something really needs to change." "I'm hoping that...."
- *Ability:* "I can do this." "This is something I do really well, so this won't be a problem."
- *Reasons/benefits of change:* "If I get control of the classroom, I think it will help all of my students to feel good about themselves and their abilities." "If this works, it will give me more time to cover the content."
- *Need/problems with status quo:* "Without some changes, I don't think I can make it through the year." "I go home every day from work just feeling exhausted." "I don't think the students are learning very much this year with all the distractions."
- *Commitment:* "I will try your suggestions." "I'm going to pay attention to my use of praise this week." "The first thing I will do is to post my new rules and teach them to the students tomorrow."

Practice

To test your ability to identify change talk, look at the following. Here, we have listed four statements. Determine whether each statement is an example of change talk and compare your answers to the ones given below the statements.

1. "I'm worried that if I don't get control of this class soon, I'm not going to make it through the year."
2. "It just seems like we're wasting a lot of time this year waiting for students to settle down."
3. "Yeah, I know it's important to have a fast pace, but you know this year I have the low group, and I worry that they won't be able to keep up."
4. "I would like to be better at setting limits with students."

Answers: (1) Yes. This is a reason to change. (2) Yes. Also a reason for changing. (3) It starts with change talk ("I know it's important . . ."), but then switches to sustain talk. (4) Yes. This is an example of goal setting.

A basic tenet of the MI approach is that people are much more likely to do things that they say that they will do versus things that they are told to do. So the role of the consultant is to ask questions that make it more likely that the teacher will talk about change (change talk) rather than spending time telling them what to do. Effective questions that serve this function ask about problems with the status quo ("What makes you concerned about your classroom right now?"), advantages of changing ("How would your life be better if you reduced disruptive classroom behaviors?"), disadvantages of not changing ("If you don't do anything, what might be some bad things that could happen?"), optimism about changing ("What makes you so confident that you can make this

> **People are much more likely to do things that they say they will do versus things that they are told to do.**

happen?"), and intentions to change ("How certain are you that you will follow through on this plan by next week?"). On the other hand, arguing about change and telling teachers the reasons they need to change generally has the opposite effect. A rule of thumb in MI is, if you hear yourself arguing for change, do something different. You want the teacher to make the arguments in favor of change.

Learning to hear change talk is a key skill that will allow you do bring MI to life. It is the metric beyond the spirit of the established consultant–teacher relationship that will tell you whether or not you are doing MI. When you have a consulting meeting full of change talk, keep doing whatever it is you are doing. That is the direction you want your meetings to go.

Why is change talk so important? Again, theory and research align with personal experience. People are more likely to believe and ultimately do what *they* say. One rationale to explain this phenomenon comes from a theory of self-perception proposed by Dr. Sandra Bem. She found evidence to support her contention that our attitudes and beliefs are directly influenced by what we do and say. When we are uncertain (ambivalent) about our attitudes, making arguments in favor of either side directly influences our beliefs. Research has shown that when people are ambivalent about changing (most of us are!), saying out loud why we think change would be good for us leads us to believe, in fact, that it is.

A series of studies by Amrhein, Miller, Yahne, Palmer, and Fucher (2003, 2004) supports these ideas in counseling sessions. These researchers were interested in studying the type and timing of change talk that occurred during counseling sessions. They carefully coded all the language in clinical sessions and then compared these language codes to actual changes in client behavior over time. They found that the level and timing of change talk during counseling meetings was in fact an important predictor of actual client behavior. When the amount of change talk increased over the course of meetings and/or if it was especially pronounced at the end of meetings, clients were likely to have better outcomes. However, their findings were more nuanced. Although all change talk is important and can move clients toward health (and at least can be a good barometer of the direction of our MI meetings), a particular type of change talk was especially important. They

> **If you hear yourself arguing for change, do something different. You want the teacher to make the arguments in favor of change.**

found that commitment language, especially during the last 5 minutes of a meeting, were most predictive of client change. So if clients were saying things like "I'm going to this ...," "I guarantee that I will ...," "I'm certain that I can ...," or "I intend to ...," they were very likely to be successful in moving forward. To have the greatest impact on helping people decide to change, it is especially important to elicit this type of language toward the end of our meetings with them. We can capitalize on this effect, by placing key questions that elicit this type of language at the end of our meetings (e.g., "How certain are you that you can follow through with this plan?").

THE RULEs OF MI

Consultants are most likely to help others resolve their ambivalence about change by resisting the righting reflex (i.e., by avoiding directly telling consultees what needs to be done), by understanding consultees' motivations, by listening, and by empowering them. These guiding principles are summarized by the acronym *RULE* (Rollnick, Miller, & Butler, 2008).

The phrase *resisting the righting reflex* refers to the need to resist the human tendency to help set people on the right course toward health and healing or self-improvement. When you see other professionals engaging in what you perceive to be poor practice, your human inclination is to tell them why they should engage in better practices. The problem with this inclination is that humans have a natural tendency to avoid persuasion. We do not like to be told what to do. In fact, we have a reflexive tendency to activate the other side of an argument when we hear an opposing view expressed. In other words, when we hear reasons why we should change, our minds automatically contemplate the reasons against such a change. In this view, when consultants tell teachers why they should adopt new classroom practices, consultants are most likely to activate all the reasons why they should *not* do so in teachers' minds.

By avoiding the righting reflex, consultants are more likely to position themselves in way that activates reasons for changing within the teacher. Essentially, they do this by asking questions or making statements that elicit change talk from the teacher. As we previously described, people are much more likely to do things that they say themselves, rather than what they are told. One of the outcomes of avoiding the righting reflex is that it allows the teacher to say out loud the reasons he or she wants to change. In turn, the teacher is more likely to tilt the balance of ambivalence in favor of changing.

> **Humans have a natural tendency to avoid persuasion. When we hear reasons why we should change, our minds automatically contemplate the reasons against change.**

Understanding a teacher's motivation for change runs parallel to avoiding the righting reflex. By getting out of the way and not arguing for others' change, the consultant is in a better position to hear and understand the reasons for change that a teacher finds most compelling. You can probably think of many reasons why a teacher should increase his or her praise rate in the classroom, but you cannot know the one reason that will compel a teacher to increase his or praise rate without asking and listening. Our most compelling reasons for tilting the balance of ambivalence in favor of changing, for changing behaviors, are generally tied to our core values. Thus, part of understanding others' motivations is learning to hear and engage them in the things they find most important in their work and in their lives. Although this may sound complicated and difficult to do, people give hints about their values through their everyday behaviors and conversations. We can also ask brief questions that give us insights into their values. Most important, we have to listen and pay attention to the "value signals" others send us. Once we are aware of teachers' values, we are better able to understand what drives them to change or stay the same.

In turn, *listening* is a central task for an effective consultant. A rule of thumb in classic MI in therapeutic settings is that the client should be making 9 of every 10 statements made—which leaves little room for clinician speech! Of course, we all think we are good listeners. Most of us have taken some basic coursework in effective listening skills and genuinely believe in the value of listening in all of our relationships. Unfortunately, very few of us are consistently good listeners. In fact, sometimes our past training as listeners interferes with our ability to be effective listeners. That is, thinking that we are already good listeners can encourage us to rush past this core component of MI. Unfortunately, there seems to be a negative relationship between amount of time spent as a consultant and listening skills; that is, the more experience and confidence we get as consultants in recognizing key aspects of classrooms that need to change, the more likely we are to rush past the listening part of our role and get to the good stuff (telling people what needs to change). As the MI literature makes abundantly clear, though, you cannot get to the good stuff without listening. People will not listen to you if you are not listening to them.

The other challenge with listening is that it is deceptively simple. Good and effective listening requires practice, focus, and patience. It is not a skill you master and then never lose. It requires persistent reflection and feedback to maintain skills as an effective listener.

The final rule of MI is to *empower* your consultee. As tempting as it is for us to take credit for all the changes that occur in classrooms and schools where we consult, it is unwise to do so. Our task is to bring teachers' own resources to bear in solving problems, to get them to see their strengths and skills, to show them what they are

> **You cannot get to the good stuff without listening. People will not listen to you if you are not listening to them.**

capable of, and to make them aware of how they make changes happen themselves. Our goal should be to put ourselves out of business so that our consultees no longer need us and instead can see and believe in their own resources to create change.

SPECIFIC STRATEGIES

Use Your OARS

Consultants are most likely to embody the MI spirit and principles when they use four basic responses summarized as OARS: <u>o</u>pen-ended questions ("What are some of your concerns?"), <u>a</u>ffirmations ("I can really see how hard you are working on this."), <u>r</u>eflective listening ("That really makes you angry when your friend says that about you."), and <u>s</u>ummarizing ("The three things I'm hearing that you really want to change about this situation are.... "). Table 4.1 provides a definition and examples of each element of OARS.

Open-ended questions are simply questions that require elaboration and more than a single word response (like yes or no). As you will see, open-ended questions are a primary tool for eliciting change talk. One strategy we use is that whenever we have an urge to tell someone what to do or share information with them, we stop and try to reframe our thought

TABLE 4.1. Examples of OARS

Open-ended questions (can't be answered in a single word):
"What are your concerns about … ?"
"Why do you want to make these changes?"
"How have you handled these problems in the past?"

Affirmations (specific and genuine):
"You're really putting a lot of thought and time into this."
"I see how hard you are working."
"You did an amazing job with praise this week."

Reflective statements (strategy of paraphrasing comments while giving special attention to the implied feelings):
"You're really frustrated by how things are going."
"You're having fun in your class."
"You just really want the best for these kids."

Summaries (two or three sentences to draw connections):
"Let me make sure I'm understanding all of the big ideas so far. You're feeling pretty worn out from all the chaos in your classroom this year and taking on new classroom strategies just seems like another burden right now. At the same time, part of you is hopeful that spending time on it now could eventually give you more time."

as a question that may elicit that answer. We ask ourselves what questions can we pose to make the person say what we are thinking. So as a consultant, if I find myself wanting to tell a teacher about all the reasons that praise can be helpful in improving student behavior and classroom climate, I stop myself and try to rephrase this thought as a question. Instead, I might ask the teacher, "What are some good things that can come from praising your students?" If the teacher veers away from identifying positive attributes of praise, I can narrow the focus of my question by asking targeted questions, such as "What might students learn by hearing you praise them (or other students)?"; "What type of atmosphere does praising students create in your classroom?"; "How do you think a student feels after you genuinely praise him or her?"; or "How do you feel after genuinely praising a student?" Essentially, these types of questions form the foundation of the Socratic method, whereby you gradually elicit insights from teachers through evocative and guided questioning.

Affirmations are verbal or nonverbal behaviors that convey acceptance, support, and encouragement for your consultee. Simple head nods, saying "yes," or giving more elaborate praise statements all fall in this realm. A requirement for effective affirmations is that they be genuine and sincere, so only affirm what you genuinely believe to be true. Otherwise, you will lose trust and credibility. It is also helpful to provide specific examples rather than global praise statements (e.g., "Good job.") because focused praise helps to prompt and reinforce that specific behavior and also because specific examples are more likely to be perceived as sincere.

Reflective listening refers to the classic counseling strategy of paraphrasing comments made by your consultee while giving special attention to the feelings implied by his or her statements or behaviors. Reflections can vary in their depth from a straight paraphrase of what was said to a guess about underlying feelings. These are best given as statements rather than as questions.

Summaries are two- to three-sentence responses that try to link together a series of ideas that were expressed during earlier parts of a conversation. Summaries can serve multiple functions. They show that you are listening and understanding a teacher's perspective. They allow you to reach agreement on what has been said to be sure that you understand the key points of a topic. You can also use summaries to highlight an ongoing theme that you have heard during a conversation. In this way, effective summaries can help teachers gain new insights into their own internal dialogues by revealing to them patterns of their thinking that they might not have fully considered before. Summaries can also serve as effective transitions to end one topic (e.g., discussing things they like about teaching) and begin a new one (e.g., discussing things they find challenging about teaching).

Practice

Try taping a segment of an upcoming consultation meeting. Teachers are often receptive to this if you tell them it is for your benefit and that no one else will listen. Alternately, you can try to tape a role play with a colleague or friend where you ask him or her to portray a teacher who is ambivalent about changing a classroom practice. Listen to the tape for your characteristic response. Do you ask open-ended questions? Are they evocative (i.e., do your questions generate lengthy responses from the teacher)? How many affirmations do you give? Are they genuine? Do you reflect any feelings? Do you do so in the form of a statement rather than a question? What percentage of time do you spend talking versus listening? Do you give any summaries? Are they brief, easy to understand, and helpful?

Take a moment to reflect on which of these response styles is most challenging for you. Some people struggle with open-ended questions or at least in asking them in an open-ended, evocative manner. Others are good at asking lots of questions to the neglect of reflective listening. Many people struggle with affirmations—that is, with giving them regularly in a way that is perceived as genuine. Others find it difficult to give concise and meaningful summaries. All of these skills take practice and ongoing reflection to perfect.

ELICITING CHANGE TALK

As you work to establish the MI spirit in your consultation relationships, the next step is to actively listen for and elicit change talk. There are many strategies for accomplishing this goal. We describe the most common ones below.

Evocative Responses

The easiest way to elicit change talk is to ask evocative questions. Evocative questions are open-ended and ask teachers to reflect on any aspect of the various types of change talk (desire, ability, reasons/benefits of changing, need/problems with status quo, or commitment). Some examples include "What makes you so confident that you can make this change [ability]?"; "What are some reasons you want to make this change [reasons]?"; and "What concerns you about the way things are going now [problems]?" The following section provides more examples of evocative questions that can be used in educational consultation. The answer to any one of these questions will be change talk. Try it out. Answer the questions yourself or ask them of a colleague and listen to the answers for change talk.

Evocative Questions That Evoke Change Talk

Desire for Change
- "What are your thoughts about how things are going in your classroom/with your teaching/with a particular student?"
- "How do you feel about [specific teaching behavior]? How much does that concern you?"
- "Tell me about things you want to be different."
- "What do you think will happen if you don't make a change?"

Ability/Optimism about Change
- "What makes you think that if you decide to make a change that you could do it?"
- "What encourages you to feel like you can change if you want to?"
- "What do you think would work for you, if you decided to change?"
- "What would make you feel even more confident that you could make a change?"
- "When else in your life have you made a big change like this? How did you do it?"
- "What personal strengths do you have that will help you succeed?"

Reasons/Benefits of Change
- "How would you like things to be different?"
- "What would be some good things about improving [specific teaching behavior]?"
- "What would you like your teaching to be like in 5 years?"
- "If you could make this change immediately, by magic, how would things be different?"
- "What would be the advantages of making this change?"

Need/Disadvantage of Status Quo/Problem Recognition
- "What makes you think that you may need to make a change?"
- "What things make you think that [specific teaching behavior] is a problem?"

- "What difficulties have you had in relation to [specific teaching behavior]?"
- "In what ways do you think you or other people have been harmed by this problem?"
- "In what ways has this been a problem for you?"
- "What makes you feel like you should do something different?"
- " What is there about [specific teaching behavior] that you or other people might see as reasons for concern?"
- "What worries you about [specific teaching behavior]?"
- "What can you imagine happening to you as a result of [specific teaching behavior]?"
- "In what ways does this concern you?"
- "What do you think will happen if you don't make a change?"

Commitment/Intention to Change

- "If you could easily make any changes, what would be different?"
- "Where are you in terms of changing your behavior at this point?"
- "I can see that you're feeling stuck at the moment. What's going to have to change?"
- "Never mind the 'how' for right now, what do you want to have happen?"
- "How important is this to you? How much do you want to do this?"
- "What would you be willing to try?"
- "What do you intend to do?"

Other evocative questions or statements that can be helpful include ones that ask about the future, the past, or extremes:

- *Looking forward or back.* Ask about a time in the past when things were different or direct the teacher forward to a time in the future when things would be better (e.g., "What will happen if things continue as they are? How would you like your classroom to be this time next year?"). Ask the "miracle question" (e.g., "If you could be 100% successful at doing this, what would be different?").
- *Querying extremes.* "What are the worst things that might happen if you don't make this change?" "What are the best things that might happen if you do?"
- *Connecting responses to values.* "This is really hard because of how much you really want to have a positive influence on these kids."

Practice

Prior to your next consultation session, memorize one or two of the evocative questions described in this section, try to ask it during your meeting, and listen for the response. If you hear change talk, you have already started doing MI!

Change Rulers

Change rulers can help make teachers' change talk more explicit and concrete by asking them to rate the importance of, and their confidence in, changing. Sample dialogue and forms are depicted in Figure 4.1. These questions can be asked at any time during a meeting, and forms are not necessary.

The basic stem of the question for the importance ruler is, "On a scale from 1 to 10, how important is it for you to [change the targeted behavior]?" After the teacher provides a number, you provide a brief summary (e.g., "An 8. Wow, so this is very important to you." Or "Okay, a 3. So, it is somewhat important."). The key to eliciting change talk comes from the follow-up question, "Why are you at __ and not a zero [or one number lower than the given number]?" The answer to this question is always change talk, usually in the form of reasons why the person wants to change.

After processing and reflecting on all the reasons the person selected the rating, it can be helpful to ask another follow-up question: "What would it take for you to go from a __ to a 10 [or to one number higher than their given number]?" The answer here can give you insights into a person's values and help you and the person develop a map for actualizing the change or for overcoming barriers to changing.

Next, it is important to gauge the person's degree of confidence that he or she can actually make the desired change happen. Recall that importance alone is not enough for someone to change. The person also needs to believe that he or she can do it. For the confidence ruler, the focus is on assessing and building self-efficacy. Following the same dialogue as you used with the importance ruler, you can ask, "On the same scale, then, how confident

---

Importance Ruler

How important would you say it is for you to _____ ? On a scale from 0 to 10, where 0 is not at all important and 10 is extremely important, where would you say you are?

| 0 | 2 | 4 | 6 | 8 | 10 |

Not at all important   Extremely important

Why are you at a _____ and not zero?

What would it take for you to go from _____ to [a higher number]?

Confidence Ruler

How confident would you say you are, that if you decided to _____ , you could do it? On the same scale from 0 to 10, where would you say you are?

| 0 | 2 | 4 | 6 | 8 | 10 |

Not at all confident   Extremely confident

Why are you at a _____ and not zero?

What would it take for you to go from _____ to [a higher number]?

FIGURE 4.1. Change rulers.

are you that you can do this?" As before, the summary and follow-up are key: "Great. A 6. So you're pretty confident. Why would you say a 6 and not a 5 [or a zero]?" The answer to this question will always be change talk, usually in the form of ability statements (e.g., "Well, because I've done this before and just need reminders"; "Because when I set my mind to do something, I can make it happen.").

These are to the two classic change ruler questions, but you can certainly use them to ask about other domains of change talk with similar effect. For instance, you can use commitment rulers ("On a scale from 1 to 10, how committed are you to making this happen?") and ask the same follow-up questions.

Timing

You can use these questions any time during a meeting that the teacher expresses interest in making a change. A particularly important time to use the rulers may be during the final minutes of a meeting. As noted earlier, research suggests that change talk toward the end of a meeting is the strongest predictor of client change. The CCU attempts to capitalize on this by placing ruler questions at the end of the meeting.

Caution!

A common rookie mistake with the follow-up question to the self-ratings is to ask why the person did not rate him- or herself one number higher. Take a moment to think about what type of response would be elicited if you mistakenly ask this type of question. For instance, "So a 7. That's important. Why *are you not* at an 8 or 9?" The answer to questions about why importance or confidence ratings are not even higher is the negative side of the ambivalence equation: resistance. For instance, you might hear a teacher respond, "Well, yes, it is important, but there are other more pressing matters right now," or "I have so many other things on my plate right now." Note how this *not* question is different from asking "What *would it take* for you to go from a __ to [one number higher]?"—which instead allows the teacher to discuss his or her values and strategies for overcoming barriers. So be cautious and be sure to ask the follow-up questions in these ways that are shown to bring about change talk. Of course, this process is somewhat self-correcting. If you find yourself using change rulers and hearing resistance statements instead of change talk, that will be a sign you may be falling into this trap.

Other Traps/Common Questions

When people first learn to use change rulers, they commonly ask, "What if someone answers '*Zero*'?" It is very unusual for an adult to give a rating of zero or even 1, especially after you have established a relationship with him or her. It is more common to hear such responses when working with teens. A response to a sarcastic teen that is usually effective is to exaggerate: "A *zero*. Oh, I was sure you were going to say negative *10*." This is usually enough to get a laugh and shift the teen out of that mode, if only for a moment. Another possible response to a very low number is to give an amplified reflection (described later), "So there is nothing in the world less important to you right now than making this change." On the other hand, the purpose of the rulers is not simply to move the teacher forward with change talk but also to assess where he or she is at in the change process. Thus, you may simply treat a very low number response as a sign that you need to revisit the selected target goal, given that the teacher is reporting that it is not very important.

In Action: Change Ruler Discussion

Below is a sample dialogue from a consultation session using change rulers.

CONSULTANT: So you've decided to focus on increasing your opportunities to respond during the coming weeks. Currently, your OTRs are at one to two per minute, and you would like to raise that to four to six per minute. Do I have that right?

TEACHER: Yes.

CONSULTANT: Great. Let me ask a few more questions to help finalize our plans. First, how important is this to you? On a scale from 0 (*not important at all*) to 10 (*the most important thing right now*), how important is it for you to do?

TEACHER: Hmm … I would say a 7.

CONSULTANT: (*Circles 7 on the change ruler form.*) Wow, 7, that's pretty high. So why would you say you are 7 and not a 6?

TEACHER: Well, like we've been talking about it, I think it will help me to keep students on task and lower some of the problems I've been having with talk-outs and disruptions. [Change Talk: Reasons]

CONSULTANT: So it will help make progress on those big goals that you have. [Reflection]

TEACHER: Right.

CONSULTANT: And how do you think OTRs will help with keeping kids on task? [Evocative Question]

TEACHER: Well, it's just the pacing. If things are going too slowly, students will get bored, but if I can keep it fast-paced and keep them all accountable, they will be less likely to drift. [Change Talk: Reasons]

CONSULTANT: That makes good sense to me [Affirmation]. I think that's a great place to start, especially given how well you are doing in other areas of the class, like your high praise rate and your great atmosphere [Affirmation]. Can you see anything that could make this become even more important, say, an 8 or 9?

TEACHER: Well, yes, if my class started getting even more chaotic. Right now, I don't like all the talk-outs, and that's why I want to do this [Change Talk: Need], but if it got even worse …

CONSULTANT: More talk-outs …

TEACHER: … I would ask you to visit my class every day!

CONSULTANT: It would become so uncomfortable you would do anything to get control of it. [Reflection]

TEACHER: Yes. But that's why we're putting so much effort into it right now. [Change Talk: Reasons]

CONSULTANT: Okay. One more important question. How confident are you that you can do this, using the same scale from 0, not confident at all, to 10, completely confident?

TEACHER: You know, I'd actually say I'm at an 8 on that.

CONSULTANT: Wow. So you are really sure you can do this.

TEACHER: Yeah.

CONSULTANT: So why an 8 and not a 5 or 6?

TEACHER: It just seems very doable [Change Talk: Ability]. All the tricks and ideas that you gave me make it easier. And the funny thing is that I know I was using more OTRs when I first started teaching. It's just a matter of getting back into that groove.

CONSULTANT: So this feels familiar. You've done it before, so this should be a breeze.

TEACHER: Well, I don't know about a breeze, but it's very doable.

CONSULTANT: And you have a lot of tools that will help.

TEACHER: That's right.

CONSULTANT: So how did you settle on four to six per minute? Is that too big a step? Maybe we should take it slower. [Coming Alongside; see below]

TEACHER: I can definitely do four to six per minute. I just need to think about it and be planful. [Change Talk: Ability]

Practice

Ask a friend/spouse to tell you about a behavior that he or she has considered changing (common topics include increasing exercise, changing diet, reducing caffeine, procrastinating). Ask the person to tell you the problem that he or she is changing. Then ask the change ruler questions. Listen for the person's responses. Reflect what you hear and then offer a summary statement at the end. Reflect on how this interaction made you feel and ask your friend/spouse the same question.

The "What Next?" Question

A finishing touch after eliciting a series of change comments is to ask what Rollnick et al. (2008) refer to as the *key question*. Essentially, you need to ask "What next?": "Now that we have all of this information on the table about why you want or need to change, what are you going to do?" The question is designed to elicit commitment or intention language and possibly to shift the person into creating a plan for change to occur. Some alternate forms of this question include the following:

> "What do you think you will do now?"
> "How are you making sense of all this?"
> "What are you going to do?"
> "So tell me the plan from here."

RESPONDING TO CHANGE TALK

Now that you are hearing change talk, what do you do with it? Fortunately, you already have the tools for responding to change talk. Rely on your OARS as your guide. When you hear change talk, your goal is to keep it going, to elicit more. You can do this by simply reflecting what you heard ("So you really want this to happen"; "This is very important to you."). By reflecting change talk, you give the person an opportunity to hear his or her own motivations again. You also invite the person to continue talking about it. After you have listened to a series of change statements, it can be helpful to summarize what you heard statements ("So what I'm hearing is that you have many reasons for wanting to improve the climate in your classroom. First, ... "). You could also respond to change talk by affirming it ("You've really put a lot of thought into why it makes sense now to work on expectations."). One other option is to invite the person to elaborate on the change statements. You can do this through statements ("Tell me more about that.") or probing questions ("What is it about talk-outs that is so disruptive for you?").

RESPONDING TO RESISTANCE

Guiding Principles

Before we describe specific strategies for responding to resistance, it is important to keep in mind some overarching principles that you can use in guiding any response to resistant comments. As always, be mindful of the righting reflex. Our gut response, when we listen to teachers tell us why they cannot or will not change, is to tell them why they *do* need to change. By now, you are well aware that this is not typically a helpful response. You have already mastered the first step: Stop yourself from responding reflexively to resistance. Pausing, waiting, and reflecting are ways to catch the righting reflex and give yourself space to move forward. Below are thoughts we find helpful in considering next steps.

Finding the Gem: Listening for Strengths, Values, and Good Intentions

A key assumption of MI is that everyone has internal treasures that we can draw out and highlight. Noted scholar and parent and teacher trainer, Carolyn Webster Stratton, has referred to this consultant skill as "finding the gem." Often,

> **Your job as a consultant is to always search for gems within others, and when you find them, to bring them to the fore of the conversation.**

people lose sight of their own strengths or become disconnected from them, especially in times of stress or challenge. Your job as a consultant is to always be searching for these gems within others, and when you find them, to bring them to the fore of the conversation. A perfect time to do this is when a person is stuck in resistance.

Sometimes the treasure is contained within a resistant statement. In this case, we simply have to listen for it, hear that part of the statement, and reflect it back to the teacher.

> TEACHER: I have tried all of these strategies that we've been discussing—building strong relationships, praising, proactive teaching. I've used them all year and with Alex, it just doesn't work.
>
> CONSULTANT: You've been really committed to making a difference for this boy, and you really wish you had seen more progress. I admire your persistence. And what a gift you have given him this year. I bet he has had few other people in his life stick with him like that. That's something that stays with children much longer than we know or see in the short term.

Other times the treasure is buried beneath the concerns or the negative talk. Here we need to ask other questions or reflect back on prior conversations what we know about the teacher's beliefs and values.

> TEACHER: We can't use incentives in our building. We use a curriculum that doesn't allow it.
>
> CONSULTANT: So what strategies do you use to encourage students in your classroom?
>
> TEACHER: Well, I write personal notes on their work.
>
> CONSULTANT: And why is that important for you to do?
>
> TEACHER: I want them to know that I notice their good work.
>
> CONSULTANT: How do you suppose that is helpful?
>
> TEACHER: They need feedback. And I don't want my class to be boring.
>
> CONSULTANT: So it is really important to you to keep students invested in learning and have fun doing it.

In either case, your task is to remain optimistic and diligent about uncovering a teacher's underlying good intentions. It is easy to get distracted by the immediate challenges of a classroom full of students and the negativity it can evoke in a teacher. Behind these frustrations, though, are the teacher's guiding values, hopes, and dreams that we need to call forth and activate. Asking good questions and listening with a "third ear" for what is truly being said, makes it more likely that you will tune into these aspirations and hear them over the noise of a crisis. When you hear these gems, reflect them and hold on to them to use in the future. An example of a consultant's statement connecting to a past gem might be the following:

> "I know how important it is to you to let your students know that you believe in them and won't give up on them, so these frustrations with this student must be especially challenging for you."

Reframe from the Child's Perspective

Another principle to help guide your response to resistance is to always keep the child's perspective near the surface of the conversation. When immersed in conflict with a student or a class, it is easy for a teacher to lose sight of what students might be thinking or learning from social interactions. Simply asking questions like "What do you think the student(s) are learning when you say (do) that … ?" or "What do you want students to learn from .. " can help teachers reconnect with their values and any discrepancies that may exist with their actions.

TEACHER: I hate to say it, but I think the only thing that gets through to Johnny is when I raise my voice and get angry with him.

CONSULTANT: You can get his attention by getting angry, but it's hard to admit because that is not how you like to be with children.

TEACHER: Yeah, I don't know. It definitely gets his attention.

CONSULTANT: So it brings him back. What do you imagine he is thinking when you do finally get his attention?

TEACHER: Hmm. Probably "Mrs. P is really pissed at me again."

CONSULTANT: Like, I really screwed up again.

TEACHER: Hmm.

CONSULTANT: What are you thinking?

TEACHER: That's probably not good.

CONSULTANT: How do you mean?

TEACHER: I mean, I don't want him to feel like a screwup, I just want him to listen.

CONSULTANT: So if there was a way to help him listen without feeling bad, you would like that better.

Another alternative path this consultant could have taken would have to been to ask the teacher to consider the perspective of other students as they watched her interactions with the target student. For instance, the consultant might have asked, "What do you think the other students are learning when they watch this?", and then followed this dialogue in a similar manner as above.

Specific Strategies for Responding to Resistance

The specific strategies for responding to resistance statements build off these basic principles (resisting the righting reflex, finding the gem, and reframing from the child's perspective). In all, Miller and Rollnick (2002) identified eight strategies for responding to resistance. Most of the responses are variations of reflective listening and build in complexity off this core microskill. Thus, the more advanced options described below (amplified reflections, coming alongside, agreement with a twist) require comfort with reflective listening and are skills to grow into as you learn MI. You may find that one or more of the options described below fit your style better than the others. It is a good idea to experiment with using one or more of the more complex or unfamiliar skills below over time as you build off the more basic or comfortable responses.

Reflective Listening

As Miller and Rollnick (2002) noted, "A good general principle is to respond to resistance with non-resistance" (p. 100). When in doubt, use a simple reflection to acknowledge the teacher's perspective or feeling. This brief acknowledgment invites further exploration, saps the energy of resistance, and avoids the trap of taking sides.

> TEACHER: I don't get why we have to do this. This is just another curriculum that will be thrown aside in a couple years.
>
> CONSULTANT: It's frustrating to put a lot of effort into doing this if people aren't going to stick with it.

Double-Sided Reflections

Double-sided reflections are excellent ways to respond to ambivalence. These responses usually take the form "On the one hand …, on the other hand, … " Double-sided reflections allow you to include a summary of both sides of the ambivalence in a single response. Note that a preceding teacher statement does not necessarily need to include both sides of the ambivalence. That is, you may be reflecting the immediate response and drawing on prior teacher responses to put together these double-sided reflections.

TEACHER: This intervention is just not going to work.

CONSULTANT: I can see your predicament. On the one hand, you're not sure how our work together can help, but on the other hand, you're really worried about how things are going in your class [prior content].

When reflecting both sides of the teacher's ambivalence, it is helpful to end with the reflection *in favor of change*, as in the example above. This encourages the teacher to elaborate on the change talk (why he or she is worried about the classroom) instead of the resistance (why the program won't work).

Amplified Reflections

Miller and Rollnick (2002) described amplified reflections as exaggerated reflections. The intention behind this type of response is to amplify a resistant statement to see how committed the speaker is to it, and hopefully, to elicit change talk as an alternative. To be effective, these comments must be delivered in a matter-of-fact manner *without any hint of sarcasm*. For instance:

TEACHER: Those studies about effective classroom management really don't prove anything.

CONSULTANT: You really don't believe research findings can be helpful to you at all.

The intent here is to highlight the extreme position implied by the teacher's statements. Regardless of the teacher's response, you will have learned something about how to proceed. Typically, the next response will soften the implied position (e.g., "Well, no—I'm interested in what some research has to say about best practices.") and add more clarification and specificity about the concerns behind the more global statement (e.g., "I just think it is more complicated when you try to put these practices in place in real classrooms."). These elaborations may give you some leverage for eliciting more change talk (e.g., "So what you believe in are research-based practices that actually work in your classroom.").

Coming Alongside (Siding with the Negative)

Miller and Rollnick (2002) found it useful to highlight a special instance of amplified reflection that they labeled *coming alongside*. This is amplified reflection in which the consultant makes a reflective statement that takes the side *against* change. Although it sounds like reverse psychology, the key is that these statements are not delivered to intentionally manipulate but instead as genuine statements that acknowledge a client's implied commitment to sustaining his or her current practices or behavior (good and deep reflective listening). The rationale is that by arguing against change through these reflective comments, the consultant creates the possibility that the teacher will respond by arguing for change. This tool should be used cautiously, especially as you are learning the method. As always, your best guide as to its efficacy is whether or not it produces change talk.

TEACHER: I don't think these strategies are going to work.

CONSULTANT: It's seems pretty hopeless, like why even try if there's a possibility it's not going to work.

Or

TEACHER: I'm going to give it a try this week and play the game every day.

CONSULTANT: (*smiling*) Hey, slow down. Are you sure you're ready to do this?

Reframing

This classic counseling strategy offers a new, more positive interpretation on a statement made by the teacher. As with all the strategies discussed so far, reframes are also a special instance of good reflective listening. From an MI perspective, these comments can be particularly impactful because they shift the flow of the conversation and thought processes away from the negative (nonchange talk) to a more positive and optimistic direction.

TEACHER: I've tried so many strategies, but none of them seem to help.

CONSULTANT: You're very persistent in trying new things that can help even when you're not seeing a lot of progress.

Agreeing with a Twist

Miller and Rollnick (2002) described *agreement with a twist* as a simple reflection with a reframe. The intent is to acknowledge the teacher's position with a slightly differently spin or direction.

TEACHER: I know how to teach these kids. No one can tell me what to do with them.

CONSULTANT: You know a lot about what works here, and really it's completely up to you want happens in your classroom. If this is going to work, you need to be the key player in this process.

Shifting Focus

Rather than pushing forward through resistance (as it often invites us to do), a better tact is to acknowledge it and then shift attention to a new direction.

TEACHER: You're probably going to be mad at me for not teaching expectations this week.

CONSULTANT: That's really not why I'm here. What do you think would be helpful for us to discuss this week?

Emphasizing Personal Choice

It's common for people to become resistant when they feel that their choices are limited or threatened. When consulting to help teachers adopt specific practices, this response is even more likely. When you sense that a teacher is threatened in this way, the best response is to simply state the obvious; ultimately, it is the teacher's decision about what to do.

> TEACHER: My principal is making me do this. She really didn't give us any choice.
>
> CONSULTANT: It seems like you have no choice here, which is frustrating. When it gets down to it, though, what you do in your classroom and how you do it is really up to you. I can't force you to meet with me. It's your decision about how we spend our time together.

Decisional Balance

A great activity for getting unstuck from one-sided thinking that uses many of these strategies described above is to use a decisional balance diagram (see Figure 4.2 for a completed example and Appendix A for a blank form). In filling out this form the person is asked to consider the pros and cons of a given behavior and/or the pros and cons of adopting a new behavior.

With teachers there are several common areas of ambivalence that consultants can anticipate as potential roadblocks to progress. For instance, because of poor training or misinformation, many educators have had bad experiences with using a time-out procedure, so they may enter consultation with a strong bias against using or trying it. Another common area of disagreement for some teachers arises around discussions related to the use of praise or incentive systems in the classroom; some standardized teaching curricula and training programs discourage teachers from using praise. For topics like these, consultants can ask teachers to consider the benefits and barriers to using these practices. It is helpful to write down their comments using a form like the one depicted Figure 4.2.

For instance, a consultant could ask, "What are some benefits to using incentives in the classroom?" The consultant then uses reflective listening and open-ended questions to draw out and pinpoint specific benefits as perceived by the teacher. As always, the consultant uses their OARS to facilitate these discussions and summarizes as needed. Next, the consultant asks "What are some barriers to using incentives in your classroom?" Aside from making this internal dialogue explicit and creating an opportunity for further exploration, this exercise commonly results in an important insight. Quite often the perceived benefits of these practices are student-centered (e.g., engenders more motivation, let's them know when they are doing well, gives them goals and targets), whereas the barriers tend to be teacher-centered (e.g., takes too much time, cumbersome, expensive). When this pattern emerges, a helpful follow-up question after writing down both sides of the debate is, "Who gets most of these benefits?" and "Who has most of the barriers?"

You can continue the decisional balance exercise by asking the teacher to consider the perceived benefits and barriers of the opposite behavior (e.g., not praising). Again,

Decisional Balance

Current Practice: _Sending to Office_

Benefits	Barriers
Good things about _sending kids to office:_	Bad things about _sending kids to office:_
It's easy.	It can become a standoff/showdown.
I don't have to think.	Seems like too big a consequence for some smaller crimes.
Gets them out of the room.	Hard to know how long to leave them out.
Less distracting.	They miss instruction.
	Sometimes they might enjoy it.

New Practice: _Time Out_

If you were to try it, what might be some benefits:	If you were to try it, what might be some challenges:
Students learn the classroom rules—respect each other.	Hard to know when to use.
Students learn to take time to think about misbehavior/calm down.	I feel powerless and uncomfortable when they won't go to chair.
Students learn that classroom is predictable—if they break a rule, there are consequences.	Other students see me struggle and will challenge me too.
Makes classroom safe.	Doesn't seem to work.
	A lot of work to remember when time is up, monitoring them.

FIGURE 4.2. Completed example of a decisional balance form.

the benefits of the status quo often favor the teacher, and the barriers or cons favor the children.

In Action: Decisional Balance

Below is a sample dialogue using a decision balance around the topic of time out.

TEACHER: I don't think time out really works. I've tried it many times, and I think kids just use it as a way to get out of classtime.

CONSULTANT: Sounds like you've had some bad experiences with time out. You've expressed some concerns about trying time out in your classroom. On the other hand, you really want to learn a strategy for dealing with kids who are aggressive. [Double-Sided Reflection]

TEACHER: Right. I'm kind of stuck.

CONSULTANT: Just so I have a better sense of your thoughts and experiences with time out, let me ask a few questions. (*Brings out decisional balance form.*) What are some of the barriers you found with using time out?

TEACHER: I just found it to be a pain. I had trouble figuring out what behaviors should be given a time out.

CONSULTANT: (*Writes these down using the words of the teacher.*) So it was hard to know when to use. [Simple Reflection]

TEACHER: Right. And the thing I hated was when kids wouldn't go to the chair. It just felt like it became this big power struggle with all the other kids watching. I hated that feeling.

CONSULTANT: So another barrier is that uncomfortable feeling, sort of powerless, when kids don't comply. [Simple Reflection]

TEACHER: Exactly. And I worried about what other kids were learning to challenge me by watching.

CONSULTANT: It seemed like it could backfire and affect your relationship with the entire class [Simple Reflection]. What else?

TEACHER: Hmm. Well, like I said. It didn't seem to work. The kids who I was using it with still were doing the same things that they got sent to time out for.

CONSULTANT: You weren't getting any benefit out it [Simple Reflection]. You mentioned before that it required a lot of work. Can you tell me more about that?

TEACHER: It just required a lot of thought and energy. Deciding when to use it, fighting to get them to do it, remembering when their time was up. You know, just a lot of mental energy. Plus it was distracting to try to continue the lesson while monitoring the kid in time out.

CONSULTANT: Okay. Let's switch to the other side for a minute [Shifting Focus]. Can you think of any potential benefits to time out?

TEACHER: Hmm. Not really. I mean, if it worked that would be great. But I just didn't see it.

CONSULTANT: Well, let me ask you this. What were you hoping to teach students when you used time out? [Evocative Question]

TEACHER: That whatever the bad behavior was, it wasn't okay.

CONSULTANT: What else? What did you hope students were learning by sitting in the back of the room?

TEACHER: I guess I wanted them to learn the rules of the classroom. That we respect each other and that if you don't respect your classmates, you have to take time to think about it.

CONSULTANT: Those sound like great things to be teaching your students [Affirmation]. What else? What would you want the students who were witnessing the time out to learn? [Evocative Question; Focusing on Child Perspective]

TEACHER: The same thing. You know, that when we break rules, we have to go away from others. We don't get to just stay in the group and continue being disrespectful.

CONSULTANT: So our classroom is predictable [Reframe]. If we violate rules, I know what will happen. There's a procedure. Almost like this is a safe place to be because I know my teacher will keep me safe, and I also know that if I make a mistake, there's a predictable response to that. [Reframing; Child Perspective, and Gem]

TEACHER: Exactly.

CONSULTANT: I've been in classes where the response to rule violations is for the teacher to yell and get angry. What do you think students are learning in classrooms like that? [Evocative Question; Child Perspective]

TEACHER: I would think the opposite: They're thinking that "my teacher gets really mad when we disappoint her, and we should feel ashamed or guilty."

CONSULTANT: Okay. So let me make sure I have this right. The potential benefits of time out are that it helps students learn the rules and makes consequences predictable and safe. Looking at this list, who are those mostly benefits for, you or the students?

TEACHER: Mostly the students.

CONSULTANT: On the other side, you listed several barriers. Looking over this list, who are those mostly barriers for?

TEACHER: Well, mostly for me. I see what you're saying.

Practice

Choose one of these advanced strategies and use it in your next consultation meeting. Listen for the teacher's response.

For more practice, try your skill by reading the sample resistance comments below for teachers A–C.

- Teacher A: "This just isn't my style of teaching; I have control over my class, and I don't need this classroom management strategy."
- Teacher B: "I don't have the time to fit this into my schedule with everything else I have going on right now."
- Teacher C: "I've tried my best and nothing is working. I am not really open to doing much more."

Next, write a response to the each resistant comment for each teacher using the advanced skills listed below. Table 4.2 provides sample advanced skill responses to each teacher:

Simple reflection: _____

_____

Amplified reflection: _____

_____

Double-sided reflection: _____

_____

Reframing: _____

_____

Shifting focus: _____

_____

Emphasizing personal choice: _____

_____

Agreeing with a twist: _____

_____

Coming alongside: _____

_____

Querying extremes: _____

_____

Looking forward/backward: _____

_____

TABLE 4.2. Sample Advanced Skill Responses

Teacher A: "This just isn't my style of teaching; I have control over my class, and I don't need this classroom management strategy."

Simple reflection: "It feels intrusive to be asked to try a new teaching style."

Amplified reflection: "These strategies feel completely different from how you normally teach." Or "You really don't have any problems in your class."

Double-sided reflection: [based on previous discussion with teacher] "On the one hand, it is uncomfortable to try to merge these strategies with your teaching style. On the other hand, you are curious how it would feel in your classroom to make it a little more flexible/fun."

Reframe: "You really are knowledgeable about how to make your classroom predictable for students. Whatever strategies that you add will have to not interfere with the structure you've established."

Shifting focus: "What do you see as your biggest strengths as a teacher, things you do particularly well?"

Emphasizing personal choice: "I'm definitely not here to try to convince you to do something you don't want to do. The only changes that will happen in your class are ones that you choose to make."

Agreement with a twist: "Right. That would be silly to not build off all the wisdom you've developed about your students this year."

Coming alongside: "Yes. It makes no sense to try anything new when things are going so well."

Querying extremes: "If things keep going as they are now, what's the best outcome you can imagine for your class? How about the flipside: What's the worst you can imagine?"

Looking forward/backward: "Look into the future and tell me what you want your class to look like at the end of the year."

Teacher B: "I don't have the time to fit this into my schedule with everything else I have going on right now."

Simple reflection: "You're really overloaded with all that you have to do right now."

Amplified reflection: "On your long list of things to do, this would be at the very bottom."

Double-sided reflection: [based on previous discussion with teacher] "On the one hand, you're feeling overwhelmed. On the other hand, you really would like to find time for making sure your expectations are clear."

Reframe: "You are really committed to doing things the right way."

Shifting focus: "Rather than focusing on taking on something new, let's talk about what is going well in your classroom so far."

Emphasizing personal choice: "I certainly don't want to add to your burden. When you get down to it, this is completely up to you."

Agreement with a twist: "There is so much going on right now that it's hard to see how this could be helpful. I'm really impressed with how you are committed to investing time in things that are going to make a difference and doing it the right way. I want to make sure that anything you decide to take on is something that has a good chance of working."

(cont.)

TABLE 4.2. *(cont.)*

Coming alongside: "Maybe this is the wrong time to work on classroom management. It just seems like a waste of time compared to your other priorities."

Querying extremes: "If things keep going as they are now, what's the best outcome you can imagine for your class? How about the flipside: What's the worst you can imagine?"

Looking forward/backward: "Look into the future and tell me what you want your class to look like at the end of the year."

Teacher C: "I've tried my best and nothing is working. I am not really open to doing much more."

Simple reflection: "It's really frustrating to put in so much effort and not see much progress."

Amplified reflection: "This has been a total waste of time."

Double-sided reflection: [based on previous discussion with teacher] "You're disappointed with our progress and yet there is still a small part of you that hates to give up after all you have invested."

Reframe: "You just want so much to make a difference in these kids lives, and it's hard to wait and see if the changes you've made are going to stick with these kids."

Shifting focus: "Before focusing on the students, I wonder if we could take a step back for a moment and reflect on all the positive changes you have made."

Emphasizing personal choice: "What we do next is completely your decision."

Agreement with a twist: "It's very frustrating not to be able to see any growth yet out of all the seeds of success you've been planting for these students."

Coming alongside: "This has become such a burden. Even these meetings feel like I'm asking you to do more and more. Maybe we need to take a break."

Querying values: "You have been working so hard on this. Remind me what was driving you so hard to make all these changes."

MI APPLIED TO EDUCATIONAL CONSULTATION

We have spent most of this chapter describing classic MI as developed in clinical contexts. There are some minor adaptations that are needed to make MI fit within an educational context. For instance, whereas MI was developed as a clinical intervention to treat behavior problems, teachers do not typically seek consultation with school colleagues to treat their own emotional problems (though, supportive listening sometimes borders on this domain). Instead, educational consultants attempt to help others (e.g., teachers) implement interventions that can change children's behavior or make their behavior problems less likely to occur. Still, the same principles apply. Some of the guidelines that have been developed for effective MI practice in clinical settings may not directly apply to school settings, however. For instance, the goal of having a 10:1 ratio of client to consultant talk may be lower in a school consultation context.

As such, MI in educational contexts may be more akin to MI in health care settings. Heath care providers commonly find themselves consulting with patients about areas outside those for which the patient originally sought consultation. For instance, a patient newly diagnosed with diabetes may expect the physician to simply prescribe medicine or an insulin regimen. Instead, the physician may want to initiate a discussion about lifestyle changes involving diet and exercise.

Elicit–Provide–Elicit

In health care settings, one simplified model that has been developed to capitalize on MI during brief social encounters is the elicit–provide–elicit (EPE) model (Miller & Rollnick, 2002). In this approach, the provider/consultant first asks what the person knows or would like to know about the topic, then provides the information in a manageable size (concise) based on what the person says or requests. Next the provider/consultant asks for the person's response to the information. A good entry question to begin the EPE process is, "What do you want to know about _____?"

Below is a sample dialogue that could serve as an alternative to the decisional balance example (above) for discussing time out with a teacher. Note that the EPE process is just an abbreviated version of MI as described throughout this chapter. All the same skills apply.

> CONSULTANT: You've had some bad experiences with time out. So that I don't give you too much information, tell me what you know about steps in the time-out procedure, the rationale, how to set it up, when to use it, how long it lasts. [Elicit] [Or "What are some challenges you had with it?"]

> TEACHER: I know that you are supposed to use it when kids are misbehaving. I just use a chair in the back of my class, and I tell kids to go to time out.

> CONSULTANT: Those things are important. What else? [Elicit]

> TEACHER: I don't know. I really had trouble getting some kids to go to time out. I had trouble remembering to end it. The times I tried it, I just gave up on it pretty quickly because it didn't seem to help. Seemed like more work.

> CONSULTANT: Would it help if I told you a bit more about how other teachers have set it up to make it most likely to be helpful? [Elicit]

> TEACHER: I guess so.

> CONSULTANT: It turns out to be a fairly precise procedure that takes practice to be most effective. One key step is to decide which behaviors will result in time out. A good place to start is to use it only for intense or aggressive behaviors, such as hitting or kicking [Provide]. Does that make sense? [Elicit]

> TEACHER: So I shouldn't use it for off-task behavior like talk-outs? I mean, some students just don't learn to stop talking out.

CONSULTANT: Great point. Other strategies are more effective for managing annoying behaviors like that [Provide]. We can talk about those as well. What would make most sense right now? Would it be helpful to hear more about setting up time out to be effective, or would you like to switch to talk about low-level disruptive behaviors? [Elicit]

TEACHER: Both are important, but let's stick with time out. I do need a tool to help me when kids are hurtful to each other. You have me curious. Maybe I haven't been doing it right all these years.

CONSULTANT: After clearly defining which behaviors will result in time out, the next step is to set up your time-out space. Sounds like you already have experience with a chair in the back of the room. The key is that it is a place that is free from distractions, a boring place. [Provide]

TEACHER: I got that. I mean, I get the big idea here, that it should be time away from attention and a time to calm down.

CONSULTANT: Exactly. See, you do know the key pieces here. I'm thinking it might just be a matter of tweaking it, because all of the pieces must be in place for it to work. Another key element is to have a simple phrase that you will use when you need to send someone to time out. It should be brief and to the point. First, name the rule violation, then give the command. "Johnny, that's hitting. Go to time out." [Provide]

TEACHER: Okay.

CONSULTANT: Time out should also be brief—no more than 5 minutes. [Provide]

TEACHER: That short. Really?

CONSULTANT: That surprises you. [Elicit]

TEACHER: Yes, some of my kids were spending ... well, let's just say a lot of time in time out. That's one reason I hated using it.

CONSULTANT: So it would be more appealing to you to have a strategy like this, that is short and gets students back in the classroom as quickly as possible. [Elicit]

TEACHER: That would be better. But I would be concerned about forgetting how long they've been in.

CONSULTANT: You've hit on another key piece. Most teachers need to use timers with a bell of some sort to remember. Because you're right, time out becomes less effective if we forget about the child or let it go on too long. [Provide]

TEACHER: Right.

CONSULTANT: So let me ask you. Is this helpful? Is this something you want to keep talking about? [Elicit]

The Check-In Question

Notice that throughout the EPE dialogue, the consultant regularly assessed the teacher's reaction to the information that was provided. Check-in questions should be used liberally throughout your conversations with teachers. The check-in question can take many forms: "What do you make of that?"; "What's your reaction to that?"; or "Would it be helpful if I ... ?" The key idea is that you want to stay in touch with how the teacher is responding to new information that you have given him or her. This skill is especially helpful during the CCU feedback session, as described in Chapter 7.

DEVELOPING YOUR MI SKILLS

MI can be taught and learned by nearly anyone with basic clinical skills; it is a deceptively simple intervention. Much like microcounseling skills, it is easy to be lulled into believing that you have mastered MI. The only way to truly learn this skill is through focused practice and consultation/supervision. To become fluent in MI requires some didactic instruction, followed by practice and ongoing supervision (see Miller, Yahne, Moyers, Martinez, & Pirritano, 2004). You have taken a first step by reading this chapter. You can practice many of the concrete skills described above in your own practice. Hopefully, this sets you on a course of further exploring MI and making it a part of your core set of consultation skills.

What is *your* next step? What do you plan on doing as your next step in learning MI? How important is it for you to commit to this next step? Why is this important to you? You get the idea ...

SUMMARY

This chapter provides an introduction to using MI in educational settings. We build on the prior chapter about characteristics of effective consultants and highlight how MI can help you embody many of these key consultant attributes. You can think of both of these chapters as laying the foundation for the CCU. The behaviors and strategies discussed in these chapters are the music behind the CCU. As you will see, we assembled the CCU with attention to all of these principles and systematically embedded many of the specific MI strategies into the CCU protocol. With this as your foundation, you are well on your way to using the CCU.

CHAPTER 5

The Classroom Check-Up
Classwide Consultation Model

The CCU was developed as a consultation model that addresses the need for classroom-level support while minimizing treatment integrity problems common to school-based consultation. The CCU is a brief intervention that utilizes MI techniques in order to engage teachers in the change process. The purpose of the CCU is to (1) target teachers' motivation to maintain current practices that are important for student success, (2) reduce teacher–student interactions that are likely to exacerbate problem behaviors, and (3) increase teacher behaviors that promote student competence and success.

> **CCU targets teachers' motivation to maintain current practices that are important for student success, reduces teacher–student interactions that are likely to exacerbate problem behaviors, and increases teacher behaviors that promote student competence and success.**

The CCU was patterned after the Family Check-Up (FCU), an assessment intervention designed for, and effectively implemented with, families of children with problem behaviors (Dishion & Kavanaugh, 2003; Rao, 1998). Like the FCU, the CCU was developed around the clear linkage between assessment, intervention, and behavior change, is derived from empirically driven theory, and is guided by MI principles and strategies (see Miller & Rollnick, 2002; Stormshack & Dishion, 2002).

CONCEPTUAL FOUNDATION

Theory of Change

The CCU builds on existing school-based consultation models by emphasizing classwide change and motivational enhancement strategies that are informed by an extensive social psychological literature base. Specific motivational enhancement strategies utilized by the CCU include giving personalized feedback to teachers on classroom behaviors, encouraging personal responsibility for decision making while offering direct advice if solicited, developing a menu of options for improving fidelity, and supporting teacher self-efficacy by identifying existing strengths and times when teachers have successfully changed classroom behaviors in the past (Miller & Rollnick, 2002). The CCU can produce effective change in classrooms when the consultant uses these strategies to forge a collaborative relationship between him- or herself and the teacher. The goal is to increase the use of effective classroom management practices. An increase in effective classroom management practices, in turn, leads to fewer classroom disruptions, fosters positive teacher–student relationships, and increases students' engagement with academic material. Providing teachers with feedback about their success implementing new practices and the link between these practices and observable changes in desired classroom outcomes (disruptions, relationships, and engagement) creates a self-sustaining cycle of positive reinforcement for maintaining the new effective practices.

FRAMES

The CCU is aligned with the core principles of effective brief interventions described by one of the developers of MI, Dr. William Miller. As he was developing MI, Dr. Miller conducted an extensive literature review about effective brief interventions to describe common elements across these strategies (see Miller & Rollnick, 2002). He identified six core principles that cut across these interventions, which he summarized using the acronym FRAMES: feedback, responsibility, advice, menus, empathy, and self-efficacy.

Most effective brief interventions include some *feedback* as part of the intervention process, but not just any type of feedback will suffice. Global feedback about what most teachers do or what research says in general is not particularly motivating. Effective feedback requires that consultants give precise, specific, and individualized feedback about the target behaviors. Daily performance feedback toward a targeted goal is one example. Telling a teacher that, in general, teachers who use behavior-specific praise in the classroom can reduce disruptive behaviors may not motivate a teacher to increase his or her behavior-specific praise. Showing a teacher his or her current rates of praise and classroom disruptions and how they co-occur over time, however, can be very motivating because it is precise and personalized feedback.

Miller also found that effective brief interventions communicated that the *responsibility* for changing rested with the individual. This is accomplished through direct, explicit, and if needed, repeated messages such as, "It's ultimately up to you if you want to do anything about the problem." Additionally, he found that *advice* can be helpful in motivating change, but only as one component of a collaborative relationship. Only giving advice and information without attending to the relationship typically produces resistance to change. But when advice is paired with responsibility statements (e.g., "As a classroom consultant, I would recommend that we start by focusing on becoming more fluent in explicit reprimands; but it is totally up to you where we begin.") in the context of a supportive consulting relationship, it can produce change. Further, when individuals express an interest in changing a behavior, giving them a *menu* of options can make it more likely that they will continue to be motivated (e.g., "There are several ways that other teachers have been successful in reducing disruptions. Let me tell you about a couple, and you let me know which one sounds best to you.").

The final two elements of the FRAMES acronym are foundational for effective collaborative relationships. Effective brief interventions all stress the importance of listening reflectively and conveying *empathy* and encouragement. Finally, interventions that tend to be motivating give a primary focus to supporting the *self-efficacy* of the consultee. That is, they support individuals' beliefs that they can indeed make the intended changes if they choose to do so. One way to foster self-efficacy is to note current successes in changing ("How did you make that happen?") and to ask about times in the past that the teacher successfully managed challenging situations ("Tell me about the last time you had a disruptive class and how you were able to get control of it.").

Based on these principles, Miller and others developed brief motivational enhancement consultation models for substance abusers. The first of these was labeled the *Drinker's Check-Up*. The purpose was to engage in a brief consultation visit with clients who had some interest in learning more about their drinking habit and to use the FRAMES principles to facilitate change. Given the success of these strategies, later efforts expanded the Drinker's Check-Up around other socially relevant behaviors. The CCU was an outgrowth of these efforts to extend effective motivational enhancement practices to teacher consultation settings.

CCU PROCEDURES

Steps of the CCU

In line with these FRAMES principles, the CCU is delivered in a series of steps: (1) assessing the classroom, (2) providing the teacher with personalized feedback, (3) developing a menu of options for intervention, (4) choosing the intervention, (5) action planning and having the teacher self-monitor implementation of the intervention, and (6) providing ongoing monitoring, which, when appropriate, includes performance feedback (see Table 5.1). Relating assessment to creating change in the classroom is a vital and unique component of the CCU. The CCU links assessment to intervention by including an assessment of the teacher's current use of critical classroom management variables, followed by feedback to the teacher and the collaborative design of a classroom intervention. Interventions are tailored to the needs of each classroom and based on objective data. Areas of need are identified (e.g., increase praise) and potential interventions are brainstormed by the teacher and consultant (e.g., teach expectations and provide behavior-specific praise to students who meet those expectations). The objective is to create individualized interventions that are important, practical, realistic, and focused on real-world effects.

TABLE 5.1. Components of the Classroom Check-Up

Step 1: Assess classroom.	• Teacher Interview • Classroom Ecology Checklist • 10- and 5-Minute Observation Forms • Overall Classroom Rating Form
Step 2: Provide feedback.	• Consultant provides feedback on assessment findings. • Feedback includes both identified teacher strengths and weaknesses.
Step 3: Develop menu of options.	• Teacher and consultant collaboratively develop a menu of options for intervening to create positive classroom outcomes.
Step 4: Choose intervention(s).	• Teacher chooses any number of interventions to implement. • Consultant provides ongoing support in the implementation of the intervention(s).
Step 5: Action planning and encourage teacher self-monitoring.	• Teacher and consultant develop an action plan for intervening. • Teacher monitors daily implementation of the chosen intervention using a self-monitoring form.
Step 6: Provide ongoing monitoring.	• Consultant conducts ongoing classroom observations. • Teacher and consultant monitor, review, and revise as needed. • Consultant provides teacher performance feedback (optional).

The CCU Process

The CCU process is depicted in Figure 5.1. First, the consultant meets with the teacher to conduct a brief informal interview. The purpose of the interview is to establish rapport with the teacher, to gather information about the management strategies currently being used in the classroom, and to identify areas for which the teacher would like additional support. Next, the consultant conducts a series of classroom observations to gather objective data on a number of critical classroom variables. These variables are outlined in Chapter 6 and align with the critical features of effective classroom management. Following the observations, the consultant prepares the assessment information and provides the feedback to the teacher. During this feedback meeting, a menu of options is developed and the teacher determines the next steps toward implementing classroom management practices in the classroom. Following this meeting, the teacher begins to implement the new practice in the classroom and monitors how well he or she is able to do so. The purpose of self-monitoring is to assess what parts of the new practice the teacher actually puts into place. Sometimes the best-laid plans do not work because the idea was not feasible, did not fit well with the classroom, or just did not make sense once the teacher tried it out. The information provided by self-monitoring the practice can lead to adjusting or modifying part or all of the intervention. Additionally, self-monitoring is a behavioral technique that, in itself, often increases the desired behavior (Johnson & White, 1971). For instance, if you were trying

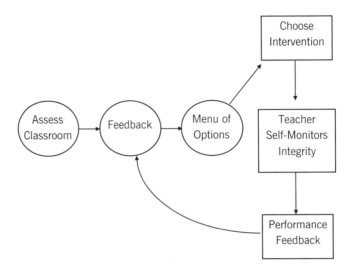

FIGURE 5.1. The CCU process.

to lose weight by watching your diet, simply keeping a diary of what you eat each day can make you more aware of your eating and increase the likelihood that you will stick to your goal of eating healthier food. Self-monitoring can increase the likelihood that the teacher will actually use the strategy in the classroom. Last, the consultant gathers data on the use of the strategies in the classroom and provides performance feedback to the teacher. For instance, if the teacher is working to increase his or her use of behavior-specific praise, the consultant observes in the classroom and then gives the teacher feedback on the number of behavior-specific praise statements provided during the observation period. This feedback can lead to a new menu of options and new interventions that are themselves monitored over time. In this way, the CCU can serve as an ongoing feedback loop consistent with well-established problem-solving models.

CCU RESEARCH

> Systematic consultation at the classroom level, as a universal prevention strategy, can create meaningful teacher and student behavior change.

Several studies have evaluated the effectiveness of the CCU consultation model. A recent study considered changes in teacher and student behavior using a multiple baseline design across four elementary school classrooms (Reinke, Lewis-Palmer, & Merrell, 2008). The CCU increased teacher implementation of classroom management strategies, including increased use of praise, use of behavior-specific praise, and decreased use of reprimands. Further, these changes in teacher behavior corresponded to decreases in classroom disruptive behavior and were maintained over time. The results are encouraging because they suggest that systematic consultation at the classroom level, as a universal prevention strategy, can create meaningful teacher and student behavior change. Additionally, Reinke et al. (2007) evaluated the effects of consultation involving visual performance feedback on teacher use of behavior-specific praise, using a multiple baseline design with three general education elementary teachers and six targeted students with classroom behavior problems. The results indicated an increase in behavior-specific praise for participating students across all teachers, relative to baseline. Additionally, teachers increased their use of behavior-specific praise with classroom peers, suggesting that the techniques produced classwide effects. Finally, Mesa, Lewis-Palmer, and Reinke (2005) reported that the CCU model resulted in a significant increase in teacher use of behavior-specific praise, which in turn led to reductions in student disruptive behaviors on a classwide level. All three studies relied on rigorous evaluation procedures, including real-time data collection of key study variables. Also, across all three studies, teachers rated the intervention as very important, effective, unobtrusive, and practical (e.g., requiring minimal time, resources, and effort to implement). Collectively, these studies indicate that the CCU model is a feasible, acceptable, socially valid, and effective method for improving classroom teacher implementation of evidence-based practices.

> **The CCU model is a feasible, acceptable, socially valid, and effective method for improving classroom teacher implementation of evidence-based practices.**

SUMMARY

The CCU is a consultation model for supporting teacher implementation of effective classroom management practices. The model incorporates effective consultation skills, including MI, use of performance feedback, and linking data to evidence-based practices. Further, the CCU is focused on changing practices at the classroom level, allowing the impact of consultation to reach beyond the individual student. The following two chapters provide a detailed description of the assessment and feedback features of the CCU. Additionally, these chapters provide case presentations outlining the use of the CCU in classrooms.

CHAPTER 6

Interview and Assessment

Assessment is a central component of the CCU. The intervention begins with a brief interview, guided by MI strategies, about the teacher's classroom experiences and practices. Following the interview, the consultant gathers direct observations of targeted classroom behaviors and climate variables. All the information from the interview and observations is collected and then presented back to the teacher during the feedback session. Data collected as part of the CCU include the Classroom Check-Up Teacher Interview, the Classroom Ecology Checklist, the Classroom Check-Up 10-Minute Classroom Observation Form, and a Classroom Check-Up 5-Minute Academic Engagement Observation Form. This chapter describes how to conduct each of these assessments. All of the forms discussed in this chapter are available in Appendix B and are reproducible.

THE CLASSROOM CHECK-UP TEACHER INTERVIEW

The purpose of the first meeting is to complete an informal interview with the teacher, provide him or her with a detailed overview of the consultation process, and collect information about his or her classroom and teaching experiences. Throughout the visit, an MI approach, described in Chapter 4, is applied.

The interview form provided in Appendix B.1 includes a series of open-ended questions across a variety of domains relevant to the consultation process. The areas include general experiences in teaching, current classroom management practices, past experiences with consultation, and specific perceived needs for support. The interview has scripted language built into it as well as specific questions and prompts for obtaining more in-depth information. However, the primary goal of this first meeting is to have a relaxed conversation with the teacher and establish a strong, collaborative relationship. Below we describe the common sequence of events before, during, and after the interview.

Prior to the Interview

You will need to clarify your role as a consultant in advance with the school administrator. It is very helpful to ensure that the school administrator supports your collaborative work with teachers while keeping the data that you gather confidential and not using it to evaluate or hold the teacher accountable. Therefore, meeting with the administrator to discuss your role prior to consulting with the teacher will avoid confusion and conflict over how information is shared. Have a discussion about why the data you gather should remain confidential. Keeping information and data collected with the teacher confidential will support a trusting collaborative relationship between you and the teacher. If for some reason this is not the case, it is imperative that you have an open discussion with the teacher about the limitations of your relationship with regard to holding information in confidence.

> **Keeping information and data collected with the teacher confidential will support a trusting collaborative relationship between you and the teacher.**

Conducting the Interview

Remember, your first meeting with the teacher sets the tone for the entire consultation process. Be sure to take time at the beginning of the process to simply engage in social conversation. Comment on the classroom or artifacts in the classroom (e.g., "That's a beautiful painting."). Don't rush into the interview. Take your time observing and getting to know the teacher. Moreover, try not to create a formal tone in the interview or deliver it in a word-for-word manner. Use the time to get to know the teacher, to gain an understanding of his or her values, experiences, and skills.

Overview

Next, provide an overview of the meeting. Begin by thanking the teacher for agreeing to meet with you. Tell the teacher the purpose of the CCU and provide an overview of its components—for example:

"Today I'm going to ask you some questions about your teaching experiences and your classroom practices. With your permission, I'll find a time later in the week to observe in your classroom. The purpose of the interview is for me to get to know you better and learn about your classroom management style."

Tell the teacher about future meetings that will be part of the process—for example:

"After I gather information from you and from the classroom observations, I will compile it. Then, we can set up another time to meet to review the information. During that meeting we will look at all the information and come up with a list of possible next steps, a menu of sorts. Together we can think about what from the menu fits best for your classroom. Then we will come up with a plan for what to do next."

Confidentiality

Once you have administrator agreement that all CCU data will be confidential, you may have a discussion with the teacher about this: "Before we begin, I just wanted to let you know that everything you share with me is confidential. I will not share information with anyone, including your school administrator. Do you have concerns or questions about this?" If administrators have not agreed to keep the data confidential, then you will need to alert the teacher of this fact.

Transition to the Interview Form

Transition the conversation to start asking questions from the Classroom Check-Up Teacher Interview: "To begin, let me ask you some questions about your experiences as a teacher." Ask all of the questions on the form, taking notes as needed. Use lots of reflective listening, affirmations, and summarizing as the teacher responds to your questions. Listen for his or her values and file these away for future reference. Listen for reasons the teacher might want to change, and for references to any successful changes he or she made in the past. Get a sense of the teacher's stage of change. For each teacher, you can use the information from the interview to help you assess whether he or she is even considering making a change, is ambivalent about making changes, or is already planning or making a change.

Sample Interview Transcript

Below we provide a transcript of a sample CCU interview to illustrate the process. This interview took place in an optimal circumstance where the teacher had enough time to complete the process in one sitting. We use it to illustrate the whole process and all the content that we try to gather in these interviews. In practice, we sometimes spread these conversations out over more than one sitting to accommodate the teacher's schedule.

The interviewee is an experienced teacher in a fifth-grade classroom. The teacher requested support for improving her classroom management skills, particularly during her math lessons. The interview takes place in the classroom, without students present, during a break in the schedule.

Interview and Responses	Comments
CONSULTANT: I appreciate your meeting with me and your interest in working together. Today I just wanted to get to know more about you and your classroom. After that, we can come up with a plan for next steps. So to begin, how long have you been a teacher?	Introduction Gathering background material
TEACHER: This is my tenth year.	
CONSULTANT: And have you always taught fifth grade?	

TEACHER: No. I taught in a resource room for a year and then in a special education classroom for 2 years. Then from there I taught in regular sixth grade, and then a couple years in third grade.	
CONSULTANT: Wow, so you've had a lot of experiences, a range of classrooms. What do you think made you want to become a teacher?	Simple reflection Open-ended question
TEACHER: Not just that I love kids, I do, but also I love to be able to explain things and see the students get it. It just is a great feeling to see and experience that.	
CONSULTANT: I can see you getting exciting just talking about that.	Reflecting positive feelings
TEACHER: Yeah. I mean, to see them learning things and what it does for them.	
CONSULTANT: Just seeing them make those connections and being part of that. When did you know that this was what you wanted to do with your life?	Reflecting values Open-ended question
TEACHER: I'm guess I've always known. I was one of those kids who played school and was usually the teacher. It's just something I always enjoyed, teaching and being part of that.	
CONSULTANT: Helping others learn.	Reflecting values
TEACHER: That, yes, and you know, I'm kind of a control freak so this was a good way to express that. (*Laughs.*)	
CONSULTANT: (*Smiles.*) So being in charge and being a leader fit naturally for you in being an effective instructor and sort of being in charge of helping kids make connections and learn.	Summary and reflection about values Keeping the fous on students
TEACHER: Exactly.	
CONSULTANT: Why elementary school?	Open-ended question
TEACHER: Well, kids here are not as jaded, they're still open. You can still change them. I mean, they might say they don't want to do something, but you can still get them to do it. And they hopefully haven't learned their limitations yet.	
CONSULTANT: You want to be a part of showing them what they are capable of.	Reflecting a gem
TEACHER: I really do. I think so many kids are left behind and never see or know what their horizons are. I love to be there when they first see who they can become.	
CONSULTANT: So those are some of your loves of teaching. What is the most difficult or hardest part of being a teacher?	Transition Open-ended question

TEACHER: Just the time. Not enough of it. You are so busy all of the time. Sometimes you just don't have time to get it all in. And I have kids who just want to tell me a story or something, and I have to say, you know, we've got to move this along. I have kids falling behind. There's just so much to do.	
CONSULTANT: That makes it hard to miss those moments when you can help kids glimpse their strengths because there's so much pressure to keep moving on.	Reflection connecting to gem
TEACHER: It's always a balance that's hard to strike and even more so now with all the testing and other intrusions into the classroom.	
CONSULTANT: How much of your lessons do you get through in a day?	Open-ended question
TEACHER: Not a whole lesson, at least not in the math class. I'm supposed to, but if I can get through a lesson in 2 days, I'm happy. I'm feeling the pressure to move forward, but I have to be sure they get it.	
CONSULTANT: How would you describe your current classroom management?	Open-ended question
TEACHER: Well (*laughs*) .. okay … hmm, sporadic. So I know the importance of being positive, but then I also have these other pressures. I know what I want, I have my plan. I use rewards, and I give gift tickets when I see behaviors I want to see. But I keep finding myself so caught up in the teaching and the content that I forget these things. I seem to do a much better job in the morning. I'm a lot more positive, and so are the kids. But by the afternoon I'm tired and they're tired, so all of our behaviors are worse.	
CONSULTANT: Everyone's worn down. So you have a good sense of how you want your management system to function, but it can be hard to track it while staying on top of the content.	Reflection and summary
TEACHER: Right. Like I said, I know positives are important, it's just remembering to do it.	
CONSULTANT: Why are positives so important to you?	Open-ended question eliciting values
TEACHER: Well, I know what the literature says. More positives than negatives. And I see it. You know, when I do track my positives and see that I'm doing more praising, I see the difference it makes. I feel the difference.	

CONSULTANT: So you like the feeling when you praise more. What differences do you see?	Reflecting and elaborating change talk
TEACHER: Kids are on track. There's less disruptions. I think I can see it makes them feel better, happier. And so do I.	
CONSULTANT: Then that makes a lot of sense why you would want to have lots of praise. You see that it makes everyone happier, it keeps everyone on task, and there are fewer disruptions—which probably means that there's more time for the important stuff, the making of connections.	Summary and connecting change to values
TEACHER: Right. Yeah, definitely, when I'm on top of it and they're on task, we do get more time for content and learning. And I know it's easier to learn in that type of atmosphere too, when people are feeling good, rather than nervous or anxious, like I'm gonna get caught or look stupid.	
CONSULTANT: Okay, right, so exactly the type of atmosphere you want to have so students can learn and grow and reach their potential. Following that, what do you see as your strengths around classroom management?	Open-ended question
TEACHER: I at least have the knowledge of knowing that if the classroom starts falling apart, I need to start looking at my strategies, and I have a plan for what to do to get the class back on track. I have a lot of experiences with kids and have been successful, so I can draw on that. I know what works. I've seen it work when I'm clear or not clear and when I'm being more or less positive, I can see the changes it makes.	
CONSULTANT: So you have good detective skills when there's a problem and can be like, *aha*, that's the problem!	Summary and affirmation
TEACHER: Right. So I feel like I know what to do and can figure it out—I just have to stick with it.	
CONSULTANT: What do you think are your weaknesses?	Open-ended question
TEACHER: This sounds really weird. I think I'm too hard on myself. Sometimes I get too frustrated with myself. I get down on myself and say I should have done this or that. And sometimes I forget to look at the good things.	
CONSULTANT: Sort of the parallel of your strength. You have this knowledge of what you want your class to be like and so you're tuned in to when it's not, and it's easy for you to criticize yourself when you're falling short of your high expectations.	Double-sided reflection

TEACHER: Yeah, when I'm not liking teaching, that's what it is.	
CONSULTANT: Right, it's hard to like teaching when you are criticizing yourself for not measuring up.	Reflective listening
TEACHER: Yeah, I can be pretty hard on myself.	
CONSULTANT: How do you think that being hard on yourself affects your ability to create the atmosphere you want to create for students?	Open-ended question focusing on students and values
TEACHER: Probably not good. It becomes, or can become, a cycle. Like if I'm not feeling good about myself, I think it comes across to students.	
CONSULTANT: And what happens to your praise rate?	Open-ended question
TEACHER: Oh, it drops. It makes it that much harder to do those things I know that I need to do. The more I'm doing what I want to do, the better the class is doing, the better I'm feeling.	
CONSULTANT: And the more they're making connections.	Reflecting the theme
TEACHER: Right.	
CONSULTANT: Tell me about your classroom rules.	Open-ended statement
TEACHER: The three I worked on at the beginning of the year were to listen, work quickly and quietly, and raise your hand. I really notice that they don't really get it, what those rules mean. As concepts, they're too big. So I've pulled out the parts I want them to focus on. And we've been practicing them.	
CONSULTANT: Do you use a reward system?	
TEACHER: I have class system reward. Individual students can earn points and then the whole class can earn points for class rewards. I used to use color spots, but I like this system much better.	
CONSULTANT: Tell me about the class reward.	Clarification
TEACHER: With a class reward they get to vote when they earn enough points. They can vote to play a social skills game or to have popcorn and juice when we sit and chat.	
CONSULTANT: That sounds fun. How's that working?	Affirmation; open-ended question
TEACHER: It works really well—better than expected. They really are motivated for either of those, or both.	
CONSULTANT: On the flip side, what disciplinary strategies do you use?	Open-ended question

TEACHER: I scream really loud. (*Laughs.*)

CONSULTANT: Yes, I've heard you down the hall.   Humor

TEACHER: No, I try to praise the kids who are doing things right. So if one kid is not paying attention, I'll praise someone close to him or her who is. Or if it's a whole-class issue, I'll stop and review the rules.

CONSULTANT: When you are working with a student with a difficult behavior, what strategies do you use?   Open-ended question

TEACHER: I try to have a respectful, caring relationship with the student. I think that is so important. And I like to give students choices and then give them time and space to make a good choice. I had this one student who would just get real agitated and act out in class, and I found that just a quick comment, "Joseph, take a minute," or something like that, would help and then I would go to him in a minute and if he was still upset, I'd give him a choice: "You pull it together or take a time out in the back." And usually he would make a good choice, and that's all he would need.

CONSULTANT: So having a strong relationship as a foundation and then giving choices and time are helpful in helping resolve those challenging moments.   Summary

TEACHER: Yes, and then sticking with it. I think the only way it works is to be sure to follow through.

CONSULTANT: Choices and consistency. What strategies have you found to be ineffective?   Open-ended question

TEACHER: Oh, well. Backing kids into a corner, not literally, but not giving them an out. So saying "You have to do this," and then when they don't, you're stuck. And just being negative. It really backfires and draws negativity out of the students. It just becomes this standoff.

CONSULTANT: So really back to that emphasis on *you get what you give*. You've seen that positive brings that out of the kids, and negative draws negative.   Summary connecting back to the theme of focusing on positives

TEACHER: Right.

CONSULTANT: What have been your past experiences with consultation?   Open-ended question to clarify expectations

TEACHER: Well, I've had kids that I referred to the behavior support team and would work with them for the entire year. And then I was the consultant for this other student in another class.

CONSULTANT: What did you find helpful?

Open-ended question to clarify expectations

TEACHER: It had to be realistic. We are so busy. So let's come up with something that I can actually do. That and listening. Coming in and saying, "Here are some ideas, what would work in your classroom?" I've seen it go the other way, where someone says, "You need to do this," and the teacher says, "No, I don't." That wouldn't work with me.

CONSULTANT: So it has to be a partnership where someone like me gives you some options, some practical strategies that might work, and you decide what you're willing to try.

Reflecting and clarifying expectations

TEACHER: Exactly.

CONSULTANT: Ideally, what would you like in working with another professional?

Open-ended question

TEACHER: I would like to get ideas to make my classroom run better. That would make it good. And something that has a good chance of succeeding. Otherwise, I get down on myself and the kids get frustrated.

CONSULTANT: So good ideas that work, or at least, are not too cumbersome. We don't want to start that negative cycle. So how often do you get a chance to reflect on your teaching?

Summary and connecting back to prior content
Open-ended question

TEACHER: Not very much. We don't get a lot of feedback. And it just goes by so quickly. I would really love to have more opportunity to get feedback and opportunities to reflect.

CONSULTANT: When you do get feedback, what does that look like?

Open-ended question

TEACHER: They tell you everything you've done, and they write it all out.

CONSULTANT: So what things do you like or dislike about receiving feedback?

Open-ended question

TEACHER: I like it. I'm a perfectionist and, like I said, a control freak. (*Laughs.*) When people are here, I know that I make a ton of mistakes, so I know it's good for me. But I can get down on myself or frustrated, if I keep hearing the same feedback, or even if I already know that I screwed up, it's kinda hard to hear again.

CONSULTANT: Okay, so if you know you already had a difficult day and say your praise rate was low, you might not want the first thing out of my mouth to be, "You're not praising enough today."

Clarifying expectations

TEACHER: Exactly. I mean, I wouldn't be mad at you, I just wouldn't find that helpful.

CONSULTANT: So is there a way I could do that so I don't repeat what you already know?

Inviting input about feedback process

TEACHER: I think if you just start by asking me how I thought it went or how I was doing, that would be a good place to start, and then you would know what I needed to hear.

CONSULTANT: Sounds like a great idea. If you were given a choice between daily face-to-face feedback or a daily e-mail, which would you prefer?

Affirmation

TEACHER: Oh, if I had the time, I'd love face-to-face, but realistically, it would be better to have something in writing that I can read on my own time.

CONSULTANT: Okay. What are some challenges around classroom management with which you would like to work?

Open-ended question and goal setting

TEACHER: I don't know how to put this. Right after lunch their motivation is low, so it's really hard for them. So I'm looking for anything to help make it interesting or more motivating. Getting them motivated and following directions right then would be a big help.

CONSULTANT: Great. Well, maybe that's a good place for me to start observing so I can come up with a better sense of what's going on there, and then we can meet again and come up with a plan.

TEACHER: Sounds great.

CONSULTANT: So just to summarize. You really love teaching and helping kids see their potential, and you have found that the best way to do that is to have a positive class, good relationships, and high praise rates. That's most likely to happen when you're feeling good about yourself. You can be hard on yourself because you know what you want your classroom to be like, and sometimes other pressures make it hard to always reach that goal. One way that I can be helpful to you is to give you feedback around these goals you set for yourself, without making you feel like you are falling short in some way. One place you would like to start is with the time right after lunch, as that is a concerning time for you right now. Does that sound about right?

Detailed summary

Check-in question

TEACHER: That's right.

As you can see, the CCU interview provides direction for eliciting important information but is delivered flexibly to allow for relationship building. The consultant follows the teacher's lead to gain a better understanding of his or her experiences, perceptions, and values. Through reflective listening and affirmations, the consultant helps build the teacher's self-efficacy and commitment to change. Additionally, by listening for gems and highlighting the students' perspective, the consultant makes it more likely that the teacher will be interested in changing key practices.

THE CLASSROOM ECOLOGY CHECKLIST

The next step following the CCU interview is to have the teacher self-assess using the Classroom Ecology Checklist (CEC). (Figure 6.1 provides a CEC completed by a consultant; Appendices B.2 and B.3 provide both a consultant and a teacher version of this tool.) Typically, we give the CEC to the teacher immediately following the interview and ask him or her to complete it over the coming week. It is also useful for you, as consultant, to complete the CEC following your observations and prior to providing feedback.

The CEC asks questions across several key classroom management domains. These domains include the physical layout of the room, expectations and routines, instructional management strategies, and behavior management strategies. The CEC is a useful tool for facilitating discussions about current classroom practices, areas of strength, or areas in need of attention. In addition to providing important information about classroom management, the tool can be used as part of subsequent discussions or during the feedback session. First, you can compare the answers from the teacher to your answers on the CEC and use any discrepancies as a point of discussion. For example: "I noticed that I scored you a bit lower on the item asking about your use of a continuum of consequences to discourage rule violation. Perhaps this is something I wasn't entirely able to observe the few times I was in your classroom. What are some of the different strategies that you use to prevent or discourage misbehavior?" Second, you can focus on areas that the teacher indicated were less than optimal for him or her and ask what he or she would like to do differently. For example: "You scored yourself less than 2:1 on your positive to negative ratio. Ideally, where would you like to be on this item? What might you do to get there?" Third, the CEC information could be incorporated into the feedback provided using the CCU feedback form. During this time, you can refer back to the answers as you review each of the domains on the feedback form. The feedback process is described in more detail in Chapter 7.

CLASSROOM OBSERVATIONS

At the end of the CCU interview, ask the teacher to identify a time of day that is most challenging with regard to managing student behavior. Schedule a visit to the classroom to collect data on critical classroom management variables during this challenging time of day. The critical classroom management variables of interest that you will observe during this

Classroom Ecology Checklist—Consultant Version

Please check the box that represents the best answer for each question based on the observation of classroom practices.

A. Classroom Structure			
1. The traffic patterns in the classroom are clearly defined and allow movement without disrupting others.	No ☐	Somewhat ☐	Yes ☑	
2. The desks and furniture in the classroom are arranged so that students can be seen at all times and the teacher has easy access to all areas of the classroom.	No ☐	Somewhat ☐	Yes ☑	
3. The materials in the classroom are clearly labeled, easily accessible, and organized to minimize clutter.	No ☐	Somewhat ☑	Yes ☐	
4. There is a system in place for students to turn in completed work and to retrieve graded materials.	No ☑	Somewhat ☐	Yes ☐	
B. Behavioral Expectations			
1. Classroom routines and expectations are clearly defined, stated in the positive, and visible.	No ☐	Somewhat ☑	Yes ☐	*Not worded in positive*
2. It is easy to figure out the classroom expectations when observing the class.	No ☐	Somewhat ☑	Yes ☐	
3. ***Ask the teacher if not directly observed***: The teacher actively teaches classroom rules and expectations several times throughout the year.	No ☐	Only once per year ☑	Yes ☐	
4. When the teacher uses an attention-getting signal, over 85% of the students respond within a few seconds.	Never responded or within 5 minutes ☐	Within a few minutes ☐	Yes ☑	Not observed ☐
5. Transitions between activities occur smoothly, without interruption caused by behavior problems.	No ☐	Somewhat ☑	Yes ☐	
C. Instructional Management			
1. The teacher gains the attention of all students at the beginning of a lesson or transition.	No ☐	Somewhat ☐	Yes ☑	
2. Based on review of the classroom schedule and observation, it appears that 70% or more of class time is allocated to academic instruction.	Less than 50% ☐	50–69% ☐	70% or more ☑	
3. A high percentage of students is observed as being engaged during classroom instruction.	Less than 60% are engaged ☐	61–89% are engaged ☑	90% or more are engaged ☐	

(cont.)

FIGURE 6.1. Example of a Completed Classroom Ecology Checklist—Consultant Version.

4. The teacher provides an appropriate pace with an optimal number of opportunities to respond while adjusting for complex content (four to six opportunities per minute for new material; nine to twelve per minute for drill and practice).	No ☐	Sometimes ☑	Yes ☐	About 2–3 per min
5. The teacher solicits both group and individual responses to questions with an effort to provide the majority of students with individual opportunities to respond (not targeting the same students for every question).	No ☐	Somewhat ☐	Yes ☑	
6. The students generally answer questions with a high rate of accuracy during teacher-led instruction.	Less than 60% ☐	61–84% ☐	85% or more ☑	
7. The teacher uses effective error corrections, such as telling, showing, or demonstrating the correct answer, rather than saying "no" or "wrong."	No ☐	Sometimes ☐	Yes ☑	Not observed ☐
D. Interacting Positively				
1. The teacher provides noncontingent attention to every student in the classroom (e.g., greeting them at the door, taking an interest in what they do outside of school).	Not observed ☐	Sometimes ☐	Yes ☑	Welcomed all to class
2. The teacher acknowledges expected student behaviors more frequently than misbehaviors (positive to negative ratio).	Less than 2:1 ☑	Less than 3:1 ☐	3:1 or higher ☐	1:1
E. Responding to Appropriate Behavior				
1. There is a system for documenting and rewarding appropriate student behavior (classwide and individual students).	No ☐	Somewhat/ Informally ☑	Yes ☐	
2. The teacher uses behavior-specific/descriptive praise to encourage appropriate behavior.	No ☐	Sometimes ☑	Most of the time ☐	
F. Responding to Inappropriate Behavior				
1. The number of problem behaviors/disruptions in the classroom is generally minimal.	No ☐	Sometimes ☑	Yes ☐	About 1 per min
2. The teacher uses a continuum of consequences to discourage rule violations (e.g., ignore, praising others, proximity, explicit reprimand).	No ☐	Somewhat ☑	Yes ☐	Did not ignore
3. There is a documentation system for managing specific behavioral violations.	No ☐	Somewhat/ Informally ☐	Yes ☑	
4. The teacher is consistent when reprimanding/ correcting misbehavior.	No ☐	Sometimes ☑	Yes ☐	
5. The teacher is calm, clear, and brief when providing reprimands/corrections.	No ☐	Sometimes ☐	Yes ☑	

FIGURE 6.1. *(cont.)*

time include (1) teacher provision of opportunities to respond, (2) correct academic responses from students, (3) teacher use of praise, (4) teacher use of reprimands, (5) classroom disruptions, and (6) student academic engagement. Each of these variables is described below, as is information about how to observe each during a classroom observation.

Once you arrange a time to visit the classroom explain to the teacher what will happen during this visit, including how long you will be there, what the teacher may want to tell the students about your presence, and what information you will be gathering. Additionally, you may want to let the teacher know that, if possible, you will check in with him or her at the end of the observation to gauge whether the teacher felt that the observation reflected a typical day. You might say something like the following:

"When I visit the classroom on Tuesday, I will plan to stay for about 20 minutes. During that time I will be gathering information about the students' behavior and your use of praise, reprimands, and opportunities to respond. If you want, you can tell the students that I am visiting to learn about what goes on in a fourth-grade classroom. Also, when I come to visit, just do what you would normally. I won't talk to any of the students or to you during the time, but I would like to check in with you at the end, if it's possible. Do you have any questions?"

CRITICAL CLASSROOM MANAGEMENT VARIABLES

Here we provide a description of the critical classroom management variables measured by the CCU classroom observation. These variables can be easily observed and, when targeted for intervention, can significantly improve the classroom environment. Following a description of the classroom management variables, each is operationally defined with specific examples and non-examples. Although you may adjust the exact definition slightly for the classroom in which your consult, once you decide upon your definition, keep it consistent and do not alter it over time. Also, it is a good idea to think about what the behavior looks like and what it does not look like. By doing so you can anticipate minimal differences in behaviors that occur in a classroom and make you question if what you observed was "it" or not. One reason for being very specific in defining what each variable looks like in a classroom is so that, over time, you collect data in a consistent and reliable manner. This careful practice allows you to compare what the classroom looked like on a particular variable prior to an intervention and after an intervention. Gathering data in the same way before and after an intervention is necessary if you want to be able to accurately say that any change is due to the intervention (e.g., a change in teacher or student behavior). If you are not precise or consistent in gathering the exact same type of data, any change you see before and after an intervention could be due to a change in how you collected the data rather than due to actual change in the classroom.

> **Gathering data in the same way before and after an intervention is necessary if you want to be able to accurately say that any change is due to the intervention.**

Each of the critical variables outlined below is tied directly to research on effective classroom management. Refer back to Chapter 2 for a review of relevant research associated with each of the variables below.

Opportunities to Respond

An opportunity to respond occurs any time a teacher provides an academic question to a student or group of students. Increasing the rates of opportunities for student responding during instruction generates more learning, provides important feedback to the teacher, and increases on-task behavior.

Academic opportunities to respond can be observed easily by counting the number of instructional questions, statements, or gestures made by the teacher that seek an oral response, recording each opportunity directed at either an individual student or to the entire class. Opportunities to respond have an academic response component to them and do not include directives that are related to behavior only (e.g., "Put your book away."). Research indicates that four to six responses (minimum of 3.1) should be elicited from students per minute of instruction on new material, with 80% accuracy, and nine to twelve opportunities to respond (minimum 8.2) should be provided during drill and practice work, with 90% accuracy (Council for Exceptional Children, 1987).

Correct Academic Response

In conjunction with directly observing opportunities to respond, the accuracy of student responses can be determined by noting the number of correct academic responses. A correct academic response occurs when an opportunity to respond is directed toward one student or a group of students and the correct response is given. To calculate the percent of correct academic responses (CARs), divide the number of correct responses by the number of opportunities provided. This allows the teacher to determine if the instruction material correctly matches the current ability of the students. If student accuracy is below 80% for new material or below 90% for drill and practice work, then a review of the material may be in order. See Table 6.1 for explicit definitions and examples of OTRs and CARs.

Praise

Praise is another important classroom management strategy that can be readily observed. Increasing positive interactions between teachers and students in classrooms can have huge effects on student outcomes. Teachers who deliver high amounts of praise experience lower off-task and disruptive behaviors from their students (Shores, Cegelka, & Nelson, 1973), allowing more time for instruction. Additionally, praise increases intrinsic motivation of students and helps them feel more competent (Cameron & Pierce, 1994).

The number of praise statements provided can be observed by counting statements or gestures that indicate teacher approval of desired academic or social behaviors. Addi-

TABLE 6.1. Definitions and Examples of OTRs and CARs

Opportunity to respond (OTR)	Correct academic response (CAR)
Definition: An instructional question, statement, or gesture made by the teacher that seeks a student response. OTRs must have an *academic* response component to them and do not include statements or directives that relate to behavior only (e.g., "Pick up your pencil."). Record an OTR for every opportunity to respond, even if the teacher repeats the same question.	*Definition:* Record a CAR when an OTR is directed at a student or group of students and the *correct* response is provided. Even if the response is delayed, record a correct response.

Examples

- "What is the capital of Kansas?"
- Teacher points to a student for a response.
- "Carter, what is 3×4?"
- "Raise your hand if you hear the sound 'tttt' in *cat*."
- Teacher nods (gestures) to a student for a response.

Examples

- Teacher asks an *individual* student for an answer to an academic question *and*
  - Student provides correct response.
  - You are unsure (including, can't hear the answer), but the teacher does not correct the student.
- Teacher: "What is 3×4?" Student: "12."
- Teacher: "What do you think about this problem, Chelsea?" Target student: Says something that is not a clear correct response. Teacher: "Well, that is one way of looking at it."
- Teacher asks *the class or a group* of students for an answer to an academic question *and more than one* person answers correctly.
- Teacher: "Class, what is 3×4?" Choral response from class: "12."

Non-examples

- "Please put your notebooks away."
- "How many people got all of the problems correct?"
- "Keegan, do you need help?"
- "Eyes on me."
- "Remember, $3 \times 4 = 12$."
- "Did everyone have a nice weekend?"
- Teacher models problems/activity—it is *not* coded as an OTR unless the teacher asks for a response during the modeling.

Non-examples

- Teacher asks an individual student for an answer *and*
  - Student does not answer.
  - Student clearly provides the wrong answer.
- Teacher: "What is 3×4?" Student: "16." (incorrect answer)
- Teacher: "Rhonda, what did you get for number 6?" Student: Says nothing.
- Teacher asks the class or a group of students for an answer to an academic question *and*
  - Only one person answers correctly.
  - Students provide the wrong answer.
  - Students provide no answer.
  - It is clear that the majority of the group is incorrect.
- Teacher to class: "What is the capital of Kansas?" Only one student responds.

tionally, praise can be separated into behavior-specific and general praise, providing more detailed feedback to the teacher.

Behavior-Specific Praise versus General Praise

Teacher praise is most effective when it is behavior-specific (Brophy, 1983). Behavior-specific praise identifies for the student the behavior for which he or she is being praised, making teacher expectations clear. Teacher praise can be counted as being behavior-specific when explicit feedback for the desired student behavior is provided (e.g., "China, I like the way you are *listening*."). Teacher praise is counted as being general if no specific feedback for the desired student behavior is provided (e.g., "Class, you are doing a great job!" or "China, nice work."). Nonverbal indicators of approval, such as thumbs up, stickers, and "high-fives," are considered general praise. See Table 6.2 for definitions of praise types and examples.

TABLE 6.2.   Definitions and Examples of Praise

Overall praise definition: A verbal statement or gesture that indicates approval of a desired behavior. On occasion, a teacher may use a pleasant tone when conveying disapproval. Praise is indicated when the interaction is based on *approval* of the student's behavior—not the teacher's overall tone.

Behavior-specific praise	General praise
Definition: Teacher provides specific feedback about the behavior being approved. *Examples* • Teacher: "Thank you for raising your hand." • Teacher: "Everyone has their eyes on me. Good." • Teacher: "Everyone is working hard on their project." • Teacher: "Table 3 students have been listening and working hard." Teacher gives the table a point toward a reward (specific statement and nonverbal gestures equals *one* behavior-specific praise).	*Definition:* No specific feedback about student behavior is provided. *Examples* • Nonverbal: Thumbs up, high-five, pat on the back, points, tokens, stickers • Teacher: "Kennedy, thank you." • Teacher: "Super job." • Teacher: "Good work!" • Teacher: "Nice work, everyone!" • Teacher: While giving a point to Table 3, "Table 3, you are doing a great job!" (nonverbal and general verbal count as *one* general praise).
Non-examples • Teacher: "Kennedy, thank you." • Teacher: "Keep it up." • Teacher: "Good work!" • Teacher: "Remember to raise your hand before you answer." • Teacher: "That is incorrect."	*Non-examples* • Teacher: "Kennedy, thank you putting your things away quietly." • Teacher: "Super. You guys finished your work." • Teacher: "Please do your best." • Teacher: "China, Dion, and Shanna are ready to share!"

Reprimands

Another important classroom management strategy utilized by teachers is the use of reprimands. The number of reprimands can be tracked by counting comments or gestures made by the teacher indicating disapproval of student behavior. Reprimands are recorded when directed to the whole class, a group of students, or individuals. Then a positive-to-negative ratio can be calculated by totaling the number of praise statements and the number of reprimands. The suggested ratio of praise to reprimands is at least 3:1. If the ratio of praise to reprimands is not optimal, a teacher can choose to increase his or her use of praise in the classroom in an effort to change the ratio. Increasing praise in the classroom has a direct link to decreasing disruptive classroom behavior. Similar to praise, reprimands can be broken into more specific categories: explicit or fluent reprimands versus critical, harsh, or emotional reprimands. Breaking reprimands into each of these two categories can be useful toward giving more specific and useful feedback for goal-setting purposes. In general, teachers should be encouraged to reduce the overall number of reprimands and move toward using more explicit and fluent reprimands versus more punitive and emotional ones. See Table 6.3 for examples and definitions of types of reprimands.

Student Disruptive Behavior

The only way to tell if classroom management strategies are working is by counting the number of disruptive behaviors occurring in the classroom. Disruptive behaviors are recorded when the statements or actions of an individual student or group of students interfere with ongoing classroom activities. It is easiest if disruptions are coded as discrete events. For example, two students fighting is one disruption; one student talking out is also one disruption. However, if two students are fighting (disruption #1), followed by the teacher stopping the fight (end of disruption), which is then followed by one of the students talking back to the teacher (disruption #2), then you would count two disruptions. Establishing rules of this kind allows you to be consistent over time when you observe in classrooms and ensures that you are documenting true change rather than simply measurement variation. See Table 6.4 for clear definitions and examples of disruptive behaviors that you can use in coding your classroom observations.

THE CLASSROOM CHECK-UP
10-MINUTE CLASSROOM OBSERVATION FORM

All of the critical classroom variables (opportunities to respond, correct academic responses, praise, reprimands, and disruptive classroom behaviors) discussed above can be tallied (frequency count) each time they are observed during a classroom visit. The Classroom Check-Up 10-Minute Classroom Observation Form was developed to assist with data collection and can be used to code these critical variables during a 10-minute observation

TABLE 6.3. Definitions and Examples of Reprimands

Overall reprimand definition: Verbal comments or gestures made by the teacher indicating *disapproval* of student behavior. The tone may be pleasant, but the interaction indicates disapproval of a behavior.

Explicit/fluent reprimand	Critical/harsh/emotional reprimand
Definition: Teacher provides a correction or reprimand that is concise (brief), in a normal speaking voice without a harsh, critical, or sarcastic tone.	*Definition:* Teacher provides a reprimand or correction using a voice louder than typical for the setting, and/or using a harsh, critical, or sarcastic tone.
Examples • Teacher: "Keith, that's talking out. Please raise your hand before you speak." • Teacher: "China, please have a seat" (when China gets out of her seat). • Teacher: "I am talking, eyes on me" (when a group of students is talking). • Nonverbal: Use of proximity, finger to lips when students are talking. • Teacher: "Class, your voices are loud. Use an inside voice." • Nonverbal: Teacher writes point on board for the class toward losing recess without stopping instruction. • Teacher: "I don't like the way this table is working." • Teacher: "China, Keith, and Shanna, please have a seat." • Nonverbal: Teacher gives a warning point to a student who talks out.	*Examples* • Teacher says nothing but slams hand down onto a student's desk. • Teacher grabs a student, using excessive physical control. • Teacher states in raised voice: "I am talking, eyes on me" (When a group of students is talking). • Teacher: "How many times do I have to tell you guys about the rules?" • Teacher: (*in a sarcastic tone*) "Wow, Jenn finally joined us." • Teacher: (*in a sarcastic tone to a student who often doesn't turn in homework*): "That's a surprise, you don't have your homework again." • Nonverbal: Teacher stops instruction to write a point on board for the class toward losing recess, using long strokes while glaring at students. • Teacher: "Everyone is doing well today except for Dana." • Teacher rolls eyes at students and sighs deeply before or after a reprimand. • Teacher makes statements using the third person, ranting: "Mrs. Smith is so disappointed in this classroom and can't understand why we just can't get this!"
Non-examples • Teacher: "No, the answer is 12." • Teacher: "Kennedy is sitting quietly, waiting for directions" (when China is talking to peer). • Teacher: "I am looking for students who are showing me they are ready to work." • Teacher: "If you are finished, you may read a book without talking." • Teacher: "Heads down on your desk when you are done."	*Non-examples* • Teacher uses proximity and gently places hand on a student's shoulder to stop a behavior. • Nonverbal: Use of proximity, hand on shoulder, finger to lips when students are talking. • Nonverbal: Teacher writes point on board toward loss of recess without stopping instruction.

TABLE 6.4. Definitions and Examples of Student Disruptive Behaviors

Definition: Any statement or action by an individual student or group of students that could be predicted to disrupt or interfere with ongoing classroom activities for the teacher and/or one or more peers.

The following are some specific disruptive behaviors:

Talking out
 Any vocalization made by the student that was not solicited or violates the classroom rule for making a comment or speaking.

Examples
- Student cries out "Me! Me! Me!" when teacher provides an opportunity to respond.
- Student asks a question or makes a comment unrelated to the academic task.
- Rather than answer a question, student tattles on another student: "He isn't working" (tattling).
- Student makes noises to gain teacher's attention (whining, grunting).
- Student hums, sings, whistles, sighs deeply, clucks tongue, or makes other noise with mouth.

Non-examples
- Coughing, sneezing, appropriate clearing of throat, or hiccups.
- Noises made by blowing of nose or any noise associated with a stuffy nose.

Noncompliance/defiance
 Not following a teacher directive.
 Refusing to participate in classroom activities.

Examples
- Student refuses to complete assigned work or answer question asked by teacher.
- Student cries "No" or puts his head down following a teacher request to come to the board.

Non-examples
- Teacher asks student to come to board to complete a math problem; the student gets up from seat, comes to board, but answers question incorrectly.
- Student leaves the room to use the restroom with permission when a new activity begins.

Negative verbal/physical interactions
 Displaying physical aggression toward another person.
 Displaying physical aggression toward objects.
 Displaying verbal aggression toward others or objects.
 Using obscene language.

Examples
- Student slams a book on desk and leaves the room.
- Student hits, pokes, bites, kicks, chokes, or throws object at a peer or teacher.

Non-examples
- Student touches the arm of a peer to gain his or her attention.
- Student accidently drops a book or other object, making a loud noise.

Note: If something seems as though it has disrupted instruction or other students, than it probably is a disruption.

(see Figure 6.2 for a completed example of the Classroom Check-Up 10-Minute Classroom Observation Form and Appendix B.4 for a blank form). For each observation, total the number of behaviors observed and calculate the rate (or number per minute) of each behavior by dividing the total by the number of minutes you observed. Additionally, you can calculate the percent accuracy for student responses and the ratio of positive to negative interactions from the data on this form as well. This information will be used for providing feedback to the teacher based on benchmarks discussed in Chapter 7.

As mentioned previously, ideally you would collect this data on at least three separate occasions. Further, it can be helpful to gather the data on separate *days*. For instance, if you gathered the data in the same classroom by coming in and out three times during the same day, you may be capturing a day that was not typical (e.g., a student with particularly

Conduct more than one classroom observation, ideally three. Further, gather the data on separate *days*.

challenging behavior was absent that day). Data collected over 3 days, either in 1 week or across a 2-week period, will likely capture typical variations in the classroom climate.

STUDENT ENGAGEMENT

Another observable outcome related to student behavior is student engagement. This variable can be measured by observing each student in the classroom for a brief moment (5 seconds) and documenting whether he or she was on or off task. These data are useful to supplement the disruptive behavior observations because in some classrooms students may be disengaged from academic material without being disruptive. Thus, we developed a separate 5-minute observation protocol to determine the overall level of classroom engagement as a separate measure from disruptive behaviors.

To conduct this observation, select a student to start with and a pattern that you can follow and remember (e.g., first row to the back going from right to left) that allows you to observe every student in the classroom. For instance, if the student desks are arranged in a U shape, you might begin at the left front corner, observing the student next to the corner student and around the group, ending with the student on the far right corner (see Figure 6.3). If you reach the end of your pattern prior to the end of the 5 minutes, simply start at the first student again, following the same pattern. You might observe some students two or more times.

Once you identify the pattern you wish to use when observing the students, begin the observation. Using a stopwatch or other device that provides you with the number of seconds and minutes, begin with the first student. When the stopwatch reaches 5 seconds, look up and determine if the student is on task (+) or off task (0). This is called *momentary time sampling* because you document the behavior that is occurring at that moment in time. When the stopwatch reaches 10 seconds look up and code whether the second student is on task (+) or off task (0). Continue until 5 minutes have elapsed. On occasion you will struggle with coding because you will notice that 3 seconds in, the student is off task, but at 5 seconds he or she appears engaged. Keep the process consistent and mark the student on task

Classroom Check-Up 10-Minute Classroom Observation Form

Teacher: Ms. Morris	Date: 10/26/10	Topic: Math Instruction
Observer: Wendy	Start time: 1:35 pm	Activity: Teacher-Directed Instruction

Type of Instruction (circle): **New Material** (**Drill and Practice**)

During the 10-minute observation period, mark a tally for each time the following behaviors are observed in the classroom. Then calculate total, # per minute (rate), % correct academic responding, and ratio of interactions (positive : negative).

	10-Minute Frequency Count	Total #	Rate: #/total minutes	% correct = CAR/OTR × 100
Opportunity to Respond (OTR)	卌 卌 卌 卌	20	2.0	(70)%
Correct Academic Response (CAR)	卌 卌 ////	14	1.4	
Disruptive Behavior	卌 卌 卌 卌 //	22	2.2	Ratio pos. to neg. = total rep/total praise = 1 : (2)
Praise Behavior SPECIFIC	//	2	0.2	Specific + General =
Praise GENERAL	卌	5	0.5	Total: (7)
Reprimand Explicit/Fluent	卌 卌 /	11	1.1	Explicit + Critical = Total: (14)
Reprimand Critical/Harsh/Emotional	///	3	0.3	

Comments:

Ms. Morris scanned the room using active supervision. The observation occurred during math instruction, which started off with fewer OTRs. Two minutes before end, she announced a quiz that the students didn't know about.

FIGURE 6.2. Example of a completed Classroom Check-Up 10-Minute Classroom Observation Form.

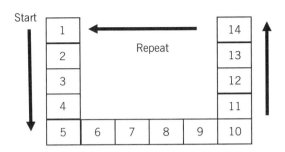

FIGURE 6.3. Example of a pattern for observing classwide student engagement.

(+). This is just a snapshot of the classroom during a brief window. It is just as likely that a student you marked as off task was on task a second before. In the end, it should all even out. Upon completion of the observation you can calculate the percent of time students were academically engaged (on task). You will use this information when providing feedback to the teacher. As with the CCU 10-minute observation, you would ideally complete three or more observations on different days. See Table 6.5 for an operational definition of student engagement. Figure 6.4 depicts a completed example of the Classroom Check-Up 5-Minute Academic Engagement Observation Form; Appendix B.5 is a blank version of the form.

OVERALL CLASSROOM RATINGS

Completing a brief overall classroom rating on several key classroom management practices can be useful to spark conversation between you and the teacher. To facilitate observation and discussion of these variables, the Classroom Check-Up Overall Classroom Rating Form can be completed following each classroom observation visit. The form allows you to rate, on a scale from 1 to 5, how well you perceived the teacher to be using specific strategies, ending with an overall rating. If you score a teacher below average on any of the items, write down a specific reason or example for doing so in the comment section. This information can then be shared with the teacher during the feedback session. The strategies coded on the Classroom Check-Up Overall Classroom Rating Form include the teacher's use of active supervision, an attention signal, and reinforcement (Was it contingent? Did it vary?); whether expectations were reviewed for both academic and social behavior; whether transitions were smooth and without much wasted time; and your overall impression of the classroom climate. For each item, the form asks you to rate the use of the strategies or your overall impressions on a 5-point scale, with 1 being poor, or not as well as other classrooms you have observed, and 5 being excellent, or better than most classrooms you have observed. Ranking an item as a 3 indicates that the teacher's use of the strategy, the classroom climate, or length of transition was average in comparison to other classrooms you have observed. Figure 6.5 provides a completed example of the Classroom Check-Up Overall Classroom Rating Form; Appendix B.6 provides a blank version of the form.

TABLE 6.5. Operational Definition and Example of Student Academic Engagement/On-Task Behavior

Definition: Student attempts or correctly demonstrates the assigned/approved activity in the absence of disruptive behavior. On-task behavior may include (1) attending to the material and the task; (2) making appropriate motor response, such as writing or looking at the teacher; (3) asking for assistance or waiting for assistance in an acceptable manner (e.g., raising hand quietly); and (4) waiting appropriately for the teacher to begin or continue with instruction.

Examples
- If the teacher is asking students to answer questions, the student is looking at the teacher and/or raising hand to offer a response.
- If the teacher is asking students to work independently, the student has a pencil out and is working on the assigned activity.
- If students are asked to wait quietly while others finish, the student is seated at desk without talking to others.

Non-examples
- Student is staring off and not working on task.
- Student is being disruptive.
- Student is working on a math assignment when he or she is supposed to be working on a specific writing activity.
- Student is doodling on the paper rather than completing the assigned task.
- Student leaves work space to sharpen a pencil and walks around the room before returning to desk.
- Student is looking at another student's paper without permission to do so.

Note: If you find yourself questioning whether the student is engaged or not, record it as *not* engaged.

FROM DIRECT OBSERVATION TO EFFECTIVE INTERVENTION

Linking assessment to intervention has become a vital part of education. The variables described above provide a feasible, efficient, and effective way of making this link. The information gathered during the classroom observation can be used to develop classroom behavior management interventions and to track whether they are working. Ideally, three to five classroom observations should be taken during teacher-led instruction. This helps avoid the problem of designing an intervention based on one particularly bad day in the classroom. Once observations are completed, a mean number per minute can be totaled for each variable to provide feedback to the teacher. Using the optimal range for the variables noted above, the teacher can develop intervention ideas targeting the areas that need improvement.

Once an intervention is developed and implemented in the classroom, several additional observations should follow. There are two reasons for follow-up observations:

Classroom Check-Up 5-Minute Academic Engagement Observation Form

Teacher: Ms. Morris	**Date:** 10/26/10	**Topic:** Math Instruction
Observer: Wendy	**Start time:** 1:55 pm	**Activity:** Independent Work/Quiz

For the next 5 minutes, every 5 seconds you will indicate if a student is on task or off task. Each box indicates two things: (1) the number of seconds into the observation that you will look up at the student to determine on task (+) or off task (0) at that moment, and (2) the interval number. Continue observing students (repeating students as necessary) until the 5-minute period is complete, for a total of 60 intervals. Then calculate the % of time the students in the classroom were engaged.

+ indicates on task (engaged)
0 indicates off task (not engaged)

5 sec	10 sec	15 sec	20 sec	25 sec	30 sec	35 sec	40 sec	45 sec	50 sec
+	O	O	+	+	+	O	+	+	+
1	2	3	4	5	6	7	8	9	10
55 sec	1 min	1:05 sec	1:10 sec	1:15 sec	1:20 sec	1:25 sec	1:30 sec	1:35 sec	1:40 sec
+	+	+	+	+	O	+	+	+	+
11	12	13	14	15	16	17	18	19	20
1:45 sec	1:50 sec	1:55 sec	2 min	2:05 sec	2:10 sec	2:15 sec	2:20 sec	2:25 sec	2:30 sec
+	+	O	+	O	+	+	+	+	O
21	22	23	24	25	26	27	28	29	30
2:35 sec	2:40 sec	2:45 sec	2:50 sec	2:55 sec	3 min	3:05 sec	3:10 sec	3:15 sec	3:20 sec
+	+	+	O	O	+	+	O	+	+
31	32	33	34	35	36	37	38	39	40
3:25 sec	3:30 sec	3:35 sec	3:40 sec	3:45 sec	3:50 sec	3:55 sec	4 min	4:05 sec	4:10 sec
+	+	+	O	+	+	O	+	+	+
41	42	43	44	45	46	47	48	49	50
4:15 sec	4:20 sec	4:25 sec	4:30 sec	4:35 sec	4:40 sec	4:45 sec	4:50 sec	4:55 sec	5 min
+	+	+	O	O	+	+	+	O	+
51	52	53	54	55	56	57	58	59	60

% on task = # interval + / total number of intervals coded × 100%

1. Total # intervals coded (+) = (45)
2. Total # intervals coded (+) + (0) = (60)
3. 1/2 × 100% = (75)%

Comments:

The first 2 minutes the students were taking a quiz. When finished with the quiz, they were supposed to complete a worksheet independently.

FIGURE 6.4. Example of a completed Classroom Check-Up 5-Minute Academic Engagement Observation Form.

Classroom Check-Up Overall Classroom Rating Form

Teacher: Ms. Morris	Date: 10/26/10	Observer: Wendy

Upon completion of an observation visit, rate the classroom on the following items on a scale from 1 to 5, with 5 being excellent compared to other classrooms you have observed, 3 being average, and 1 being poor. For items you rate below average (1 or 2) write down reasons for the lower rating in the comment section provided. For items you rate above average, write your reasons for doing so as well.

Please circle the most appropriate rating for each item using the following scale:
5 = excellent; 4 = above average; 3 = average; 2 = below average; 1 = poor; NO = not observed

Item	Rating	Comments
Use of Active Supervision	5 **(4)** 3 2 1 NO	Teacher walked around room while providing instruction
Use of Attention Signal	5 4 3 **(2)** 1 NO	There were one or two occasions a signal would have been useful
Followed the Schedule	5 4 **(3)** 2 1 NO	
Reinforcement Was Contingent	5 4 **(3)** 2 1 NO	
Variety of Reinforcement Used	5 4 3 **(2)** 1 NO	Used verbal praise only
Reviewed Academic Expectations	5 4 **(3)** 2 1 NO	Unexpected quiz, but instructed on how to complete and what to do after
Reviewed Social/ Behavioral Expectations	5 4 3 **(2)** 1 NO	At times it was unclear if calling out was okay or not
Transitions Were Smooth	5 4 3 **(2)** 1 NO	The transition to taking the quiz took about 4 minute—a bit long
Overall Climate Was Positive	5 4 **(3)** 2 1	
Overall Rating	5 4 **(3)** 2 1	Focus on increasing variety and use of positive reinforcement

Additional Comments:

This is the first of three observations. Ms. Morris did not use an attention signal. Transitions may have been smoother with a signal. Also, expectations for how students should gain teacher attention were unclear. She actively supervised by walking around the classroom and scanned for students needing attention. Also, use of praise was contingent on student behavior. Having a few other strategies to give attention to appropriate behavior could be useful—thumbs up, token system …

FIGURE 6.5. Example of a completed Classroom Check-Up Overall Classroom Rating Form.

1. Continued observations allow teachers to see if they have actually changed their rate of targeted variables (e.g., praise is increasing). This is known as *performance feedback*, and it is a powerful tool for changing behavior. Studies have documented the effectiveness of performance feedback in facilitating behavior changes in teachers (Noell et al., 2000; Reinke et al., 2008).
2. Continued observations allow teachers to see if classroom disruptive or off-task behavior is decreasing as a result of the intervention. In other words, is the intervention working? If there is no change in student behavior, then the intervention will need to be rethought or changed slightly. This tweaking process should continue until the desired change is seen in student behavior.

SUMMARY

This chapter describes the assessment procedures utilized by the CCU to inform intervention development. A sample transcript of the CCU interview highlights the use of MI strategies to facilitate motivation and engagement in the teacher participating in the process. Additionally, the critical classroom management variables are described and defined, and methods for gathering precise and useful data are detailed. The data collection methods described in this chapter link directly to the design of effective classroom-level interventions. The next chapter focuses on compiling the data gathered from the classroom observations, the CEC, and the CCU interview into a user-friendly format for providing feedback, developing a menu of options, and creating an action plan linked to effective classroom management interventions. Additionally, the next chapter discusses in greater detail the use of performance feedback to support teachers as they implement new strategies in their classroom.

CHAPTER 7

Feedback and Beyond

You have an abundance of information after completing the CCU teacher interview, the CEC, and the classroom observations. Now what? The next step is to compile all of the rich data you have gathered and present it in a manner that can be easily understood and useful in guiding intervention planning. This chapter describes the process of compiling the data, providing feedback to the teacher, developing a menu of options, designing an intervention based on the specific needs of the classroom, and creating an action plan for next steps. This chapter also reviews the process used for ongoing progress monitoring and for giving performance feedback. We conclude the chapter with a troubleshooting guide for using the CCU and handling common questions or concerns. Chapter 6 focused on Step 1 of the CCU (see Table 5.1, p. 73). This chapter focuses on Steps 2–6.

PREPARING FOR THE FEEDBACK SESSION

Taking the data you have gathered from your interview, measures, and observations and preparing them for presentation to the teacher requires a combination of professional judgment and a reference to the CCU feedback guidelines provided in Table 7.1. An important part of the process is to spend time integrating your findings into a comprehensive classroom conceptualization.

Begin by compiling the information you have gathered into concrete, quantitative data. In other words, review the data collected during classroom observations and generate the following: (1) the mean rate of opportunities to respond, (2) the mean percentage of student accuracy, (3) the mean rate of classroom disruptions, (4) the mean rate of praise, (5) the mean rate of reprimands, (6) the ratio of positive-to-negative interactions, (7) the number of behavior-specific praise statements versus general praise statements across observations, and (8) the number of explicit/fluent reprimands versus critical/harsh reprimands.

TABLE 7.1. CCU Feedback Guidelines

Indicator	Red	Yellow	Green
Percent correct academic responding	Less than 75% new material Less than 80% drill and practice *or* Material too easy (100% across observations)	75% new material 80% drill and practice	80% new material 90% drill and practice
Time on task (academic engagement)	Less than 80%	80–89%	90% or more
Opportunities to respond	Fewer than 1 per minute	1–3.9 per minute	4 or more per minute
Ratio of interactions	Less than 1:1 or less than one praise statement per minute	At least 1:1 consistently	At least 3:1 consistently
Specific versus general praise	No praise	More general praise than specific praise	More specific praise than general praise
Quality of interactions	Raised voice, targets individual child More than two harsh/critical reprimands	Any negative tone, criticism, sarcasm in voice One to two harsh/critical reprimands	Always positive
Disruptions	10 or more in 10 minutes or 1 per minute	5–9 in 10 minutes or 0.5–0.9 per minute	Fewer than 5 in 10 minutes or less than 0.5 per minute

After making these calculations, review the teacher interview to identify areas that the teacher was interested in targeting for intervention. Also, review the interview for areas in which the teacher felt he or she was doing well, and current practices already in place. Then, review the CEC for specific information you may want to discuss during the feedback session, including the items that you rated highly (teacher strengths) and the items that may need attention. Last, review the Classroom Check-Up Overall Classroom Rating Forms completed following each observation. These forms provide you with talking points across important classroom management practices. Additionally, the comments section on this form may provide you with some anecdotal information that was captured at the time of your observations. For instance, you may have jotted down a particular behavior-specific praise statement and its effect on the classroom that you want to share with the teacher, or perhaps you wrote a reprimand statement that you heard the teacher make, which could have been more explicit or fluent. Specific examples of positive and negative classroom attributes are helpful as you present the data to the teacher because the teacher can think back to the moment and reflect on that practice, how he or she may have handled it differently, or how it felt to him or her at the time. Appendix C provides information on how to calculate the data that align with the CCU feedback guidelines.

Conceptualization

Once you complete calculations for the observational data listed above and have reviewed the CCU interview and CEC, you are ready to begin conceptualization. First, review the CCU feedback guidelines provided in Table 7.1. Recall that the CCU process begins with a comprehensive ecological assessment of the classroom, including a consideration of needs and resources. Prior to creating the feedback form, it is important to take time to integrate all the findings from this assessment into a comprehensive conceptualization. *The goal of this process is to define the problem in a very specific and solvable way and to identify malleable factors that can solve the problem.* Essentially, you are asking yourself this question: What are the most pressing needs for the teacher and the classroom, and what are their most important assets and resources? By first taking time to reflect on these data and identify the one or two most pressing issues, you will be better prepared to create the feedback form and deliver the feedback session.

Figure 7.1 provides a visual guide for integrating and considering all the information gathered prior to feedback. You can see that when providing feedback to a teacher, it is important to consider the data that you have collected from the teacher's own report, from your classroom observations, and from the interview within the context of the resources and support available, the systems operating within the classroom (individual students) and in which the classroom operates (the school and community), as well as the cultural context across these systems. Lastly, your own impressions are important as you conceptualize providing feedback to the teacher. The entire process is guided by theory on building effective

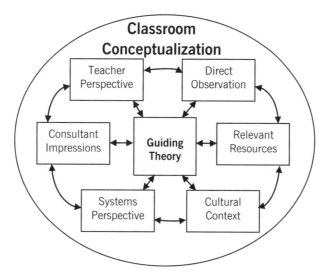

FIGURE 7.1. Factors related to conceptualizing the classroom.

> **The goal of conceptualizing the classroom and preparing the feedback to provide the teacher is to define the problem in a very specific and solvable way and to identify malleable factors that can solve the problem.**

classroom environments. Once you have spent time reflecting on the important domains that inform conceptualization, you can begin to fill out the Classroom Check-Up Feedback Form (see Figure 7.2 for a completed example and Appendix C.3 for a blank form).

The Classroom Check-Up Feedback Form

The Classroom Check-Up Feedback Form is a tool for efficiently communicating results from your assessment to the teacher. The form also helps you to present the information in an objective, nonconfrontational manner. Rather than you as consultant being the person communicating any negative feedback, the form becomes the communication tool, and much like a medical test result on paper, is hard to dismiss or argue against the objective data.

The form capitalizes on a color coding system that is fairly universally recognized: the red–yellow–green colors of traffic signals. Many teachers use a similar color system as part of their classroom discipline plans, so they know intuitively that scores in the green mean *keep going or doing what you are doing* because you're doing it well; scores in the yellow mean *slow down and reflect* about doing something differently; and scores in the red mean *stop and do something differently*. We provide this explanation when we first show teachers the form, and they get it. (See Appendix C.3 for information on how to obtain a color version of this form.)

The Classroom Check-Up Feedback Form breaks down the key elements of classroom management systems into four categories and then subdomains within these categories. The form depicted in Figure 7.2 contains the traditional categories that we have used with the CCU. But note that the form is adaptable to different contexts or skill areas that you want to emphasize. In the final chapter of this book you will see one adaptation we have made to the form for application in settings where teachers are being asked to implement particular programs (e.g., the Good Behavior Game or a socioemotional curriculum).

Completing the Classroom Check-Up Feedback Form

Appendix C.2 provides details about the sources of information you may use for each CCU feedback domain as well as some general guidelines for determining feedback. The next step is to simply place an X along the row of each subdomain within each category. Remember, if an X is in the green, that means that this is a strength of the classroom and something the teacher should continue doing or build upon; an X in the yellow is something the teacher

> **When preparing the feedback form, attend to the strengths and resources. Be sure to identify these strengths and include them on the feedback form.**

may want to consider changing or improving; and an X in the red is something to definitely pay attention to and try something different. The continuum from green to red allows you to emphasize certain findings during the feedback session. If you put something far over to the left in the green, as far as it can

Classroom Check-Up Feedback Form

Teacher: Ms. Morris Date: 11/02/10

Classroom Structure

Physical Layout	X
Classroom Rules	X
Classroom Routines	X
Smooth Transitions	X
Other: *Well organized*	X

Area of Strength — Needs Attention

Instructional Management

Schedule Posted and Followed	X
Academic Objectives Clear	X
Pacing	X 2 per minute
Student Accuracy	X
Student Engagement	X 81% on task
Other:	

Area of Strength — Needs Attention

Behavior Management

Behavioral Expectations Clear	X
Active Supervision	X
Use of Praise	X
Use of Reprimands	X
Positive to Negative Ratio	Ratio 1:2 X
Used Variety of Reinforcement	X only praise
Other:	

Area of Strength — Needs Attention

Classroom Climate

Use of Noncontingent Attention	X greeted all students
Interactions with Students	X
Level of Disruptive Behavior	about 1 every other minute X
Other: Positive Climate	X

Area of Strength — Needs Attention

FIGURE 7.2. Example of a completed Classrom Check-Up Feedback Form.

go, you are communicating that this is a special strength of the classroom and the teacher's current practices. If you put something to the far right in the red, as far as it can go, you are communicating that this is a serious problem area that needs immediate attention. You can also use orange as an indication that a certain area is getting close to becoming a serious problem. Use the continuum to your advantage by emphasizing certain red zone scores over others. This is where your professional judgment and consideration during conceptualization come into play. Below we describe some general decision rules we have developed for placing *X*'s on the form.

Attending to Strengths and Resources

As you craft the feedback that you will deliver to the teacher, think about the main areas of concern. Ensure that these key areas are highlighted on the form. However, be sure that the feedback form reflects both strengths and areas in need of attention. Every form should contain indicators in the green. If this is not reflected in the existing categories, identify an area and write it into the "Other" category. In a similar vein, if an area of concern was identified that does not fall under the feedback categories, write the area of concern into an "Other" category. This is particularly important if you think that the concern is a major contributor to classroom misbehavior. For instance, teachers who are experiencing high levels of personal stress may struggle with managing classroom behavior. If this is something that would benefit from discussion and potential intervention, write in "level of stress" in the "Other" category and put an *X* in the red zone. This will generate a conversation about the level of stress the teacher is experiencing and how that might impact the students.

Preparing Specific Examples

After calculating the indicators found on the Classroom Check-Up Feedback Form, review the teacher interview, the CEC, and Classroom Check-Up Overall Classroom Rating Form for specific examples. During the feedback session it is helpful to give concrete examples of the most important areas of concern. For example, if the quality of interactions indicator is considered in need of attention (red), recalling a specific example can be useful in reviewing the feedback. Similarly, you might reflect on the moment with the teacher when he or she provided a particularly harsh reprimand to a student. An example of a conversation may look like this:

> "The interaction with student category is getting at the tone or quality of some of the reprimands that you use in the classroom. It is in the red because on two occasions during a classroom observation, you raised your voice a bit and seemed frustrated. On one occasion you said something like, 'If anyone in the classroom had done their homework, then they would not be so worried about having to take this quiz.' I wonder if you recall that day. What are your thought about that?"

The consultant invites the teacher to reflect on this particular instance. Clearly, this could be a sensitive topic about a critical leverage point in the classroom. Presenting a specific example in a matter-of-fact manner brings the topic to the forefront and initiates a conversation that could lead to evocative questions about how the teacher was feeling during these times, how children might perceive these episodes, and alternative responses that the teacher might use in the future. Likewise, it is also important to provide specific examples when reviewing items in the green. Specific examples make affirmations seem sincere and give the teacher guides for exactly what he or she is doing well.

Summary and Guiding Principles

Following are key points to remember as you prepare for the feedback session:

- Do not spend a lot of time fretting over the precise placement of *X*'s on the feedback form. The form is intended to be delivered as part of a conversation, not just as a laboratory report. Use it to stimulate discussion and evoke change talk.
- Plan what message you want to send to the teacher based on your case conceptualization and strategically place *X*'s where you want the teacher to focus his or her attention/efforts.
- Use the Classroom Check-Up Feedback Guidelines in Table 7.1 to determine whether an area is red, yellow, or green. However, remember, if you feel that one area needs particular attention, you can place the *X* as far to the right in the red as possible, whereas, other areas may be red, but not as far out on the continuum. Use the entire scale to communicate the full picture.
- Come prepared with specific examples of the most important areas you want to highlight.

PRESENTING FEEDBACK TO THE TEACHER

Introduction and Overview

Set up a time to meet with the teacher to present the feedback and start planning for next steps. Ideally, you will complete the feedback and action planning phases in a single meeting, so try to find a 45- to 60-minute block of time for this meeting. In practice, it can be difficult for a teacher to have this much time to devote in a single block, so if needed, you can break the session into two 20- to 30-minute meetings.

Social Conversation

As before, take time at the beginning of your visit to engage in social conversation. Pay attention to your pacing; that is, try not to rush the social conversation or push to get started on the feedback immediately. Allow time for you and the teacher to get settled into the conversation before transitioning to the feedback. Do not bring out the feedback form until you are ready to begin sharing that information.

Introducing the Procedures

As you move toward providing the feedback, explain to the teacher what is about to happen. A conversation explaining the process might go like this:

> "Lori, thanks for meeting with me. I have compiled all the data from the classroom observations I conducted over the last week or so. It was really helpful to observe the classroom, and I think I got some good information. What I have done is to summarize all of this information into a simple graphic, so that we can look at it together to see where we might want to focus. The form shows us what is going well and where we might want to think about trying something new. But before we take a look at this form, let me ask you what you learned from filling out the Classroom Ecology Checklist or from our discussion last week?"

What Did You Learn?

Begin by asking teachers to reflect on what they learned from the assessment process. Often the interview and assessment questions create new insights for teachers that they had not previously considered. Asking the teachers about any learning they experienced will provide you with valuable knowledge about where he or she is in the change process and any specific ideas the teacher may already have developed for changing. These ideas can be revisited during the menu-of-options phase. If teachers say that they did not reflect upon the assessment process, their admission may tell you that they are in an early stage of change, or it may simply be an indicator of their overall work and stress load. After the teacher's response to your question, you might provide the following kind of transition:

> "That's great. I'm glad that you were able to reflect on our conversation and come up with some ideas for new classroom strategies. When we go over the feedback form, we can see where those ideas align with the information I gathered over the last week."

Identifying Relative Teacher Strengths

Again, be sure not to rush the conversation about teacher strengths. Take time to pause and reflect. Two key elements of effective discussions about strengths include being specific and sincere. Note that these comments should be based on both your observations as well as objective data. Some critical aspects of being perceived as genuine include spending enough time with the teacher and in the classroom and giving specific examples of strengths you have observed. Consider the following explanation:

> "Let me begin by noting all the great things I noticed about your classroom. The atmosphere is very supportive. It's clear that you really care about your students and helping

them be successful. You have a great interpersonal style. You really get down on their level when speaking to them and use gentle touch to remind or redirect. I really sense that every student in that room knows that you care deeply for him or her and want the best for all of them. The other thing that really stood out to me is how much time you put into planning each day to be successful. These are important strengths of yours that we will want to capitalize on and keep going as we consider any changes you would like to make."

Introducing the Feedback Form

Next, tell teachers what red, yellow, and green signify on the form and that you will take notes of areas where they may want to focus to help plan for next steps. It can be helpful to begin by showing the teacher a blank feedback form. Showing a blank form first allows you to explain what the color coding indicates without the teacher getting distracted by focusing on his or her specific marks. Explain that areas in green are areas of strength, things that the teacher will want to keep doing. Yellow areas are in the warning zone and represent areas to consider changing. Those areas in the red indicate practices that they will want to stop and think about. These are practices that should be given attention when thinking about ideas for what to change. Following is a sample explanation:

> **Showing a blank feedback form allows you to explain what the color coding indicates without the teacher getting distracted by focusing on his or her specific marks.**

"On this form you'll notice that there are different categories. Under each category is a specific area for feedback. Next to each area, I have marked an X along a continuum that goes from green to yellow to red. Now, if something is marked in the green, that is something that is going well—it's a strength of the classroom. We don't want to change anything about this, but we may want to build off of it. If something is in the yellow area, that is something that we might want to give some attention to, and if something is in the red, that means that this is an area we definitely need to focus on changing. As we go along, if you see something that you want to target, let me know and I will jot it down and we can come back to it. Do you have any questions? Okay. Let's take a look."

Delivering the Feedback

After providing an overview and introduction to the feedback process, you are now prepared to "walk through" the feedback form. We use one of two approaches when providing feedback, based on the personal preference and style of the consultant and the anticipated needs of the teacher.

> **One point of the feedback session is to engage the teacher in a dialogue about topics that may be difficult to discuss or that he or she had not really thought about previously.**

Approach 1: Starting with the Positives

"Let's begin by looking at what is going well."

One possible approach is to begin by covering the feedback form with a blank sheet of paper, then slowly moving the blank paper to the right to reveal only those areas in the green. This allows you to review all of the positives associated with the classroom first. Next you move the blank paper further to the right to show the areas in the yellow, and then finally the ones in the red. There are pros and cons to this approach. For one, the teacher receives a high dose of positive reinforcement up front and may be more receptive to feedback that is less positive as you move along. However, the feedback is spread across different domains and may seem disjointed when presented in this manner (rather than covering one domain at a time). Additionally, although it is great to have all of the positives delivered upfront, it also means that all of the more negative feedback is delivered together as well, without positives to break it up. Thus, when using this approach, it is a good idea to refer back to the strengths within each domain as you reveal areas that need attention.

Approach 2: Starting at the Top and Moving Down the Page in Order

"The first domain on this list is the overall classroom structure. The first item is the physical layout of the classroom. Let's start here and move down the page."

A second approach to providing the feedback is to start at the top of the feedback form and simply go in order from top to bottom. Again, there are pros and cons here. This approach allows the feedback to occur within domains and may help center the conversations around these topical domains better than the strengths approach described above. Additionally, both positive and negative feedback are interspersed throughout the session. However, if the first sections of the form are all in the red, you may find yourself beginning the conversation with only negative feedback. In practice, we use both methods, depending on the classroom and circumstances. The key is just to be mindful of the strengths and limits of each approach.

Checking in to Create Dialogue

One point of the feedback session is to engage the teacher in a dialogue about topics that may be difficult to discuss or that he or she had not really thought about before. Therefore, it is important to check in with the teacher over the course of the feedback meeting. After each feedback point, ask the teacher for his or her reactions to the feedback (or reflect it): "What do you make of that?" "Does that fit with your perceptions?" "That surprises you." When possible, give specific numbers and reference points as part of the feedback. Provide specific information on the rate of opportunities to respond, the percent of students engaged during instruction, the ratio of interactions, and the rate of disruptive behavior. This information can ground the conversation in ideas for change. For instance, you might inform the teacher of his or her current ratio of interactions compared to what research suggests is the optimal ratio. Following is an example of how these points might be explained:

"In looking at the form, we see that your ratio of interactions is in the reddish-orange zone. This is because during the classroom observations, I tallied the number of praise statements and reprimands you provided and then calculated the ratio of positive to negative. Your ratio was 1:2, meaning that you provided two reprimands for every praise statement. Ideally, your ratio would be more positives than negatives. What are your thoughts on that?"

Providing Ample Summaries

Be sure to summarize each section of the feedback form and give the teacher plenty of opportunity for reflection about what the feedback means and how he or she is interpreting the findings. Regular summaries provide the time and space for absorbing all of the feedback details.

Sample Feedback Session

The following provides a brief example of a portion of a CCU feedback session with a fifth-grade teacher. The meeting took place in a single 45-minute session, with the action planning dialogue continued in the next section.

Feedback Session Dialogue	Comments
CONSULTANT: Thanks so much for meeting with me. I've really enjoyed observing your classroom. There are so many positive things that I noticed that you do. I really appreciate how much work you put into your class preparation and how thoughtful you are about getting to each student. It's just a very positive atmosphere in there, and that's hard to do.	Affirmations
Now that I've had some time to observe your class and put together the things we talked about, I'm going to show you this feedback form. These marks represent where you are within each of these categories. As you might guess, if you have something in the red, that's something that is in need of attention; if it's in the yellow, we may want to think about changing it; and the green means keep doing whatever you are doing. Make sense?	Summary and preview
	Check-in question
TEACHER: Sure. Like the color system we use in my class.	
CONSULTANT: Right. So let's start here. You can see that the percent of correct responses is in the green. The students are getting about 91% of opportunities correct. Anything above 85% is good.	Personalized feedback Affirmation Strategically starts with a positive
TEACHER: But am I asking questions that are too easy?	
CONSULTANT: Well, so you want them to have a certain level of success, otherwise they will get frustrated. For new material	Provides requested advice

it can go a bit lower, like 85%, but for review you really want it to be about 90%.

TEACHER: That's good to know.

CONSULTANT: Now I put you in the yellow for opportunities to respond, and I think you said you thought your pacing was a bit slow. What did you guess your rate would be?

TEACHER: Four per minute or so.

CONSULTANT: On average, you are at two per minute.

TEACHER: Oh, so that's slow.

CONSULTANT: That surprises you.

TEACHER: Yeah. See the challenge is, they just aren't keeping up. I just see them falling behind.

CONSULTANT: Right, and still, you seem like you were expecting to be faster than that.

TEACHER: Yeah, I guess I did. I certainly try to keep the pace because I know how important it is for learning but also to keep them on track.

CONSULTANT: Well, research says to shoot for four to six for new material and bump it up to nine to twelve when you are reviewing. I wonder, what would happen if you boosted it a bit?

TEACHER: It would be interesting to see and to get feedback on it, because it is hard for me to know except just by guessing how fast I'm going.

CONSULTANT: So it would be helpful to have some ongoing feedback about that.

TEACHER: Yes. And I have a question. Do you think it would be better to go through some direct instruction, say, of math facts, to give them more opportunities to respond. Would that be a good thing?

CONSULTANT: That's a great idea. A lot of teachers find that helps. But for now, would this be something we could add to our menu of options? Then we can come up with a specific plan for that, if you'd like.

TEACHER: That would be very helpful.

CONSULTANT: Here's another area in the yellow: student engagement. But these are related, like you said. Slower pacing can lead to off-task behaviors or disruptions. So you're at 81% for student engagement. You want to be around 90%, so that's not bad.

Marginal annotations:

Personalized feedback

Open-ended question to keep teacher engaged

Feedback

Feeling reflection

Avoids arguing against why pace is important and instead focuses on teacher surprise; elicits change talk

Open-ended question picturing future change

Reflection

Affirmation and adds to menu for further discussion so that feedback process can continue

Personalized feedback

TEACHER: And the rating was done right after lunch, so that's pretty good.

CONSULTANT: And that's the time you wanted to work on improving. — Connecting to prior content and goals

TEACHER: Yes.

CONSULTANT: Should we add that to our menu for further discussion? — Getting agreement to emphasize collaboration

TEACHER: Sure.

CONSULTANT: Okay. Look here at the praise category; this is in the yellow. Now the reason it is yellow is not because you don't use praise. You do. However, you use a lot more general praise, like saying, "Good job," than behavior-specific praise, which includes why the student is being praised—like, "Good job raising your hand." What do you think about that? — Personalized feedback / Affirmation / Open-ended question to clarify understanding and reaction

TEACHER: Oh, yeah. I know I should be doing that. That is something I would like to improve. — Change talk

CONSULTANT: The other area here is your ratio of praise to reprimands. You can see it's in the red. Your ratio was about 1:2. — Personalized feedback

TEACHER: Yikes.

CONSULTANT: That's really shocking to you. — Reflection

TEACHER: Yes. I suspected it was low, but I can't believe that I give more reprimands than praise.

CONSULTANT: What about that is so concerning to you? — Open-ended question eliciting change talk

TEACHER: I just know how important that ratio is, and I really try to attend to it. I know some days it's hard, and I can really feel the difference.

CONSULTANT: It feels different when you praise less. — Reflection

TEACHER: Absolutely. *I* feel different, and I know that the students can feel the difference too.

CONSULTANT: This ratio is shocking to you because you really know how helpful it can be to be more positive, and you always try hard to do it. — Summary highlighting change talk

TEACHER: Right, but I mean this is very helpful to have someone giving me this specific, detailed feedback.

CONSULTANT: On a positive note, your fluent use of reprimands is in the green. You are really good at staying calm and being — Personalized feedback and affirmations

clear about what students were doing wrong. Does that all sound right?	Check-in question
TEACHER: Yes, I try to pay attention to those things.	
CONSULTANT: As far as monitoring, you keep an eye on them. And your transitions are smooth.	
TEACHER: That's one I really work on. I spend a lot of time preparing them for transitions.	
CONSULTANT: Yes, and that goes back to your expectations, which are very clear. Students know what you want and what will happen if they don't do it. And your transitions are great. I don't think you are losing much time at all. Your classroom climate is great, very positive. I don't think the students are afraid of you or anything like that. (*Laughs.*)	Personalized feedback and affirmations

Humor |
| TEACHER: Not yet. (*Laughs.*) | |
| CONSULTANT: Quite the opposite. They look comfortable and seem to respect you and each other. It feels like a very positive and safe place to be. And your organization and structure fit with that. I notice how you have set up paths for students to follow, and they really get that. That level of predictability goes a long way toward helping everyone feel safe and good. The social environment seems very good. I haven't seen kids picking on each other or teasing each other. Does that all fit? | Affirmations

Check-in question |
| TEACHER: Yeah, I think that's all in line with how I think of my class. | |

TRANSITION AND ACTION PLANNING

Transition to Planning

After reviewing the Classroom Check-Up Feedback Form, provide a summary of the feedback and a transition to start talking about next steps. It can be helpful to ask the teacher to summarize his or her take-home points from the feedback. For instance, you might ask, "Based on all the information we've covered so far, what stands out to you the most?" or "What do you see as the most important thing we've discussed so far?"

As you start moving toward discussing next steps, ask the teacher to identify his or her greatest area of concern or the topical area to work on first; "Where do you want to start?" or "What is your biggest concern right now?" or "What do you think is the most important thing to focus on first?" Spend some time reflecting the teacher's comments back to him or her, as all of these questions will yield some form of change talk.

Menu of Options

It is helpful to take notes about important points or topics the teacher was interested in addressing during the feedback session. Next, it is important to generate a list that can serve as a menu of options for how to proceed. Use the Classroom Check-Up Menu of Options (see Figure 7.3 for a completed example and Appendix C.4 for a blank form) to help with the process. The top of the form begins by asking the teacher on what areas he or she would like to work. Additionally, there is a column in which you can write ideas you develop together. The form also has a general list of ideas and ongoing support that can be useful. Here, the process is very collaborative and should include brainstorming to identify potential solutions. Invite the teacher to offer suggestions for addressing the problem.

You should actively contribute to constructing the menu. Recall that during the conceptualization phase (prior to this meeting), it is helpful to come prepared with your idea of the main issues and also some ideas for intervening. However, ensure that you do not simply impose your own plan, but build a collaborative menu of possible options for targeting the areas identified by the teacher as most important. Write all the ideas that you develop during the meeting down on the Classroom Check-Up Menu of Options. A few standard options are provided as well to help with planning.

> **When transitioning into next steps, ensure that you build a collaborative menu of possible options for targeting the areas identified by the teacher as most important.**

After the options have been exhausted, transition to the Classroom Check-Up Action Planning Form (Appendix C.5). You might transition by stating something like the following:

> "Okay, we identified several ideas for next steps. Let's take a moment to identify one or two of these ideas that we want to put into action. We are going to use this action planning form to come up with the next steps. When we finish, I will make a copy to leave with you and take one with me so that we know what we planned to do before our next meeting."

The Classroom Check-Up Action Planning Form

After compiling a list of options on the Classroom Check-Up Menu of Options, next present the Classroom Check-Up Action Planning Form to the teacher. We recommend that you be the one who writes out the plan on the form. This helps keep the discussion moving and gets good information written on the page. Also, you guide the process to make the plan concrete and ensure that it is doable. In other words, try to come up with a plan that is specific and likely to be successful. For instance, if the teacher does not use behavior-specific praise, set a specific goal for how often the teacher will use behavior-specific praise, how this will be measured, and during what time frame. The goal should be realistic. Using the baseline observation data as a reference point is helpful when setting a realistic goal. See Figure 7.4 for a completed example of the Classroom Check-Up Action Planning Form. You might say something like the following (see p. 121) to support the action planning process:

Classroom Check-Up Menu of Options

Teacher: Ms. Morris   Date: 11/02/10

Target Areas for Improvement:
Based on the feedback, on what areas would you, as the classroom teacher, like to focus?
1. Pace of Instruction—math
2. Increase use of behavior specific praise and improve positive to negative ratio
3.

Menu of Options to Increase Effective Classroom Management Strategies:

Collaborative Ideas	Strategy Starters	Ongoing Supports
Hang a prompt to signal to praise students who are meeting expectations.	To improve positive to negative ratio (goal = 3:1), identify strategies to increase praise and reduce reprimands.	Conduct weekly check-in.
Target some behaviors, like raising hand, and use behavior specific praise when it occurs.	To improve classroom climate: Increase noncontingent positive reinforcement.	Model strategies in classroom.
Do some drill and practice in math. Beat the timer. Ask individual and group questions.	To improve pacing of lessons: Identify strategies to break down complex into smaller chunks and ideas for providing more questions to more students.	Observe and provide performance feedback.
Give 2 minutes on math questions in the box, then have whole group give answer.	To improve use of reprimands: Identify strategies for knowing when to use reprimands and when not, as well as ideas for making the reprimands concise and fluent.	Schedule a visit to observe another teacher using strategies.
	To improve correct academic responding: Review lesson material to determine if above or below current level of students. Teach to mastery.	Videotape and review together.
	Identify behaviors of concern and develop a hierarchy of consequences to increase consistency.	Books:
	Develop a lesson plan for teaching classroom expectations. Teach the expectations regularly.	Resources:
	Other:	Other:

NEXT STEP: Identify from the menu one or more strategies to put into place. Complete the Action Planning Form to identify the specific goal (e.g., increase use of behavior-specific praise from 5 to 10 per lesson).

FIGURE 7.3. Example of a completed Classroom Check-Up Menu of Options.

Classroom Check-Up Action Planning Form

Teacher: Ms. Morris   Grade: 5th   Date: 11/02/10

Those things going well in my classroom:	Areas I would like to focus on improving in my classroom:
Very positive; students know expectations and routines	Increase pace of instruction during math and use more behavior-specific praise than reprimands

Specifically, my goal is to: Provide four opportunities to respond per minute during math instruction. To use behavior-specific praise and have a ratio of interactions of 2:1.

What actions will I take to meet this goal?

Task: What needs to be done?	Description of Plan	Resources: What is needed to get it done?	Timeline
Provide drill-and-practice math problems.	To increase rate of opportunities to four per minute during math instruction, the following will occur:	Ms. Morris will create flash cards with review math problems.	Complete by 11/03/10
Beat the timer during box math review.	1. Will begin instruction with drill and practice of review math problems for 2–5 minutes.	Ms. Morris has a timer that she can use for beat the timer strategy.	Complete
Use a prompt to remind to provide behavior-specific praise.	2. Will play beat the timer, giving students 2 minutes to complete the box math problem, then have whole group respond.	Ms. Morris will create a yellow smiley face sign and tape it below wall clock.	Complete by 11/03/10
	3. Following group response, I will ask individual students to answer problems.		
Focus on a behavior that I want to see more of (raise hand).	To increase use of behavior-specific praise and improve ratio to 2:1, the following will occur:	Wendy will observe during math instruction and give feedback.	11/03 11/05
Ignore talk-outs.	1. Place a prompt (smiley face) under clock to remind me to praise.	Ms. Morris will self-monitor using the strategies.	Ongoing
	2. Target students who raise their hand to answer a question for specific praise: "Thank you for raising your hand."	Ms. Morris and Wendy will meet to see if plan is working.	11/11
	3. Ignore students who call out—don't reprimand.		

FIGURE 7.4. Example of a completed Classroom Check-Up Action Planning Form.

(cont.)

Classroom Check-Up Action Planning Form *(page 2 of 2)*

How **important** is it for you to meet this goal in your classroom?

0   1   2   3   4   5   6   7   8   (9)   10
Not Important   Very
at All   Important

The **most** important reasons for making this change and meeting this goal is:

I know that when students are engaged, they are learning.

When I'm positive and their engaged, everyone's happy.

How **confident** are you that you will meet this goal in your classroom?

0   1   2   3   4   5   6   7   (8   9)   10
Not Confident   Very
at All   Confident

Some reasons that **I am confident**:

Done it before. I know I can do it.

You will be giving me feedback and support.

Is there anything that could get in the way of meeting this goal?

I could get behind in the lessons if I spend too much time doing drill and practice stuff.

I could forget to ignore talk-outs.

What can I do to help make sure this doesn't get in the way?

I could set the timer during the drill and practice to only 5 minutes so that we don't get behind.

If you observe me using reprimands for student talking out or not ignoring them to call on someone with a hand raised, you could remind me.

FIGURE 7.4. *(cont.)*

- "Now, let's talk about next steps. On this form, let's first think back to what is going really well or what is a strength for you and the classroom. Whatever plan we come up with should be sure to use this strength to ensure success."
- "Next, we just talked about some ideas for areas to improve. Which do you think is the most important to target at this time?"
- "Now let's come up with a specific goal to work on for this week."

Be sure to elicit specific, observable, and realistic goals from the teacher. One way to do this is to ask clarifying questions including who, what, where, how often questions. For instance, if the teacher says "more opportunities," ask him

> **When creating a plan of action, be sure to elicit specific, observable, and realistic goals from the teacher.**

or her what that would look like. How would you know? What would be different that you could see? How often would you see him or her doing it?

Below, we continue the dialogue from the feedback session with the fifth-grade teacher described above. Notice the summary and transition from feedback to planning at the start of the dialogue.

Action Planning Dialogue (Continued from Above)	Comments
CONSULTANT: So there's a ton that's going well in your classroom. You have clear expectations and a positive climate. It is predictable. Students know the rules and how you will respond when they violate them. The two areas that stood out as possible ones to work on were increasing your pacing and your praise. So our next step is to come up with a plan for what to do next. Which areas stand out to you from this menu?	Summary Transition to action plan Next step question
TEACHER: The opportunities and praise. Did you have ideas or did you want to brainstorm?	
CONSULTANT: Let's brainstorm. We already started a bit on opportunities. You had said that at the start of a lesson, you could provide some drill-and-practice opportunities. What else have you thought about doing?	Structuring Open-ended question about solutions
TEACHER: Well, like today, we did a lot of these little box exercises. They started on it doing independent work. But they have a tough time with these exercises. If I put them up on the overhead, though, I can tell they don't really do the problems with me. If we do the exercises all together, then I lose a lot of kids because only some kids are answering, unless I pick from the jar. So I haven't figured it out.	
CONSULTANT: If you are working on providing opportunities to respond, you probably want to have everyone work on one	Summary elaborating teacher's own solution

box at a time. Give them 2 minutes and then say, "Okay, everyone, what's the answer?"

TEACHER: I like that. I have a timer and could do that.

CONSULTANT: And then you can alternate individual versus group turns. You can do the first one together: "Everyone, what is 92 plus 3?" And then randomly call on individuals: "Now, Tommy, what is 91 plus 5?" | Elaborating solution

TEACHER: Right. So random calling will help keep them all on task. | Clarifies expectation

CONSULTANT: So you like this idea? And it's realistic? | Open-ended question

TEACHER: Absolutely.

CONSULTANT: Let's write this down. What are the things you are going to work on?

TEACHER: Providing opportunities to respond by doing some drill and practice, like for 5 minutes. I used to do it on entry slips, so I can do this. I'll either do a written entry slip or an oral multiplication drill. I'm also working on their engagement by giving them opportunities and giving them tickets.

CONSULTANT: So how does that work? | Clarifying question

TEACHER: Well, I have tickets in my pocket, and I start giving them out for starting on time. I can also start giving them out for participation. And so for opportunities, we'll race the clock. And then use sticks for individual turns.

CONSULTANT: And so you'll do race the clock and then ding: Everyone responds. And then you switch to individual turns. | Summary

TEACHER: And then it takes less of my time. I like that.

CONSULTANT: And what was the other area of concern? Oh, yeah, praise. And these two go together. Increasing opportunities will increase students' engagement, which will also give you more chances to praise them. You do pretty well with your praise. But many teachers need a signal. What would work for you? | Affirmation

Open-ended question

TEACHER: I'm trying to think if I could make a little smiley face and put it in a place where I would see it. | Generating ideas

CONSULTANT: That's great. Places people have put it is like the corner of the overhead.

TEACHER: Oh, I know, I will put it above the clock. Every time I look up, which is constantly, I'll see it and remember to praise.

CONSULTANT: Great idea! So here's our plan? (*Reviews action plan.*) Do these meet your first criteria you gave me the other day of being practical and likely to work?	Affirmations Connecting to prior material
TEACHER: Absolutely, I like it.	
CONSULTANT: Okay, then. Let's use our rulers here for review. How important is it, using this scale (*pointing to sheet*), for increasing your opportunities and praise this week?	
TEACHER: I'd say a 9. I'm really stoked.	
CONSULTANT: Great. And so why a 9 and not say a 7 or 8?	Open-ended question
TEACHER: I just know how helpful it can be. It's back to what we talked about before. When I'm positive and their engaged, everyone's happy.	
CONSULTANT: And learning.	Prior value content
TEACHER: Right.	
CONSULTANT: And now this one. How confident are you that you can do it?	Open-ended question
TEACHER: I'd say an 8 or 9 again.	
CONSULTANT: So really confident. Is it the same for praising and opportunities?	Clarifying
TEACHER: Hmm. I think so. Yeah.	
CONSULTANT: So why so confident?	
TEACHER: You know, I've done it before. I know I can do it, especially with you giving me feedback and support. I've done it before on my own, so this should be easy with your help.	
CONSULTANT: You're really committed to making this happen.	Statement eliciting commitment language
TEACHER: Definitely.	

Importance and Confidence Rulers

The second page of the Classroom Check-Up Action Planning Form has questions and rulers to elicit and measure how important the plan for change is and how confident the teacher feels in implementing it. Once a specific plan has been developed, be sure to ask the teacher to answer the questions on the importance and confidence rulers. Recall that these are key MI strategies. We placed these questions at the end of the meeting because research has shown that the most important type of change talk (that best predicts whether people actually follow through on change) is the type that occurs during the final minutes of a session. In particular, the more commitment language that is expressed (e.g., "I'm going to do this."), the more likely it is that people will actually *do* what they say.

Begin by asking the importance question on the form: "On a scale from 0 to 10, with 10 being *very important* and 0 being *not important at all*, how important is it for you to meet this goal in your classroom?" Regardless of the number the teacher selects, ask them why that number and not one less. For instance:

TEACHER: I'd say a 6.

CONSULTANT: Great. That's pretty important. Why a 6 and not a 5? [You could also go lower " … a 3"].

Be sure to reflect the teacher's responses here, as this will almost certainly be change talk. If a teacher says *0*, you can amplify and exaggerate by saying, "So this is the least important thing in the world right now to you." This kind of rating would also be a sign that you need to start over and select a new goal.

Next, ask: "What would it take to go from a 6 to a 7? What would have to happen?" You can then "walk" the teacher up to a *10*. Write down things that the teacher says above the numbers he or she gives. If a teacher says, "If I got a reprimand from my principal" to get a 7, write *principal reprimand* above the number 7 on the form. Throughout, continue to use active listening and reflection. You can also prompt the teacher to tell you all the reasons why making this change or meeting this goal is important by simply asking him or her. You can write down the answers in the box next to the importance ruler on the form. The more the teacher talks about why using the new strategy in the classroom is important, the more committed he or she becomes to actually implementing the strategy.

> The more the teacher talks about why using the new strategy in the classroom is important, the more committed he or she becomes to actually implementing the strategy.

Repeat this process with the confidence ruler: "How confident are you that you can make this change and meet this goal in your classroom?" Be sure to follow up with the "one-less" question and then with the "one-more" question. Lastly, discuss potential barriers to meeting or working on the goal and brainstorm ways to avoid or overcome these barriers. Then give the teacher a copy of the Classroom Check-Up Action Planning Form and keep a copy for yourself as well.

Teacher Self-Monitoring

One final step before ending the meeting is to develop a quick and easy tool for the teacher to self-monitor the implementation of the action plan. Self-monitoring can be helpful in assisting with the implementation process for two reasons. First, the act of self-monitoring is an intervention in itself. Self-monitoring makes the teacher more aware of his or her behavior and serves as a reminder to follow through on the plan. Second, self-monitoring data can be used to document whether the plan is working and modify it as needed. As the teacher tracks which parts of the plan actually get implemented, this information can guide the problem-solving process. For instance, a teacher may find that a part of the plan is not really feasible or does not fit well with his or her classroom, and therefore, he or she does not do it. The Teacher Self-Monitoring Form (Appendix C.6) can provide this information and initiate a conversation about what needs to be modified for the teacher to be able to do it or select and plan a new intervention that is

> An intervention can be effective only if it is actually carried out in the classroom.

more feasible. An intervention can be effective only if it is actually carried out in the classroom. If parts of a plan are not being carried out, you can brainstorm with the teacher to problem-solve and come up with a solution or another plan altogether. Figure 7.5 provides a completed example of the Teacher Self-Monitoring Form.

STEP 6 OF THE CCU MODEL: ONGOING MONITORING

Monitor, Review, and Revise

At this point, you and the teacher have already put in a great deal of work and effort to come up with the plan and prepare to implement it in the classroom. Don't stop here. Sometimes when people expend effort in creating a beautiful document of next steps, it feels like the real work has already been done. However, this is not the case. It is only the beginning. Once the teacher goes back to the classroom and begins implementing the new strategies, it is important to continue the consultation relationship.

Once the intervention is developed and the teacher is self-monitoring the implementation, conduct several follow-up classroom observations using the CCU observation forms. The information you gather will allow you to determine if the new strategies are doing what you and the teacher had hoped. In other words, is it working? If you find that after a few classroom observation visits the data are not going in the correct direction (i.e., disruptions down, engagement up), then it is time to revisit and revise the plan. As mentioned earlier, the self-monitoring information can be useful because it can reveal if the lack of change is simply due to the teacher's failure to fully use the new strategies. However, if the strategies are being implemented but no change is occurring, then it may be time to revise the plan.

Ongoing Performance Feedback

Collecting follow-up data through classroom observation can also allow you to provide the teacher with ongoing feedback. For instance, if a teacher is working to increase his or her use of behavior-specific praise, you can observe in the classroom and then let the teacher know whether or not he or she has actually increased behavior-specific praise. As noted previously, this is called *performance feedback*, and it is a particularly powerful consultation tool. Studies have documented the effectiveness of performance feedback on behavior change with teachers (Noell et al., 2000; Reinke et al., 2007). There are several ways to provide ongoing performance feedback. One that we have found useful is to graph the number of student disruptions along with the targeted teacher behavior that the teacher is trying to increase (e.g., behavior-specific praise). The graphs can be created in a computer graphing program, such as Excel, or they can be hand-created. The graph showing both student and teacher behavior allows the teacher to see how changing his or her behavior directly

Teacher Self-Monitoring Form

1. Write in the date for each day this week. 2. Write in the strategies to be used. 3. Check off those strategies that you use each day. 4. Provide comments about any challenges encountered.					
Strategy:	Date: 11/03	Date: 11/04	Date: 11/05	Date: 11/06	Date:
Provide drill-and-practice math problems 2–5 minutes beginning of math	☑	☑	☑	☑	☐
Play beat the timer during box math review (2 min.), then have group respond	☑	☐	☑	☐	☐
Use a prompt to remind to provide behavior specific praise	☑	☑	☑	☑	☐
Ignore talk-outs and provide behavior specific praise to students with hand raised	☑	☑	☐	☑	☐
	☐	☐	☐	☐	☐
Comments: 11/06 is Friday. Will start with new form on Monday. Didn't have time for beat timer 2 days.			Forgot to ignore a few times		

FIGURE 7.5. Example of a completed Teacher Self-Monitoring Form.

impacts student behavior. Figure 7.6 illustrates an example of this type of performance feedback for a teacher. For performance feedback to be effective, you need to ensure that (1) you meet with the teacher to explain how you will be graphing the data and to make certain that he or she understands how to interpret the data on the graph, and (2) you provide the graph to the teacher as soon after the observation as possible (ideally, the same day). The reason for getting the information to the teacher as quickly as possible is so that he or she can easily recall the moment that you collected the data and think of ways to improve. If

Step 1: Conduct observation and graph the data. Give the teacher the graph to review.

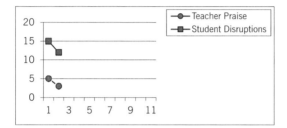

Step 2: Conduct another observation, graph, and leave for review by teacher.

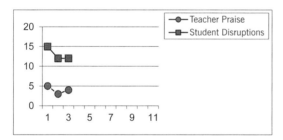

Step 3: Continue providing performance feedback until the teacher is successful.

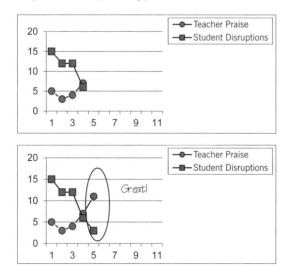

FIGURE 7.6. Example of ongoing performance feedback with teacher to increase praise.

> **Ongoing performance feedback is a great tool to pull out with a teacher who needs extra support to get new strategies integrated into daily practice.**

he or she receives the performance feedback a week later, the teacher may not be able to recall the day of the observation. If you are working with a teacher who is struggling with increasing praise or providing opportunities to respond, performance feedback may be an option that you discuss to help support him or her in the classroom. Although ongoing performance feedback may not be feasible in all situations, it is a great tool to use with a teacher who really needs that extra support to get new strategies integrated into his or her daily practice.

NOTES FROM THE FIELD: HELPFUL TIPS, TROUBLESHOOTING, AND CASE EXAMPLE

The purpose of this section is to consider common issues or questions that arise as consultants first start using the model. Additionally, we describe case examples of working with teachers who are ambivalent about changing.

Helpful Tips

Avoid Uninvited Advice Giving

By now, you know that giving uninvited advice may actually induce resistance. We felt the need to repeat it one more time, because it is such a compelling trap. Even after giving trainees extensive support in learning MI and using the CCU, we regularly see them fall back on this reflexive consultant response of giving advice when they get stuck. It's easy to fall into the trap of giving advice or information in response to a resistant statement (e.g., "Research has shown that …"). The problem with this response is that it is a subtle (or sometimes not-so-subtle) trap of taking sides. Essentially, the message this response sends is, "If only you knew a little more, you would feel differently"—which is a presumptuous, if not condescending, message. The most likely response to uninvited advice or information given after a resistance response is further resistance ("Yes, but …"). If anything you want to be the one saying, "Yes, but …," not the teacher. On the other hand, invited or well-timed advice or information giving can be helpful.

Be Sure to Ask the Check-In Question When Giving Feedback

When people first start delivering feedback, they tend to talk through the feedback and then give possible advice or suggestions. Sometimes this occurs because of the inevitable time pressures that are part of the school setting; sometimes, however, this occurs because the interviewer is uncomfortable with the feedback. Regardless, try pausing a bit after you give the feedback to get the teacher's impression. The question "What do you think about that?" can be helpful. You cannot linger with all feedback items in this way, but you should do it with a least a couple items—the ones that you want to emphasize.

In a similar way, be sure to check that a teacher agrees with anything you write on the form. If you wrote that the classroom rules and expectations were well laid out and an obvious strength, double-check with the teacher: "I think you do a great job of.... Do you think so too?" or "Does that sound right to you?"

After the teacher agrees with your feedback, you might try following it up with questions about specific examples of what he or she is doing well or asking why he or she thinks something is important. Engage the teacher further by letting him or her come up with the plan.

Remember to Summarize Frequently

Get in the practice of providing regular summaries of different sections of the interview and feedback meetings. There are some natural places to do so. For instance, you might summarize at the end of domains on the feedback form, as you transition to the menu, and then again to the action planning form. But any time you feel that a lot of information has been discussed it is a good time for a summary. You might even ask the teacher to help with this aspect of the process as a strategy for keeping him or her engaged. It is fine to ask a teacher to summarize what he or she has heard so far. This also checks his or her understanding of the feedback you are giving.

Be Careful Not to Dismiss the Data

It is a fine line between giving information tentatively and inadvertently communicating that the data are unimportant. Given that it can be uncomfortable to give negative feedback, consultants sometimes have a tendency to back away from, or minimize, the negative. This can be subtle; be aware of, and pay attention to, any time you notice yourself explaining away negative feedback. One common way of "dodging" a piece of negative data is for the consultant to send a message that the data may not be accurate (e.g., "This was merely one observation, on one day"). Dismissing relevant data in this manner also diminishes the effect of the feedback overall and the likelihood that other information will be taken seriously.

Come to the Feedback Session with a Flexible Plan

As you reflect on the data and the classroom, try to identify one area you think would make a difference and intentionally highlight that in the feedback. This selection requires some reflection on your part prior to beginning any feedback session and might even help with the time pressure as well. By focusing on one or two areas you really want the teacher to become aware of, you can then quickly move through the other components. This is all part of the conceptualization process. But remember, your plan and leverage need to be flexible. Ultimately, it is the teacher's decision about what, if anything, he or she wants to do.

> **Any plan that you propose needs to be flexible. It is the teachers' decision about what, if anything, they want to do.**

Try Strategies for Building Teacher Self-Efficacy

Creating mastery experiences is the best technique for building self-efficacy. As we discussed in Chapter 3, supporting teachers so that they effectively implement good practices and then allowing them to see how these practices improve their classroom is key to fostering self-efficacy. In addition, there are social strategies for building the belief that a teacher can be successful in the practice even before he or she tries it. For instance, when a teacher comments on how she has done something successfully in the past or had positive experiences, it can be helpful to note that he or she is a great problem solver. Ask lots of "How did you do that?" sorts of questions when you notice a particular strength. Additionally, help the teacher see the connections between changing practices and the impact those changes are having in the classroom. For instance, give specific observation feedback about the connection between when the teacher has used a strategy and the degree of on-task student behavior observed.

Remember to Ask Teachers to Elaborate Their Ruler Ratings

One common mistake we see with the ruler question is that consultants sometimes fail to capitalize on opportunities to affirm teacher ratings and get them to elaborate their change talk. For instance, if a teacher gives a high rating, such as a *9* or *10*, be sure to celebrate that rating with them. You might say, "Wow, this is super important to you!" When you ask the follow-up question ("Why a 9 and not an 8?"), be sure to elicit all the reasons that the rating was so high by asking "What else?" or "What other reasons make this so important to you?" You can even ask the teacher to elaborate further: "Which parts seem most important?" With all of these questions, you are asking the teacher to elaborate his or her reasons for changing. Also, be sure to draw links between these reasons and prior goals and values that the teacher has expressed. For instance, if a teacher said, "It will help create a peaceful environment," you could respond by saying, "So having a positive, calm classroom is one of your biggest values as a teacher, and you think that these changes you want to make will help you to continue building that environment." Or "Doing this is really consistent with the core values you try to promote in your classroom."

Another common mistake we see is when consultants let teachers discount their own Ruler ratings after being asked the follow-up question. For instance, a teacher might respond, "Well, it is important because it has been a challenging year, but it will be really hard to focus on this right now." In this example, the teacher ends her statement by supporting the status quo (not change talk). Here, be sure to go back and ask for why it is important again, because the teacher did not really answer the question.

> CONSULTANT: So, there is a lot going on right now. But let me be sure I'm clear. You rated the importance as a 5. Does that feel right to you?
>
> TEACHER: Yes.
>
> CONSULTANT: So tell me the reasons it is important to you—say, why you would say it is a 5 and not a *1*?

Finally, when asking follow-up questions using the confidence ruler, be sure to elicit self-motivational statements and not just circumstantial reasons the teacher is confident in changing. For instance, some teachers will say they are really confident that the plan will work but attribute the reasons to something outside of themselves: "My students are really good this year, and they are still impressionable at this age" or "The principal really thinks this is important." The key language you want to elicit when asking the follow-up question about confidence is self-efficacy language, that is, "Why I [the teacher] can do this." To shift the conversation in this direction, you might say, "So those are reasons you think that this will impact the kids, which is great. I'm also thinking about your confidence in doing the plan. What are some reasons you are so confident in your ability to follow through with this?"

Troubleshooting Common Motivational Issues

Appendix C.7 provides effective MI strategies and types of personalized feedback that can be particularly helpful in addressing common motivational areas when consulting with teachers. Note that all of these suggestions draw on the big ideas of prior chapters.

A Teacher Reluctant to Discipline

Below we provide an extended example of a feedback session with a teacher who was initially unmotivated to change a key behavior to highlight some of the principles in helping a teacher move toward action planning. The teacher worked in an urban school district with a large number of children from very low income families. She viewed her role as providing primarily a nurturing influence in these children's lives and was reluctant to provide needed structure and discipline strategies in her classroom. Throughout the dialogue below, note how the consultant skillfully reflects back to the teacher's own stated values to build a vision of a structured classroom that would be consistent with those values. Note also how initially the teacher distracts the flow of the interview, but the consultant provides gentle structure to keep the feedback session moving forward.

Feedback Session Dialogue	Comments
CONSULTANT: Basically what I'm going to do is go over all the information I've been gathering. The way the feedback form is set up is, you have an overarching category and then the subcategories. And the way this works is that if it's in the green, keep doing what you're doing because it's awesome. If you are in the yellow, that's something you might want to think about doing something different, and if it's in the red, it's like a stop sign. It means you definitely want to think about doing something differently.	Summary and preview
TEACHER: Okay (*looking at the form*), so these are the categories.	Teacher jumps ahead

CONSULTANT: Yes.

TEACHER: And opportunities to respond is in the yellow. Needs some improvement.

CONSULTANT: Right, what do you make of that? | Check-in question

TEACHER: I notice with these kids, I answer more than I do in other classes. I haven't decided if I do it because I want to pull it out of them. So I can see that I could be down in the yellow for that.

CONSULTANT: So you're not surprised to see that as an area to work on. | Reflection focusing on change statement

TEACHER: No, I would have guessed that.

CONSULTANT: I put you in the yellow because your average rate is two opportunities per minute. And generally you want to be at four to six for initial learning, and for practice and review it should be nine to twelve. | Personalized feedback

TEACHER: So do you give us feedback on how to improve this thing?

CONSULTANT: Is that something you would like to spend time on? | Question emphasizing personal responsibility

TEACHER: Yes, I mean it seems like something that's low, and I would need help to change it, especially with these kids.

CONSULTANT: Okay, well, how about if I put this on our menu and after we discuss these different areas, we can look over the final list and you can decide what you want to work on. | Setting aside topic for future discussion / Emphasizing personal responsibility

TEACHER: Sounds good.

CONSULTANT: On the correct opportunities, you are in the green. They are right at 85%, so they are right about where you want them to be. | Affirmation / Personalized feedback

TEACHER: That's good to hear, because I worry that they are not getting it. So 85% is the comfort zone?

CONSULTANT: Eighty-five percent indicates that most of the kids are getting it, and they're getting most of it. And that's okay for new material. For review, though, or for things you send home, you want them to be more like 90%, so they can do it and they don't get frustrated. | Providing requested information

TEACHER: Okay.

CONSULTANT: So on engagement, we do a classwide student engagement measure.

TEACHER: (*looking at form*) It's actually higher than I thought it would be.	Jumping ahead
CONSULTANT: You thought that would be lower.	Reflection
TEACHER: This class especially seems to be off task a lot.	
CONSULTANT: Right, and when I watched them, for the most part, they are paying attention to you. I put you in the yellow because it's a little below the optimal range; they're at 84% on task and you want them at 90% or higher. And your range was 76–90%.	Personalized feedback
CONSULTANT: So here's the praise-to-reprimand ratio.	
TEACHER: This one's in the yellow.	
CONSULTANT: Yes, so the praise we're looking for is very specific because you tell them exactly what they are doing well. This one is in the yellow because you give a lot of praise, but it is general—"Nice Job," "Good."	Personalized feedback
TEACHER: Yes, I know I do that, and I try to catch myself, but it's such a habit.	
CONSULTANT: When I look at the data, you are more than 10 times likely to give general praise then specific.	Personalized feedback
TEACHER: Yeah, and in the math class I think I'm so focused on getting the content that I don't want to spend a lot of time praising them, but for that group they probably need it the most.	Change talk
CONSULTANT: Tell me more. Why do you think that praise would be especially important for these kids?	Open-ended question
TEACHER: Well, the kids in this class don't get a lot of positive attention at home.	
CONSULTANT: So this is the one place you can be sure that they can get positive attention.	Reflection and connecting to prior content
TEACHER: That's one thing I always want to give them. A safe and positive place. And even if they're late, I tell them I still want them here.	Change talk
CONSULTANT: That really comes across.	Affirmation
TEACHER: I'm glad.	
CONSULTANT: But still you said it is a bad habit to be giving general versus specific praise.	Eliciting change talk

TEACHER: Well, it just can sound monotonous, maybe even not genuine, to only be saying things like "Good job."	
CONSULTANT: So being more specific in your praise is another way to let students know you genuinely care about them.	Reflecting values
TEACHER: I think so, yes.	
CONSULTANT: How else can behavior-specific praise be helpful to students?	Open-ended question
TEACHER: It lets them know exactly what I expect of them. And they respond to positive praise when they know what I'm talking about.	
CONSULTANT: How do you mean?	Open-ended question
TEACHER: When I use specific praise, I can see it makes a difference in their paying attention.	
CONSULTANT: Which is important. One area that I also put in the yellow was disruptions (*pointing to the form*). You have about three per minute.	Personalized feedback
TEACHER: That doesn't surprise me.	
CONSULTANT: No?	
TEACHER: I know there are a lot of talk-outs in my math class, and it seems we really struggle with transitions from one task to the next.	
CONSULTANT: So you're aware of the disruptions. How do you feel about how frequently they occur?	Open-ended question eliciting reasons for change
TEACHER: I don't like it. I would definitely like it to be lower.	
CONSULTANT: How do you think fewer disruptions would be helpful?	Open-ended question
TEACHER: Well, you know, it's distracting, for me and for everyone. It just makes it harder to teach and to learn when there are so many interruptions.	
CONSULTANT: How does that fit with the type of classroom you want to give these students—a safe and positive place?	Open-ended question referring back to values
TEACHER: It all fits. I mean, part of being safe and positive is being respectful.	
CONSULTANT: What do you think students are learning when there are a lot of disruptions?	Open-ended question drawing on student's perspective
TEACHER: Well, they are not learning a lot because it leaves less time for instruction.	Connecting to values

CONSULTANT: Uh-huh. And if there were fewer disruptions, what message would that send to students? In this class, we value …

TEACHER: We value each others' time. And also there's a time for work and a time for play.

CONSULTANT: So reducing disruptions, in addition to making your job easier, can also send a powerful message to students about the type of safe and positive place this is.

Summary connecting to values

TEACHER: Right.

CONSULTANT: Okay, the final piece of feedback I'll give you today, and I'm going to cover this up and ask you to guess this one, is about how clear your classroom expectations and rules are. Where would you put yourself, from green to red, on that one?

Open-ended question eliciting engagement

TEACHER: Hmm. I'm not sure. I think okay.

CONSULTANT: Another way to think about this is to ask yourself "How well do all of my students know exactly what I expect of them throughout the day for each task or transition?"

Providing information

TEACHER: Okay, I would say probably the yellow, about here then (*pointing to the form*). I do tell them the rules, but I could probably do it more often and practice them more. And we do struggle with our transitions.

CONSULTANT: That's about where I put you to. You do have your rules posted but it's just a matter of reviewing and practicing.

Personalized feedback

TEACHER: I do need to do that more often. I see, Alex [another teacher in the building] with his class, and I'm like, man, I need to do that. His students stay in line and listen. So I see that this is important. I need to practice.

Change talk

CONSULTANT: You look at Alex and how he teaches and practices his rules as an example of how you would like to be.

Reflection elaborating change talk

TEACHER: Yes, I have seen him practice lining up his students and other things, and it definitely seems to make a difference.

CONSULTANT: Putting this all together, what are the big ideas you are going to take from all of this feedback (*pointing to the form*)?

Eliciting summary from teacher

TEACHER: The ones that stand out to me are the disruptions and praise. And the rules.

CONSULTANT: Can you see how all those go together?

Open-ended question

TEACHER: Yeah, I mean, if I'm clearer with the rules and we practice them, it seems like there will be fewer disruptions.

CONSULTANT: And how can behavior-specific praise support that? | Open-ended question

TEACHER: If I teach the rules and refer back to them with praise statements, it just reinforces the practice. | Summary

CONSULTANT: Those all great points. You know that there's a lot going well in the classroom. You really have a nurturing and supportive style, and the kids can feel that. So that's a big part of what you want to give them. And now the other key piece of that safe and positive environment is to teach them respect for you and each other by teaching and practicing the rules, and giving them behavior-specific praise. | Affirmations Connecting change back to values

In this example, the consultant highlighted three interrelated areas as potential targets (increasing behavior-specific praise, decreasing disruptions, and clarifying and repeating expectations) in improving the classroom environment. The consultant had conceptualized these areas as critical leverage points to bring about change in this classroom. Based on prior conversations, he knew that the teacher was reluctant to view herself as a disciplinarian and thus resisted having much structure in her classroom. He attempted first to show how a positive strategy (behavior-specific praise) is actually a key element of creating a structured environment that is entirely consistent with the classroom environment she hoped to provide for these students. Building off that insight, he then helped the teacher draw connections between disruptive student behaviors and the need to more clearly articulate her expectations to them. At the end of this process, she was now open to taking steps toward improving these areas.

SUMMARY

In this chapter we review the feedback and action planning process that can be so helpful for engaging teachers in the change process. After delivering feedback and enhancing the motivation of a teacher to work toward specific goals, the consultant is in a position to help the teacher create a plan for achieving those goals. At this point, when a teacher is ready to plan for change, the consultant can draw on the vast literature about behavior change technologies in the classroom. The next chapter provides a primer on effective classroom management interventions and ties them to the feedback provided as part of the CCU.

CHAPTER 8

Developing Effective Strategies
for Classroom Change

The CCU procedures that were outlined in Chapters 6 and 7 support a productive consultation process by which teachers feel supported as they carry out new strategies for creating change in their classrooms. The purpose of this chapter is to describe effective interventions for improving any areas that were identified during the CCU as needing attention. The chapter focuses on research-based methods for increasing the use of classroom management practices based on the critical features described in Chapter 2. However, the methods described below are not rigid and will need to be adapted to fit the needs and skill level of the teacher who will be carrying out the strategies in the classroom. All classrooms are unique, and effective interventions need to be sensitive to the contextual fit of the classroom and school setting where they are implemented. Furthermore, the chapter does not provide an exhaustive list of all possible interventions. Rather, we describe strategies that are well documented as effective in addressing the most common areas of concern for teachers. View these as instruments in your portable tool kit that you can use as you discuss action planning with teachers. Recall, though, that effective consultants are knowledgeable, resourceful, and flexible. Thus, the interventions that you co-create with teachers are most likely to work for them in their classrooms if you remain attentive to the big ideas or principles of effective practices as defined by solid theory and research.

> **View these strategies as instruments in your portable tool kit that you can use as you discuss action planning with teachers.**

CHARACTERISTICS OF EFFECTIVE INTERVENTIONS

Effective interventions share several specific qualities. When selecting and adapting strategies in collaboration with a classroom teacher, be sure that the intervention is (1) based on empirical evidence, (2) consistent with an ecological perspective, (3) likely to produce socially valid and measureable outcomes, (4) proactive, and (5) feasible and minimally intrusive within a typical classroom setting.

First, when working to design effective classroom interventions, consider the evidence available indicating that the practice will result in meaningful change in classroom behavior. (See Chapter 2 for a review of classroom practices that have been evaluated and shown to improve classroom behaviors and enhance academic outcomes for students.) Beginning with practices that have been researched and shown to be effective increases the likelihood that your intervention will be impactful in a given classroom. Likewise, avoiding practices that have been tested and shown not to work can minimize the chances of frustration and possible failure of your consultation.

Second, focusing on internal child deficits as the cause for problematic student behaviors provides little to no information about how to design classroom interventions. Instead, viewing problem behaviors from an ecological perspective, or as a discrepancy between the current classroom environment and the capacities of the student(s), leads to a broader and more useful range of classroom-based interventions. Keeping the focus on environmental factors that can be modified to produce successful student behavior should be emphasized when designing interventions.

Third, interventions should be designed to produce measurable and socially valid outcomes. A socially valid outcome is one in which students are treated with respect and dignity and benefit as a result. An intervention designed solely for the purpose of controlling student behavior without benefiting the student would *not* be socially valid. An extreme example would be a first grade teacher who expects students to sit quietly at their desks for extended periods of time and sends students out of the classroom who are fidgeting or out of their seats. In this example, students do not benefit because they are removed from instruction for a very minor misbehavior. More socially valid outcomes could be achieved if the consultant helped the teacher create guided opportunities for movement, adjust the schedule to allow for briefer periods of time in which students are expected to sit quietly, teach the expectation for staying seated, and praise those students who are meeting the expectation. Some or all of these interventions optimize learning, promote positive teacher–student relationships, support student self-regulation, and are more likely to produce socially valid change. Likewise, it is most helpful if interventions target concrete, observable behaviors that can be objectively measured over time. Measureable goals are required if you are to determine whether the intervention is effective or needs to be modified or discontinued.

Fourth, proactive interventions are helpful because they place an emphasis on preventing problem behavior rather than waiting to respond to or punish behaviors after they occur. Prioritizing strategies that help teachers create learning environments that prevent problems increases the amount of time available for learning by reducing the time spent correcting misbehavior. Proactive strategies allow teachers to spend more time teaching and less time putting out fires.

Fifth, effective interventions are also feasible and minimally intrusive. Interventions should capitalize on resources that are already present in the typical classroom or that can be prepared with minimal cost and effort. Practices that are feasible, cost-effective (in terms of both time and expense) are more likely to be used and maintained (Witt, Noell, LaFleur, & Mortenson, 1997). Intrusive interventions—those that disrupt the flow of regular classroom routines for the teacher and/or the students—are not likely to be used over time. For instance, removal from the classroom is a very intrusive intervention, as compared to more proactive strategies that focus on modifying classroom routines, teaching expectations, and praising students when they are meeting the expectations.

Consider an example. A high school teacher has a student who exhibits a pattern of disrespectful outburst during instruction. An intrusive intervention would be for the teacher to do nothing until "reaching her wit's end," and then removing the student from class any time he is disruptive in the future. A less intrusive series of interventions would be to meet with the student after only one or two such disruptions, let the student know the expectations, and provide the student with guidance on when and how to use humor in the classroom. If that approach was not effective, the teacher could begin a frequency count of disrespectful outbursts and provide that information regularly to the student and parents, while concurrently teaching the other students in the class not to encourage any behavior of a classmate that is not in that classmate's best interest. If that were ineffective, the teacher could then share the frequency count regularly with school counselors and administrators with the request that additional help be provided to help the student be successful. Any and all of this series of interventions would be more likely to change the student's behavior and less intrusive of the student's education than removing him from class.

INTERVENTION HIERARCHY AND MENU GUIDE

In this chapter we organize interventions based on a hierarchy, with proactive, less intrusive interventions serving as the foundation, or building blocks, before other more reactive, intrusive interventions. As depicted in Figure 8.1, the hierarchy implies that interventions on the lower steps should be used liberally and repeatedly, whereas interventions at higher steps should be used less frequently and only after the strategies at the foundation are in place. This chapter reviews ideas for each level of the hierarchy.

Below we describe each of the interventions as an option that could be generated for the Classroom Check-Up Menu of Options based on the areas of concern derived from the observations and feedback. Table 8.1 provides useful guidelines for starting points within domains needing attention. However, the table is not an end point or an exhaustive list of all possible interventions, just a list of critical leverage points that are often helpful in creating positive changes in classrooms. Importantly, teachers who are struggling with managing student behavior will need a continuum of supports for increasing appropriate behavior

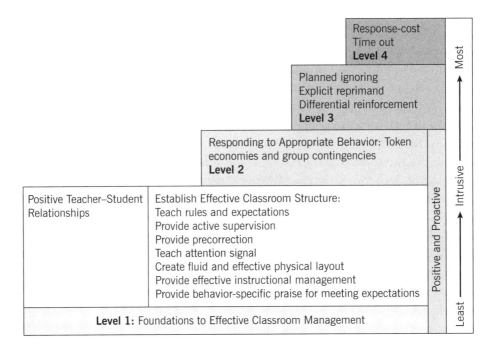

FIGURE 8.1. Hierarchy of classroom interventions.

and decreasing inappropriate behavior. Thus, when consulting with a classroom teacher, determine which strategies are already in place and which can be strengthened. Then, work toward assisting the teacher in building a range of effective strategies and a solid foundation in positive proactive classroom management. At the end of the chapter, we provide a brief list of other resources that you may find helpful in considering a broader range of effective interventions for classrooms.

INTERVENTION IDEAS
FOR IMPROVING CLASSROOM STRUCTURE

There are several ways to determine if classroom structure is an area that needs attention. For instance, when you visit a classroom to conduct observations, you may notice that the schedule or rules are not posted, that students take a great deal of time transitioning from one activity to the next, or that the classroom is cluttered and without clear paths. A tell-tale sign is when you, as observer, are not sure what the teacher is expecting of the students from moment to moment. If you observe any of these examples, you should bring up classroom structure as an area in need of attention when discussing possible interventions with the teacher.

> **A telltale sign is when the observer is not sure what the teacher is expecting of the students from moment to moment.**

TABLE 8.1. Intervention Menu Guide

Critical area in need of attention	Corresponding menu of intervention strategies
Correct academic responding above or below optimal level	1. Adjust academic material to match student ability. 2. Use evidence-based instructional practices.
Time on task (academic engagement) below optimal level	1. Actively teach classroom rules and expectations. 2. Use active supervision and proximity. 3. Use an attention signal. 4. Provide precorrections. 5. Increase opportunities to respond. 6. Use opportunities to respond strategically. 7. Increase behavior-specific praise for on-task behaviors.
Opportunities to respond less than optimal	1. Increase opportunities to respond.
Ratio of interactions more negative than positive	1. Teach rules and expectations. 2. Teach behavioral routines. 3. Improve teacher–student relationships. 4. Increase behavior-specific praise. 5. Use planned ignoring. 6. Provide explicit reprimands.
Behavior-specific praise not used or is less than optimal	1. Increase behavior-specific praise. 2. Teach rules and expectations. 3. Teach behavioral routines. 4. Improve teacher–student relationships.

Disruption levels higher than optimal	Strategies from across the critical areas can be used. Begin with and rely heavily upon these strategies:
	  1. Improve teacher–student relationships.
	  2. Improve classroom structure.
	  3. Attend to appropriate behavior.
	
	Move into interventions for responding to inappropriate behavior once positive proactive strategies have been put into place.

Classroom Rules and Expectations

In classrooms with high levels of disruptive behaviors and teacher reprimands, focusing on classroom rules and behavioral expectations can produce positive outcomes. When classrooms have poorly constructed rules or no established rules, the first step is to work with the teacher to determine behavioral expectations for the classroom and develop effective classroom rules. For classrooms with appropriate rules but low rates of student compliance, the best starting point may be to teach and review the rules, practice the expected behaviors, and reinforce the appropriate behavior at high rates. Below, we review the development of effective classroom rules and expectations and then describe procedures for teaching these rules to the students.

It can be important to discuss with teachers the difference between *expectations* and *rules*. Expectations are global qualities that we would like students and adults to uphold. For instance, we would like students to be *responsible*. A rule, on the other hand, is specific and observable. For example, *coming to class with a completed work assignment* is the specific and observable form of being responsible. Ideally, schools have schoolwide expectations in place that a teacher can easily link to her classroom rules. For instance, many schools use Positive Behavior Interventions and Supports (PBIS) as a schoolwide behavior program. Often schools using PBIS have schoolwide expectations that include "be safe, be respectful, be responsible." Classroom rules can be developed that directly align with these global school expectations. For instance, "keeping hands and feet to self" is a classroom rule that aligns with being "safe." Table 8.2 shows examples of school-wide expectations and corresponding classroom rules. Notice that the classroom rules are positively stated, specific, observable, concisely worded, and kept to a minimum.

> In classrooms with high levels of disruptive behaviors and teacher reprimands, focusing on classroom rules and behavioral expectations can produce positive outcomes.

In collaboration with the teacher, give some thought to the most common classroom misbehaviors. Take into consideration the grade and developmental level of the students in the classroom. Create a list of positively stated rules. You may work with the teacher to identify the rules, or the teacher may want to include the students in developing the rules. Regardless of how the rules are developed, they should describe what the students are expected to do rather than what they should not do. To create positively stated rules, think first of the misbehavior (e.g., hitting) and think of the opposite of this misbehavior (e.g., keeping hands and feet to self). Next, work with the teacher to put the rules in writing and post them in the classroom where all the students can see them. For preliterate and early literacy students (i.e., preschool, kindergarten, and first grade) it is helpful to develop a visual prompt that depicts the rule in conjunction with written text. For visual prompts, some teachers have students demonstrate a behavior that complies with the rule and take a photograph to display the behavior next to the rule. For example, the teacher could take a photograph of students sitting with their legs crossed and hands in their lap during circle

TABLE 8.2. Classroom Rules Aligned with Expectations

	Schoolwide expectations		
	Be safe	Be respectful	Be responsible
Classroom rules	Keep hands and feet to yourself.	Raise your hand and wait to be called on to talk.	Come to class on time.
		Listen to your teacher.	

time to post alongside the rule "keep hands and feet to self." The rules should be clear and posted in such a way that any person who enters the classroom would be able to see and understand them.

Simply listing and posting classroom rules is not sufficient to develop and maintain appropriate student behavior. It is important to actively teach and reteach the rules to students. Teaching the classroom rules communicates to students exactly what is expected while providing teachers with the opportunity to reinforce behavior consistent with the rules. Teaching classroom rules as a lesson, similar to teaching reading or any other academic subject, is an example of a proactive intervention. Once rules are identified and posted, work with the teacher to develop a lesson for teaching the classroom rules. A lesson is most effective when it includes teaching the rule and why it is important, modeling positive and negative examples of the rule, having the students practice following the rule, and verbally praising or acknowledging the students for following the rule. We use the following motto to help remember these important procedures: "Teach, model, practice, and praise." Figure 8.2 provides a lesson plan for constructing procedures to teach the classroom rule, "Raise your hand and wait to be called on to talk." (See Appendix D.1 for a blank Teaching Classroom Rules template).

Behavioral Routines

An effective strategy for decreasing disruptive behavior and increasing time spent on instruction is to teach expectations for student behavior during classroom routines. Similar to teaching classroom rules, behavioral routines can be actively taught to students by teaching, modeling, practicing, and reinforcing the appropriate behavior.

First, it is helpful to develop a list of the behavioral routines that occur throughout the day. Typically, students are expected to make numerous transitions and navigate a variety of expectations within and across classrooms. Some common routines that would appear on the list

> **Behavioral routines can be actively taught to students by teaching, modeling, practicing, and reinforcing the appropriate behavior.**

you develop in collaboration with the teacher include arriving at and leaving the classroom, transitioning to new activities or settings, working independently or in groups, distributing materials and turning in assignments, requesting help from the teacher, returning from recess or another class, and experiencing interruptions such as fire drills or substitute teachers. Next, work to define clear and consistent behavioral expectations for all regularly scheduled classroom activities. Use these behavioral expectations to develop a lesson plan for each routine, beginning with those routines or activities that are most challenging for students. For instance, if students are often confused about how to obtain teacher help during small-group reading instruction, create a lesson plan for teaching the expectations for this routine first. Ultimately, by preparing a lesson plan for each behavioral routine, teachers can greatly increase the likelihood of success in the practice of these routines with their students. An example of a lesson plan for lining up to leave the classroom can be found in Figure 8.3 (see Appendix D.2 for a blank form).

Teaching Classroom Rules

Rule
Raise your hand and wait to be called on to talk.

Teach
Provide a verbal description of the rule and why it's important: "We raise our hand and wait to be called on before talking. This is being respectful because it allows everyone to have a turn and to let me know when you need something."

Model
Provide a positive example by showing the students the behavior: "This is how we raise our hand to wait to be called on to talk." Raise hand straight above head.   *Provide a negative example by exhibiting the incorrect behavior:* Raise hand and shout out "I know, I know!" Then, ask the class, "Was that the responsible way to get the teacher's attention?"

Practice
Have a student or students demonstrate the rule: "Kennedy, show us how we raise our hand and wait to be called on to talk."

Praise/Reinforce
Provide specific praise to the student or students who demonstrated the rule: "Great job raising your hand, Kennedy."   *Devise a plan for reinforcing students who follow the rule:* During class instruction, especially during reading, I will look for and "catch" students when they raise their hand and wait to be called on before talking. I will attempt to provide specific praise to students with hands raised each time I call on them. "Thank you for raising your hand."

FIGURE 8.2. Example of a completed lesson teaching the classroom rule "Raise your hand and wait to be called on to talk."

Teaching Behavioral Routines

Routine
Lining up to leave the classroom

Teach
Provide a verbal description of the routine and why it's important:
Lining up correctly is an important skill for smooth transitions. Tell students: "When we all line up correctly—this means that our eyes are forward, voices off, and hands and feet are to ourselves—we make more time for learning, fun activities, and recess. Lining up correctly is helping us to be safe and to follow directions. When it is time to line up, I will stand at the door and say, 'It is time to line up.' I will call each of your table groups one by one. When I call your table number, quietly stand up, push in your chairs, and walk to line up at the door, keeping your hands and feet to yourself."

Model
Provide a positive example by showing the students the behavior:
"Table 3, please show us how to line up correctly." Students from table 3 quietly stand up, push in their chairs, and walk to the door without touching one another. "Great job, table 3. That is lining up correctly."
Provide a negative example by exhibiting the incorrect behavior:
"Tell me, class, is this lining up correctly?" Teacher sits at a desk, then stands up without pushing in the chair and runs to the door. "What did I forget to do?" The class answers that the teacher did not push in his or her chair and did not walk safely to the door.
"What if, when I called on a table to line up, everyone stood up and went to the door? Would that be lining up correctly?" Solicit from students what to do instead.
"What if when we lined up, everyone was bumping into each other or talking?" Solicit from students what to do instead.

Practice
Have a student or students demonstrate the routine correctly:
Give all students a turn to practice by asking each table of students to line up. Praise each group for doing so correctly.
Play the "Lining Up Game." The class practices lining up correctly. Every time students line up perfectly, the class gets a point. Play until the class gets 3 points in a row.

(cont.)

FIGURE 8.3. Example of a completed lesson teaching the behavioral routine "lining up to leave the classroom."

Teaching Behavioral Routines *(page 2 of 2)*

Praise/Reinforce
Provide specific praise to the student or students who demonstrated the routine correctly:
"Keisha, thank you for walking slowly to the line!" Provide more attention for appropriate behavior than for misbehavior.
Devise a plan for reinforcing students for demonstrating the routine correctly:
Each time the class lines up, I will give behavior-specific praise and attention to students who are lining up right. Additionally, we will play the "Lining Up Game" at every opportunity to line up. I will keep the score on the board. Once the class reaches a predetermined point goal, they will earn a celebration (preferred activity, extra minute of recess, sticker, etc.).

FIGURE 8.3. *(cont.)*

Active Supervision

Research has shown that the more time teachers spend behind their desk, the more disruptive and off-task behaviors occur in the classroom. Active supervision involves getting out from behind the desk, walking around the classroom, scanning (both visually and auditorily), and using proximity to support positive student behavior. There are several reasons why active supervision is an effective proactive classroom management strategy. First, as teachers move about the classroom, they can praise and give feedback to the group and individual students as they complete their work. Second, by proactively monitoring student work and behavior, the teacher can catch problems early and provide help or redirect misbehavior before it becomes too disruptive. Additionally, active supervision allows teachers to identify students quickly who need more support in their learning efforts, leading to less frustration, improved comprehension, and fewer disruptions. Last, the use of proximity, or simply moving closer to a student or group of students displaying misbehavior, can function as a powerful corrective strategy. Think about yourself driving down the highway. You look up to see a highway patrol officer on the roadway. What is the first thing you do? In my case (W.M.R.), I tend to take my foot off the pedal and check my speedometer. Proximity works on the same rationale. Moving alongside or toward a group of students misbehaving prompts them to stop the misbehavior and start displaying the desired behavior. In addition, the teacher who has built positive relationships will find that the students want to demonstrate their best behaviors when he or she is circulating, to show that they are living up to the teacher's high expectations.

When working with a teacher toward increasing his or her use of active supervision, recall that effective supervision requires that the classroom be structured in a manner that allows easy movement around the room. If it is not, the structure will serve as a barrier to active supervision. Identify areas of the room that could be altered to improve the physical layout. Then brainstorm with the teacher about when and how he or she might use active supervision. Perhaps the teacher typically uses small-group work or independent work time as a period in which to plan lessons or grade papers. However, during your observations you notice that many of the students are off task during these times. You can suggest that the teacher try using active supervision during this time as a way to increase on-task behavior and student engagement. Of course, this will mean that the teacher will need to find other times or generate other ideas for lesson planning and grading, but the benefits of active supervision for both students and teacher are valuable.

Precorrection

For classrooms in which rules and expectation are clear but students still have difficulties with certain transitions or activities, using precorrection can be a useful strategy. The first step is to identify times when students could benefit from a brief reminder of the expectations. A precorrection makes it more likely that students will meet these expectations. Next, develop explicit statements with the teacher that clearly describe what the students should do following the precorrection statement. Come up with group and individual behavior-specific praise responses for students who meet the expectation. It can be helpful to talk about which students in the classroom may need more support for the behavior routines identified as problematic. The teacher can target those students to give individual behavior-specific praise statements. At times, precorrections can be targeted to individual students who particularly struggle with the behavioral expectation. In these cases, suggest that the teacher offer any individualized precorrection discreetly (i.e., go over and tell student in a quiet voice) following a group precorrection. A completed example of a Precorrection Planning Form is provided in Figure 8.4 (see Appendix D.3 for a blank form).

Attention Signal

Getting and holding the attention of students is an important management tool for any teacher. Use of an attention signal can help decrease the number of disruptions that occur during transition periods in the classroom. Attention signals are beneficial across many situations. For instance, imagine a teacher who is actively walking around the class and monitoring student work and discovers that the students do not fully understand the assignment. Using a signal that has been well practiced, the teacher can get the attention of the entire class within seconds to clarify the directions and answer any new questions. Without the signal it could take several minutes of yelling over the noise in the classroom to get everyone's attention.

To support teachers in successfully using an attention signal, begin by identifying what the teacher would like to use as a signal. Combining an audible and visible component to the signal can be helpful because if students miss one cue, they may notice the other. One effective method for gaining attention is to say in a firm, loud voice (but not shouting),

Precorrection Planning Form

Step 1:	Identify a behavioral routine for which students are likely to have difficulty meeting expectations without a reminder.
Step 2:	Write the specific precorrection and behavior-specific praise statements that will be used.
Step 3:	Determine if the precorrection procedure was effective.

Behavior Routine:	Lining Up for Lunch
Precorrection Plan	At 10:45 a.m. provide a 5-minute warning. Use attention signal. "We are about to line up for lunch. Remember to push in your chairs and stand quietly at your desk. When I call on your group, you will walk with hands at your side and line up at the door."
Behavior-Specific Praise for Group	"You all pushed your chairs in quietly. Good job." "Excellent. Everyone is quietly standing behind their chairs ready to line up."
Behavior-Specific Praise for Individuals	"Carter, you stood right up and pushed in your chair. Great job." "I see that Joni is ready. She is standing at her desk quietly."
Did 85% of students meet expectations?	(YES) NO
If no, develop a plan to explicitly teach the behavior routine to the class.	

FIGURE 8.4. Example of a completed Precorrection Planning Form.

"Class, your attention please," while swinging your right arm in an arc straight out from your side and holding your arm above your head until all students are looking at you with their hands raised. Another popular attention signal used by teachers is rhythmic clapping. For this attention signal, the teacher claps out a rhythm and the students clap back the same rhythm in response and then look quietly at the teacher. Both of the signals mentioned have advantages. For instance, they can be given from any location in the classroom, in the hall-way, or on a field trip. Other attention signals that we often see teachers use include flicking the lights in the classroom on and off, using a bell, a harmonica, or music. The signal should be developmentally appropriate. For instance, high school students may consider clapping back as part of the signal to be childish, whereas students in elementary school may find a clapping attention signal to be fun and effective.

Regardless of the signal used, teachers should be able to get the attention of the entire class within 5 seconds. For this to occur, students must be taught the signal and how to respond to it. The signal can be taught to the students just as classroom rules and behavioral routines are taught. First, introduce the signal and explain when it will be used. Next, tell the students what the expectation is after the signal has been given (e.g., raise their hands and quietly look at the teacher). Last, practice the signal with students, providing them with feedback and praise as appropriate. Continue to practice until the signal gains the attention of the entire class within 5 seconds. A well-practiced signal helps teachers achieve quick transitions of students between tasks, creating additional time for academic activities.

Physical Layout

One fairly simple change that teachers can make in their classroom to bolster classroom management is to ensure that the physical layout of the room promotes positive teacher–student interactions and prevents disruptive behavior. Some aspects of classrooms cannot be changed (e.g., oddly shaped rooms, columns that obscure sight, size and location of windows), and not all teachers have control over the physical layout of the classroom. However, brainstorm with the teacher to figure out what can be changed to make the best of what cannot be changed. Work together toward the following goals:

1. Ensure that the teacher has full access to all parts of the room.
2. Arrange student desks in a manner that maximizes the needed structure and the type of instructional activities that occur in the classroom.
3. Minimize disruptions in high-traffic areas.
4. Have a system for how students hand in completed work and retrieve new work.
5. Ensure that everything in the classroom has a place.

Active supervision is an important component to classroom behavior management. Therefore, positioning student desks in a manner that allows the teacher full and easy access to all parts of the room is vital. When teachers can move easily about the room, they can more easily provide corrective feedback to students who are off task, provide positive feedback to those who are doing well, and answer questions as needed. Further, the use of physical proximity can be a very effective strategy in decreasing disruptive behavior. In classrooms that allow the teacher to provide active supervision, students are constantly aware of the teacher's proximity to them. Simply moving closer to a group of students can bring them back on task without the need for a comment or reprimand.

Effective classrooms arrange student desks in a manner that optimizes the type of structure and common instructional activities that occur in the classroom. For instance, arranging desks in clusters or pods is excellent for cooperative learning activities and easy access to all students, but students could be easily distracted in the small groupings and engage in more off-topic conversations. On the other hand, arranging desks side-to-side in rows is good for frequent whole-class instruction because it directs attention to the front of the room and makes student interactions more difficult due to spaces between desks. When determining the best layout, you should discuss the pros and cons of each design, keeping in mind the types of activities that most commonly occur and the level of structure the students in the classroom will benefit from the most.

When thinking about the design of the classroom, identify the high-traffic areas, or those areas that students need to use the most frequently to move about the classroom. For instance, students will need to access some areas regularly to throw away trash, sharpen pencils, get supplies, turn in work, or join small-group discussions. Help the teacher design the classroom so that these areas are free of desks or other barriers so that students can get to them without having to move objects (e.g., don't store classroom equipment in front of the pencil sharpener). Work together with the teacher to identify these high-traffic areas and then do a walk through to make sure those areas are free of obstacles and far enough away from student desks to prevent distractions and disruptions.

If student work completion is a chronic problem, examining the current classroom system with this particular area in mind can be helpful. Collaboratively review and revise procedures for assigning, monitoring, and collecting student work. Create a system that students use to determine assigned work, file completed work, pick up graded work, and access needed materials. Work with the teacher to identify a permanent place in the classroom where students can look to determine what needs to be completed. If there is no plan in place for students to keep their own record of assigned homework, come up with a strategy (e.g., writing assignments into planner) and a lesson plan for teaching the students how to use the strategy. Spending time and effort up front to create simple, easy-to-understand systems for turning in work, picking up work, retrieving work, getting new assignments, and accessing materials can reduce wasted time and keep students on task.

Last, clutter and disorganization can lead to chaos. To avoid these, it is important to create a space for everything. If the classroom has materials in piles on desks or the floor, work toward building a system where the piles are transferred into neatly organized files placed into a cabinet; old or unnecessary items are placed into storage boxes and moved out of the classroom; and books and other materials are placed on clearly labeled shelves. In other words, work with the teacher to develop an organizational system in which materials and information can be readily stored and located.

Daily Schedule

The daily schedule is a critical component of classroom structure because it informs both teacher and students about the type of activities that occur each day in the classroom. A key question to ask is whether the classroom's schedule allows for a balance of teacher-directed work, independent work, and group-work activities. To determine this, have the teacher create a list of subjects taught and the length of time allotted for each subject/class. Then ask the teacher to list the activities that typically occur within each subject area and the amount of time these activities take. Last, determine if the activities are teacher-directed work, independent student work, or student group work. After generating this list, for example, a teacher may notice that 60% of the classtime is teacher-directed, 20% independent work, and 20% cooperative group work. The next step is working with the teacher to decide if this is a good balance for his or her classroom, or if adjustments are needed. Although there are no absolute rules, a good rule of thumb is that no particular activity should last longer than 20 minutes, and the more variety, the better. In addition to determining the appropriate balance of these types of activities, it is also helpful to consider how the different activities impact student behavior at different times of the day.

Modifying the schedule can often have a positive impact on a class that has high rates of problematic behaviors. For example, in an elementary classroom, if the teacher typically schedules independent work during the last part of the school day and finds that students are engaging in a great deal of off-task behavior during this time, then a shift to more interactive or teacher-directed tasks might be beneficial. To use a secondary example, a teacher may have classes of freshman English both first period and seventh period. Although the content will be the same for both classes, to keep students engaged during seventh period may require that the teacher run a more active and structured schedule compared to the morning. Reviewing times and activities in which students are highly engaged versus off task can lead to intervention ideas that include changing instructional format and activities to increase student engagement. Additionally, it helps to identify times when students will benefit from precorrective statements that quickly remind them of the expectations for an activity and how they can meet those expectations before problem behaviors occur (see upcoming section on Precorrections for more information).

INTERVENTION IDEAS FOR IMPROVING TEACHER–STUDENT RELATIONSHIPS

Positive relationships between students and their teachers are essential. Why? The most obvious reason is that a positive teacher–student relationship is built on trust, understanding, and caring, and as a result, fosters student cooperation and motivation to learn and achieve in school. Students who feel valued by their teachers internalize the values and goals that teachers hold for them (Connell & Wellborn, 1991). They are more motivated and work harder to solve challenging tasks. Furthermore, research indicates that students from less fortunate backgrounds who establish a close relationship with a teacher or counselor have much better long-term outcomes than students who do not establish a close relationship with an adult (Comer, 1993). Given these important reasons for building positive relationships among teachers and students in classrooms, almost any classroom is likely to benefit from interventions that enhance the teacher–student relationship, particularly if behavior problems present themselves fairly regularly. *The power of all other strategies mentioned in this chapter is enhanced when students trust and respect their teacher.*

Effective and positive classroom management and positive teacher–student relationships go hand in hand. Positive classroom management strategies help students feel an emotional connection to their teachers and their school (McNeely, Nonnemaker, & Blum, 2002). Therefore, supporting teachers in the use of positive, proactive classroom management techniques will foster positive teacher–student relationships. This makes sense. Think about an effective classroom environment in which the expectations are clear, routines and procedures are understood, students are reinforced for meeting expectations, and consequences for not meeting expectations are fair and consistent. In such a classroom students feel safe and valued. In a classroom where rules are unclear and inconsistently reinforced, however, students may feel confused and unfairly treated, feelings that strain teacher–student relationships. In the next section we provide additional strategies with which to create positive teacher–student relationships. Many of these can be easily employed by any teacher who feels that his or her classroom environment would benefit from improved relationships.

> **The power of any other strategy mentioned in this chapter is enhanced when students trust and respect their teacher.**

Increasing Noncontingent Interactions

Noncontingent interactions or noncontingent attention builds personal relationships with students. Essentially, teachers who use noncontingent attention take an active interest in the lives and happiness of their students, interacting with them in positive ways, without this interaction being dependent on student behavior. Examples include greeting students at the door, asking them about their weekend or what activities they enjoy doing outside of school, tying in the activities they enjoy with instruction, and using their name in a greeting when passing them in the hallway. These very simple strategies can have a significant and lasting impact on future interactions between teachers and students. To support teachers in increasing their use of noncontingent attention, you might ask them to think of a teacher from their past that made them feel valued and important. Have them identify what that particular teacher did that made them feel this way. It may help to share your own reflections about an outstanding teacher from your past to help generate ideas and discussion. After identifying behaviors that support the feeling of being valued and important, describe strategies that would foster these behaviors and that the teacher would be comfortable integrating into the classroom (e.g., standing at the door and greeting each student by name, sharing a story about him- or herself with the class).

Because building positive relationships with students is the cornerstone of effective classroom management, it can be helpful to discuss some of the challenges and issues that arise as a teacher sets forth to improve relationships with students. It is important to discuss with teachers that there will be students who are more challenging than others and that these students may not outwardly show appreciation when acknowledged by a teacher. However, despite the challenge presented by these students, persistence tends to pay off. Sometimes the most difficult-to-reach students are the ones who benefit the most from a positive teacher–student relationship. We have found in practice that it is often the student who outwardly shrugs off a greeting or positive gesture that inwardly genuinely appreciates the act and feels valued and important. Avoid giving up on providing this important type of attention to these students. It may be necessary to find less public ways to interact with the student who seems to react when provided with a public greeting.

Further, it is a good idea to mention that the teacher does not need to be every student's favorite teacher, nor does the teacher need to be every student's friend. The teacher will want to be relatable and knowledgeable about his or her students, but it is not necessarily appropriate for the teacher to use slang language or follow student trends. Rather, a teacher who establishes clear expectations, remains fair and consistent, creates opportunities for students' success, and communicates that they care about the individuals in their classroom as both a student and a person, will produce positive outcomes. It is important to remember that noncontingent attention has a place and time in the classroom. Opportunities to provide noncontingent attention are most likely to occur as students enter the classroom, at the end of class, or in the hallway. On occasion, noncontingent attention will find its way into instruction (e.g., "Nick, great answer. By the way it's great you are feeling better and back in class.") but these moments should be brief. Teachers should avoid having long discussions on tangential topics during teacher-led instruction or when monitoring independent student work. If it becomes a habit, the students may go out of their way to lead the teacher off topic.

INTERVENTION IDEAS
FOR IMPROVING INSTRUCTIONAL MANAGEMENT

Given that one of the primary purposes of proactive classroom management is to increase the amount of time that students engage in relevant and rigorous academic instruction, some time needs to be spent on examining the relationship between student behavior and instruction. There is a direct link between how instruction is delivered in a classroom and the behavior of students in that classroom. When instructional tasks are too difficult, students become frustrated and disengaged. On the other hand, when instructional tasks are too easy, students become bored and disengaged. Further, when an activity goes on too long and a group is having difficulty maintaining attention, more of a teacher's time is spent sustaining attention and less of the students' time is spent thinking about the material. In order to maintain appropriate student behavior and strengthen academic efficacy in the classroom, teachers need to provide students with mastery experiences. When tasks are too easy, success holds little value to students. Yet when tasks are too difficult, students experience failure, which undermines academic efficacy. Finding a balance in which student learning is maximized by keeping lessons moving at a good pace and using strategies to maintain student engagement in the material will also help to decrease disruptive behavior. The following section provides some useful strategies for improving instructional management in the classroom. For classrooms in which high levels of disruptive behavior or low academic engagement occurs during structured or semistructured instructional activities, guiding teachers on how to effectively intersperse these strategies throughout their daily instruction can be beneficial.

Increasing Opportunities to Respond

The use of brisk pacing during teacher-led instruction is one variable that has been shown to decrease problem behavior and increase academic achievement. Off-task behaviors can occur when students become disengaged from instruction (Lewis & Sugai, 1999). Increasing the rate of opportunities for active student response during instruction generates more learning, provides important feedback to the teacher, and increases on-task behavior. An opportunity to respond occurs any time a teacher presents an academic question to students, either as a group or individually (e.g., "What is the square root of 49?").

> **Brisk pacing during teacher-led instruction has been shown to decrease problem behavior and increase academic achievement.**

Strategically Using Opportunities to Respond

In classrooms in which the teacher finds that student attention tends to wander during instruction, increasing the use of opportunities to respond can be an effective strategy. Several techniques can be useful. One is to incorporate variety and unpredictability into question asking, so that students learn that they may be called on at any time. Teachers should question students at random, on occasion questioning students again after they have answered an earlier question or asking them to comment on another student's answer (e.g., "Cheryl, do you agree with Steve's answer?"). It's important to note that this technique should be used to stimulate interest, challenge the class, and avoid predictability. It should not be used to simply catch inattentive students as punishment or to make them feel embarrassed. If misused in this way, students may become resentful, causing damage to the teacher–student relationship.

Teachers can further foster classwide attention with the effective use of wait time: The teacher poses a question to the entire class and then allows time for students to think before calling on an individual to answer (e.g., "What is the square root of 49? [*wait time*] Okay. Kyan, what is the square root of 49?"). If there is a possibility that any student might be called on, each student is more likely to think about the answer. In contrast, if the teacher states the name of someone to answer before the question is asked, the other students in the class know that they will not be held accountable for answering and are less likely to stay engaged and think about the question.

You may also advise teachers to track their use of opportunities to respond. Tracking helps to (1) ensure that all students are given opportunities to respond and (2) determine the level of accuracy of student responses. Brighter or assertive students are often more likely to seek response opportunities, and teachers may find it to be more reinforcing to call on these students because they give the right answers. To avoid this pitfall, teachers can keep track of who has responded and who has not, so that they can distribute opportunities evenly over time. You could support the teacher by identifying a feasible system for tallying and tracking response opportunities—for instance, using a log book with a simple coding system that allows the teacher to track both who has responded and the success rates of students in answering questions of varying difficulty levels. Additionally, tracking student accuracy is useful in determining the appropriateness of the instruction content. For instance, if during teacher-led instruction the teacher provided 20 opportunities to respond, but only 10 of those opportunities were answered correctly, or a 50% accuracy rate, the teacher may take this low rate as a sign that the material needs additional review because it was not understood by half the class. Further, a teacher who gets 20 correct responses for 100% accuracy may recognize that high rate as an indication that the material is too easy and that more challenging materials can be presented. Helping teachers set up a system that allows them to gather this important data in a way that helps them make good decisions about instruction can significantly impact student achievement and behavior.

Increasing Pacing of Instruction

The Council for Exceptional Children (1987) provided guidelines for the optimal rate of student responding. These guidelines state that four to six responses (minimum of 3.1) should be elicited from students per minute of instruction on new material, with 80% accuracy, and nine to twelve opportunities to respond (minimum 8.2) should be provided during drill-and-practice work, with 90% accuracy (Council for Exceptional Children, 1987; Gunter, Hummel, & Conroy, 1998). When working with teachers in which the number of opportunities to respond is less than optimal, you may suggest some fairly simple strategies that they may find useful. The following provides some ideas that teachers may incorporate into practice. However, the list is far from exhaustive. In collaboration with the teacher, you may develop additional ideas that are more individualized and work better for that teacher in their classroom.

> **Four to six responses should be elicited per minute of instruction on new material, with 80% accuracy, and nine to twelve opportunities to respond should be provided during drill-and-practice work, with 90% accuracy.**

In an effort to increase the number of opportunities provided during teacher-led instruction, the teacher may find the following approaches to be helpful:

1. Break complex problems down into smaller chunks, having students provide the answers to each chunk of the problem.
2. Ask drill-and-practice questions from a deck of questions made up on note cards, to which students provide brief choral responses interspersed with individual student responses.
3. Provide questions and have students quickly write their responses on a small white board, holding it up to show the answer. Other ideas for having students respond to group questions include having students turn to a neighbor to share an answer; having students hold up a two-sided card with yes–no, true–false, agree–disagree; having students display thumbs up or down to a question; and having students stand up if they believe an answer is true or stay seated if it is false.
4. Mix into every lesson a session of brief, fast-paced teacher-directed review of previous material, asking for both individual and group responses.

5. Use a seating chart, checking off each time a student is called on individually to ensure that everyone gets a chance.
6. Ask a question, allow think time, and then call on a student without having students raise hands.
7. Ask a question and then draw a stick with a student's name out of a jar. Once all the students have answered a question, put the student names back into the jar.
8. If a student who is called on does not know the answer to a question, give some think time before asking for a classroom choral response or before allowing a student to "phone a friend" for help in answering the question. Then return to that student in a few minutes with the same question.

Regardless of which strategy a teacher uses to increase his or her rate of opportunities to respond, it is important that the questions are relevant, meaning that they are important and applicable to student experiences, and that they have the appropriate level of rigor for the students in the class.

Increasing student opportunities to respond has a positive effect on student achievement and behavior. Additionally, the more opportunities that a teacher provides for students to respond the more times that a teacher can provide praise or positive feedback (e.g., TEACHER: "What is the square root of 49?" CLASS: "7." TEACHER: "Great thinking, that's correct."). Therefore, implementing and maintaining proactive classroom management by utilizing effective instructional practices lends itself to both an increase in opportunities to respond as well as an increase in overall student engagement.

USE OF EVIDENCE-BASED INSTRUCTIONAL PRACTICES

There are several evidence-based instructional practices that teachers can use to increase student engagement and maximize achievement. In addition to increasing student opportunities to respond, teachers can utilize direct instruction techniques, peer tutoring, computer-assisted instruction, and guided notes. We briefly describe these practices here. (For a more thorough review, see Simonsen et al., 2008.) First, direct instruction is an approach to teaching that is characterized by clear presentation of content with use of signals that is carefully sequenced to allow for seamless and progressive mastery of skills. Instruction uses high rates of opportunities to respond, review of content, systematic feedback, and ongoing progress monitoring, and students learn concepts and skills to mastery (Engelman & Carnine, 1982). Second, classwide peer tutoring pairs students together with the roles of tutor and tutee. Students provide each other with instruction and give each other immediate error corrections (Delquadri, Greenwood, Stretton, & Hall, 1983; Fuchs, Fuchs, & Burish, 2000). Third, computer-assisted instruction uses technology to provide students with one-on-one instruction, including frequent opportunities to respond and immediate corrective feedback, using material tailored to the appropriate instructional level of the student (Jerome & Barbetta, 2005; Silver-Pacuilla & Fleischman, 2006). Fourth, guided notes are provided to students by the teacher; they outline lectures or chapters and contain the main ideas and spaces for students to fill in additional details (Lazarus, 1993). The idea is that students become active rather than passive learners. Each of these practices could be employed by teachers wanting to increase the effectiveness of their instruction while increasing academic achievement, student academic efficacy, and student engagement.

INTERVENTION IDEAS
FOR RESPONDING TO APPROPRIATE BEHAVIOR

Every teacher needs a toolbox of strategies for how to respond when students meet expectations. If you are working in a classroom with a low ratio of positive-to-negative interaction, exploring strategies for improving this ratio will be important. A ratio of *at least* three positive for every one negative is optimal in the classroom (Sprick, Booher, & Garrison, 2009).

Increasing teacher use of strategies for responding to appropriate behavior can be helpful in several ways. First, when students are reinforced for expected behavior, they are more likely to repeat it in the future. Second, responding to appropriate behavior indicates to students that the expectation is important and valued by the teacher. Third, other students who observe their peers being reinforced for appropriate behavior are more likely to engage in that behavior in the future because they learn the expectation and the positive consequence associated with it. Last, teachers who respond positively to students exhibiting expected

> **A ratio of *at least* three positive for every one negative is optimal in the classroom.**

behavior are supporting effective positive teacher–student relationships. Supporting teachers in developing a continuum of strategies to respond to appropriate behavior enables them to function as positive proactive classroom managers.

Increasing Behavior-Specific Praise

Three characteristics make it more likely that praise will be a successful reinforcer: contingency, specificity, and sincerity (Brophy, 1981). That is, effective praise needs to be contingent on performance of the desired behavior, specifically state the characteristics of the behavior being praised, and sound credible to the student being praised. Praise is considered behavior-specific when explicit feedback regarding the desired student behavior is provided (e.g., "China, good job lining up quietly."). Behavior-specific praise can be given to individual students ("Kennedy, thank you for raising your hand."), to groups of students ("Table 3 students are working quietly at their seats."), or to the whole classroom ("Everyone has eyes on me, ready to learn."). Behavior-specific praise is cost free, takes little physical effort to implement, is time-efficient, and is not intrusive in the classroom.

Used proactively, behavior-specific praise can eliminate many problem behaviors and is effective with even the most challenging students. It accomplishes two important goals. First, behavior-specific praise includes a statement of the desired behavior, thus making the expectations clear to all students in the classroom. Second, the use of behavior-specific praise reduces the need for reprimands and increases positive interactions with students

(Reinke et al., 2008). For example, if a student in the classroom is calling out answers without raising his or her hand, the teacher may provide behavior-specific praise to a student who *has* raised his or her hand (e.g., "Thank you for raising your hand, Juan. What is your answer?"). This reminds the student calling out, and everyone else in the classroom, of the expectation to raise one's hand without the teacher reprimanding the student or giving attention to the problem behavior. Increasing the use of behavior-specific praise in the classroom promotes healthy, positive classroom environments while reducing problem behavior.

There are several strategies that may be utilized to support teachers in increasing their use of behavior-specific praise. First, you should begin by simply having a discussion with the teacher about how behavior-specific praise could be incorporated into the current classroom. One idea for doing this is to have the teacher identify a few disruptive behaviors that commonly occur in the classroom and interfere with instruction. Write these behaviors down and identify the opposite, desired student behavior. Next, generate a list of behavior-specific praise statements that the teacher could use when the correct student behavior is being demonstrated. The teacher should then identify a time of day to "catch students being good" (see Figure 8.5 for an example of a completed Catch Students Being Good form and Appendix D.4 for a blank form). During this time, the teacher can utilize the behavior-specific praise statements that you developed together when the appropriate behavior is seen. This will give the teacher a focus and help him or her become more fluent in behavior-specific praise. Over time, you can work with the teacher to identify other behaviors and times of day to help the skill generalize across the school day.

Another strategy is to have the teacher develop a stimulus prompt to help him or her remember to use behavior-specific praise in the classroom. For instance, many teachers we've worked with, who use overhead projectors simply wrote on a sticky note *"Look up and use behavior-specific praise."* Upon noticing the note, the teacher looks up to find a student or students displaying appropriate behavior and provides them with praise (e.g., "You all have your eyes on me. Great work!"). Another teacher placed a smiley face sign directly below the classroom clock because she regularly glanced at the clock throughout the day. When she looked up at the clock, the smiley face reminded her to provide behavior-specific praise to a student or students in the class who were behaving appropriately.

> **Have the teacher develop a stimulus prompt to help him or her remember to use behavior-specific praise in the classroom.**

One other strategy to support teachers in increasing behavior-specific praise is to observe them in the classroom and provide them with performance feedback. To do this most effectively, identify a time when the teacher would like you to observe. Next, as you observe, keep a frequency count of how often the teacher uses behavior-specific praise. It can also be helpful to keep a tally of general praise, or praise that does not explicitly describe student behavior (e.g., "Good job!"), and reprimands. This information can give you and the teacher an idea of his or her ratio of positive-to-negative interactions as well as relative rates of behavior-specific to general praise. Following the observation, meet with the teacher to discuss his or her use of praise. We recommend that feedback be given fairly soon after the observation to allow the teacher to more accurately gauge his or her use of behavior-specific

Catch Students Being Good Form

Step 1:	Identify a time of day to "catch" students being good. A time when disruptive behavior is fairly high can be a good target.
Step 2:	Write down the common disruptive behaviors that occur during this time.
Step 3:	Write down the behavior you would like to see more of.
Step 4:	Write down a list of behavior-specific praise statements to use when you "catch" the students displaying the behavior you would like to see more of.

Remember that behavior-specific praise is praise that tells students exactly what they are doing correctly (e.g., "Thank you for raising your hand.").

Time to "Catch" Students:

In the morning during the first 20 minutes of reading instruction.

Problem Behavior	Behavior to "Catch" *This is the behavior you want to see more of. It is often the opposite of the problem behavior.*	Behavior-Specific Praise
Sample: Talking Out	Raising hand and waiting to be called on.	"Thank you for raising your hand and waiting patiently."
Wandering around the classroom.	Working quietly at their desks. Transitioning from circle time to small groups quietly and quickly.	"[Student name] is working hard at his [or her] desk." "I see [student name] getting right to work at his [or her] desk."
Talking to peers about things unrelated to the assigned work.	Being on task during group work.	"The group in the back got to work right away. I can see that group [xx] is getting their work done."

FIGURE 8.5. Example of a completed Catch Students Being Good Form.

praise. There is also value in letting a teacher estimate his or her use of behavior-specific praise before giving the feedback. Additionally, it can be helpful to graph the number of behavior-specific praise statements for a teacher over several observations. This way, teachers can compare times when they use more or less behavior-specific praise. In the end, the goal is for the teacher to become comfortable and fluent in using behavior-specific praise.

Use of Group Contingencies and Token Economies

Group contingencies and token economy systems are often used in combination and are most frequently implemented at the elementary and middle school levels. In a token economy system students exchange earned tokens (e.g., sticker, chips, marbles) for a reinforcer. Group contingencies occur when the teacher provides a group of students with reinforcement contingent on appropriate behavior for the entire group. An example of a group contingency program using a token economy that often works well in classrooms is the "Success Behavior Bank." To set up this program, the teacher informs students that each time he or she catches them showing success behaviors, the class will earn a marble or other token. Each earned token is then placed into a medium-sized canning jar or other transparent container, allowing students to track how many tokens they have earned. Once the jar is full of marbles, the entire class earns a reward (e.g., extra recess, popcorn party). Each time the teacher places a marble into the jar, he or she provides a brief behavior-specific praise statement to announce the success behavior (e.g., "I see everyone at table 3 hard at work. That's a success behavior."). Group contingency programs can be set up to reinforce the entire class, small groups of students, or pairs of students.

Typically, group contingencies are established to increase positive behaviors by giving attention to the behavior that the teacher wishes to increase (e.g., raising hand, completing assignments on time). However, group contingencies also have been used to reinforce the absence of problem behaviors. This form of group contingency works to teach students to inhibit problem behavior while increasing on-task behaviors. One example of a group contingency intervention that works to inhibit behavior is the Good Behavior Game. The Good Behavior Game was developed in 1969 by a classroom teacher and has an extensive research base showing that it increases on-task behavior and decreases disruptive behavior (see Embry, 2002, for a review). To set up the Good Behavior Game, the teacher splits the classroom into small groups or teams. For instance, if the students are seated in tables clustered together, each cluster would be a team. Next, the teacher explains that each time someone from within their group misbehaves, the group will earn a point. Of course, for the game to be effective the teacher needs to make explicit those behaviors that are considered misbehaviors (e.g., talking out, off task, out of seat). On the board, or in some area of the classroom visible to the students and easily accessible to the teacher, each team has its name written and a space where tallies of misbehavior can be marked by the teacher. The teacher informs the class that teams who earn 5 or fewer points during a specified period will earn a reward. The teacher may want to gather baseline information about the number of misbehaviors that occur regularly in a classroom and set a goal so that fewer occur during the game. For instance, if the teacher finds that 20 or more misbehaviors occur in a 10-minute time period, then setting the goal for 7 or fewer points initially and reducing this amount over time may be more appropriate. Thus, the number of points that earns a reward can be adapted to reflect the skills and needs of the classroom.

Next, the teacher announces the start of the game and how long it will last. It is most effective if the teacher starts the game out in relatively short intervals (i.e., 5 minutes) and builds up to longer games. During the game, the classroom routines and activities continue as usual. For instance, the teacher may be leading a classroom discussion or providing direct instruction. However, when the teacher notices a misbehavior, he or she calmly and briefly announces it (e.g., "Red team, that's talking out") and marks a tally for the offending team. After the designated time lapses for the game ends, the points are counted for each team. Teams that meet the goal (e.g., 5 or fewer points) earn a brief and immediate reward that is reinforcing (i.e., students enjoy it) and developmentally appropriate (e.g., standing up and doing a little dance as a reward for primary age children; with middle school students, the winning team might get a slightly reduced homework assignment such as doing five fewer homework problems than originally assigned). Teams who have points in excess of the goal (e.g., 6 or more) do not earn a reward. Quick prizes for good behavior allow the teacher to pause instruction for only 30 seconds to a minute to provide the winning teams with the prizes. Below are some ideas for prizes for younger and older students.

Younger Students

- Stickers
- First to line up
- Everyone on team wears paper crown
- Goes across hall to be applauded by the class across hall
- Gets class mascot (stuffed animal)
- Gets to sing a fun song (e.g., the Hokey Pokey)

Older Students

- Released from class 1 minute early
- Free time while rest of class works
- Note home to parents
- Gets to work outside
- Gets to choose to work at desk, stand, or sit on floor
- Gets reduced homework assignment

Setting Up Token Economy Systems

When working with a teacher who wants to establish a token economy system, either for groups of students within the class or for individuals, adhering to a few principles will make it more likely that the system will be successful. First, the system should be as simple as possible, using readily available materials. If it becomes too complicated and materials are hard to obtain, the system will become burdensome and the teacher may discontinue it because it is impractical. Second, it can be helpful to identify one or two behaviors that the teacher would like to see more often in the classroom and begin by reinforcing these behaviors among students. Third, be sure that students understand the specific, observable behavior that will earn a token. Fourth, the reward system needs to be clear and precise. The teacher and students may want to create a chart that includes the rewards that can be earned and the tokens needed for each reward. The chart should be posted in an area where everyone can see it. As a non-example, a vague system might be explained by a teacher like this: "When you do what I ask, then you can earn some points that you can use to get a prize." This explanation does not inform students about how many points need to be earned or what the prize would be. Fifth, the rewards, while they should be inexpensive and feasible, also need to be something for which students in the class are willing to work. In other words, the prizes need to be reinforcing. Additionally, having a variety of options for rewards is helpful because inevitably students will become tired of earning the same reward, and choice itself can be reinforcing. Last, the system should be fun for all. Both the teacher and students should enjoy giving/earning point and rewards.

> **The system should be as simple as possible, using readily available materials.**

There are many examples of token economy systems that you and the teacher can emulate. Teachers often create the best systems when they are invited to be creative while adhering to the overarching principles noted above. Some schools utilize a schoolwide reinforcement system in which students earn tickets or "gotcha bucks" that can then be used to purchase items from a school store. Teachers can simply use these ticket tokens in their classroom. If no schoolwide program exists, teachers could set up their own store and implement this strategy in their classroom by using tickets to reinforce behaviors they would like to see more often. Other tokens that have been used successfully are colorful armbands that are given to students for appropriate behavior, stickers on a chart, simply marking an *X* or drawing a smiley face on a chart, poker chips delivered into a container, filling a tube with water 1 inch at a time, or coloring in spots or squares from a picture or table taped to the students' desks. The form of token is not important, other than it should be obvious to the student that the token was earned for appropriate behavior, and it is feasible for the teacher to implement.

Identifying rewards that are successful in reinforcing students is key to an effective token economy system. To develop a menu of rewards that are appropriate and reinforcing, begin by brainstorming ideas with the teacher and then bringing these ideas to the students. It is helpful to have some ideas already prepared prior to talking with students so that the teacher does not feel pressured to use rewards suggested by the students that are not feasible or in line with his or her values. Rewards can be social reinforcers (e.g., student recognition), activity reinforcers (e.g., special privileges, jobs, computer time), or material reinforcers (e.g., tangible items). Generating a few ideas from each category can be helpful. You may want to use the Incentive Selection Form provided in Appendix D.5 to support brainstorming across these different domains (see Figure 8.6 for a completed example). It is important that rewards be developmentally appropriate. Although brainstorming with the teacher is helpful, encourage the teacher to remain open to students' suggestions, as they may identify rewards that are simple and easily delivered that you or the teacher never considered.

Incentive Selection Form

Identify several potential incentives from each of the domains listed below.

Work to add to the number and variety of reinforcements in each column to increase positive student behavior in your classroom.

Social Reinforcer	Activity Reinforcer	Material Reinforcer
Kid of the Day Award (comes with special privileges like lining up first, leading the morning routine). Positive letter home to parents. Pin on badge: "I am a good learner." Be a teacher's helper for the day. Earn privilege to take home "classroom pet" (stuffed dog) overnight.	5 minutes of computer time 5 minutes of listening to music Opportunity to help a younger child in another class Get to sit in an adult computer chair at desk Eat lunch with teacher Disco time	Scratch-and-sniff stickers Pencils, erasers, markers Small notepad Baseball cards Bubbles Crackers, sugarless gum, jelly beans

FIGURE 8.6. Example of a completed Incentive Selection Form.

INTERVENTION IDEAS FOR RESPONDING TO INAPPROPRIATE BEHAVIOR

During classroom visits, you might observe that a teacher delivers corrections inconsistently, uses harsh and prolonged reprimands, applies more intrusive interventions (e.g., sending a student to the office or time out) than less intrusive responses (e.g., planned ignoring or fluent corrections), or gives different consequences to two students demonstrating the same misbehavior (e.g., Johnny is sent to office; Jane is given a verbal reprimand). On the other hand, you might observe a high level of disruptive behaviors or little on-task behavior in a classroom with little or no response from the teacher to correct the behavior. Any of these scenarios could lead to a discussion with the teacher about developing a continuum of responses to inappropriate behavior that match the varying degrees of misbehavior.

One effective strategy toward building a plan for a continuum of responses to inappropriate behavior is to work with the teacher to develop a list of classroom misbehaviors and their consequences. One way to do this is by using the Discipline Planning Form (see Figure 8.7 for a completed example and Appendix D.6 for a blank form). In the left column, have the teacher list com-

> **Work with the teacher to develop a list of classroom misbehaviors and their consequences.**

Discipline Planning Form

Step 1:	Develop a list of misbehaviors that occur in the classroom, beginning with the behaviors that are the *least* disruptive or concerning, and ending with the *most* disruptive or concerning. Be sure that behaviors are specific and observable.
Step 2:	Identify a response to each misbehavior.

Misbehavior	Response to Misbehavior
Talking out	Ignore misbehavior and praise students who raise a hand or are working quietly. For repeated talking out, give correction. "That's talking out. Please raise your hand."
Getting out of seat without permission	Give a correction. "Please have a seat."
Socializing with peers during class time	Praise other students who are on task. Redirect the students to the task on which they are supposed to be working.
Swearing or verbal aggression	Provide a correction with response cost. "That language is not okay. You lose a point."
Defiant, not complying with directive	Ignore misbehavior and praise student with appropriate behavior. "I like how Lauren is quietly getting out her homework to hand in."
Throwing objects	Provide a correction with a consequence. "Throwing things is not being safe. You lost 5 minutes of recess today."
Hitting a peer	Send to time out. "That's not being safe. Please go to the safe seat and take a time out."

FIGURE 8.7. Example of a completed Discipline Planning Form for developing a continuum of responses to inappropriate behavior.

mon classroom misbehaviors. In the right column, work with the teacher to create a list of appropriate responses to each misbehavior. By completing each column, the teacher anticipates common misbehaviors that occur in the classroom and reflects on how she or he would like to respond. As a result, when a particular misbehavior occurs in the classroom, a plan is already in place for how the teacher will respond. A structured plan is helpful in that it makes it less likely that the teacher will panic or react emotionally to misbehavior or treat students differently. It is a good idea to review the list with the teacher to assess his or her level of comfort in actually using the responses identified on the form and making sure only strategies that the teacher is able and willing to do are on the list. For those strategies with which a teacher feels less comfortable or competent, you could work together to practice the skill and develop additional strategies to support implementation in the classroom setting.

Planned Ignoring

In classrooms where you observe a large number of reprimands, particularly for classroom misbehaviors that are reinforced by teacher attention, planned ignoring can be an effective intervention to decrease disruptions and the number of negative interactions between the teacher and students. This is a great way to improve the positive-to-negative ratio for teachers. Ignoring attention-seeking behaviors and praising students who exhibit appropriate behaviors will lead to higher rates of positive interactions and fewer negative interactions.

First, work with the teacher to make a list of misbehaviors that can be ignored. It can be helpful to use the Discipline Planning Form (see completed example in Figure 8.7) to determine a response for each behavior. Keep in mind, it is not effective to ignore behaviors that students use to avoid activities (e.g., walking around the room when they should be seated, talking to peers during independent work, or any off-task behavior). Additionally, dangerous or highly aggressive behaviors cannot be ignored. Also, when identifying the behaviors to be ignored, evaluate whether each behavior is truly attempting to gain teacher attention or if it is more likely a behavior to gain peer attention (e.g., making silly comments that cause other students to laugh). Once you and the teacher have decided on those misbehaviors that can truly be ignored, develop a plan for implementing the practice.

Planned ignoring sounds fairly simple until you actually try to do it. It is easy to fall into a well-set trap by acknowledging the student who eagerly calls out correct answers even though he or she should have raised a hand. Planned ignoring is an extinction strategy. In order for it to work, the behavior must be completely ignored (i.e., never acknowledged). Planned ignoring can be challenging because when first implemented, the target behavior will actually get worse before getting better. In other words, the level of disruptions will increase initially before decreasing. For instance, in a classroom where calling out once met with teacher attention, a student will continue to call out. As ignoring continues, the same student may call out again at a more frequent pace; the student may test the new contingency to be sure that the rules of attention getting have really changed, given that the strategy worked so well in the past. It is important to educate teachers about these response bursts and help them anticipate them as they initiate planned ignoring strategies. Otherwise, they may become discouraged and give up prematurely—which would only serve to reinforce the more intense behavior responses of students that immediately preceded their attending. If a teacher provides attention at the peak of this increase, the students learn a new rule: In order to get the teacher's attention, we just need to call out even more frequently, loudly, or disruptively.

When implementing this strategy, the teacher should tell the class about the new rule; that when the target misbehavior occurs (e.g., calling out), the teacher will ignore these responses. Additionally, it is important for the teacher to tell students what to do instead (e.g., "Please raise your hand and wait to be called on."). The teacher should plan to provide behavior-specific praise to students who use the appropriate behavior (e.g., "Thanks for raising your hand."). Given that planned ignoring can be a difficult skill to learn, providing the teacher with performance feedback can be a useful tool to support his or her learning. Plan to conduct an observation during a time that the teacher has identified as the prime time for the target misbehavior to occur. Track the number of times that the target behavior was displayed, how often the behavior was ignored, and how often the teacher provided praise for the alternative behavior. Debrief with the teacher as soon as possible to praise his or her effort and give feedback on how well it went.

Explicit Reprimands

An explicit reprimand is a brief, respectful, clear verbal statement delivered within close proximity (rather than from across the room) that states the expected behavior to a student or group of students displaying inappropriate behavior. An explicit reprimand is the flip side of behavior-specific praise. The reprimand tells the student exactly what he or she should be doing in place of the misbehavior. For example, "Kim, eyes on me, please," rather than, "Kim, please stop playing in your desk." It may be useful to have a discussion about the use of reprimands to support teachers in improving their use of effective classroom management. For instance, during an observation if you notice that the teacher uses reprimands that are ineffective because they are too long, harsh, and/or used too frequently and not in conjunction with other proactive strategies, you may mark the use of reprimands as needing some attention during the feedback session. Provide the teacher with specific examples of ineffective reprimands you observed in the classroom and how an explicit reprimand might be used instead.

On occasion, a teacher may find him- or herself relying more on the use of reprimands than on proactive behavior management strategies. Taking some time to reflect on how reprimands are used in the classroom can be helpful. You may first want to broach the topic by sharing that it can be challenging to manage student behavior, particularly if the teacher is frustrated by that behavior as reflected in the tone of reprimands used in the classroom. This discussion may lead to clarifying classroom expectations, establishing rules, teaching the rules, and reinforcing positive behavior. Keep in mind that, on occasion, teachers do need to provide explicit reprimands. Therefore, discussing how to effectively use reprimands can be valuable.

It can be helpful to use the Discipline Planning Form to identify times when the use of an explicit reprimand is warranted. For example, the teacher may experience a situation where students do not stop talking after he or she used proximity as a cue. In this situation a reprimand could be used to redirect them (e.g., "Kent and Erin, raise your hand and wait to be called on if you have something to say."). It could also be helpful to develop a list of common reprimands with the teacher and determine if they are effective, explicit reprimands, or not, and if not, rephrase them in a way that makes them explicit. For instance, if the teacher reports that he or she tends to say, "Please *stop* talking [or other behavior]," you can inform him or her that this is a brief, clear, and respectful reprimand, but it does not tell the student what the expected behavior is. You can work with the teacher to rephrase the reprimand to be explicit: "Please raise your hand [or other expected behavior]."

In addition, discuss strategies for handling situations when the teacher may need to talk with a student about misbehavior in a way that is more detailed and lengthy than a simple reprimand. For example, if a student is disrespectful to a peer during a lesson, the teacher may want to discuss the importance of treating others with respect with this

> **Provide the teacher with specific examples of ineffective reprimands you observed in the classroom and how an explicit reprimand might be used instead.**

student. However, stopping the lesson to have a lengthy discussion would disrupt the flow of instruction and interfere with student learning. Finding a neutral time outside of instructional activities to have the discussion would be best. There are several reasons that having a discussion immediately after a misbehavior tends to be ineffective: (1) Other students in the classroom are left waiting; (2) giving the student immediate attention for the misbehavior could actually increase the behavior if the student finds the attention affirming; and (3) it is much more effective when the other students are engaged in another activity, and the discussion can occur privately. Discuss the importance of these issues with the teacher, and identify types of problems that may be better handled by meeting with a student privately and discussing how the student could use better strategies to handle a similar situation in the future. As with explicit reprimand, student discussions about misbehavior are most helpful when they teach the student the expected behavior to replace the misbehavior.

Differential Reinforcement

Differential reinforcement uses positive reinforcement to differentiate or separate appropriate student behavior from inappropriate behavior by increasing one while decreasing the other. Overall the goal is to increase appropriate behavior while decreasing inappropriate behavior, typically by not reinforcing the inappropriate behavior. We have outlined various strategies for differential reinforcement in Table 8.3 to provide a primer for considering the best approach for supporting teachers toward using this strategy with students in their classroom.

Differential reinforcement combines several of the prior strategies already discussed, including planned ignoring, praise, and token economy systems or group contingencies, on occasion. It can be helpful to review these sections as you and the teacher work toward implementing differential reinforcement. The first step toward implementing differential reinforcement is to define exactly what the problem behavior is and what the teacher would like the students to be doing instead. The next step is to collect data on how frequently the problem behavior occurs. These data provide the information needed to set goals with regard to reducing the behavior. Next, a menu of incentives should be developed to reinforce the students for appropriate behavior. Finally, determine a time interval in which the differential reinforcement procedures will occur. The time interval can vary from a few seconds to hours; however, it is generally more effective if the time intervals start out small and increase over time.

Differential reinforcement procedures can be applied to the whole classroom, groups of students, or individual students struggling with challenging behaviors. Table 8.3 provides examples of classroom-level procedures. The exact procedures and criterion will change based on the type and level of problem behavior experienced in the classroom. When devising a plan for differential reinforcement with a teacher, you will want to discuss some of the potential problems. First, as with planned ignoring procedures, the problem behavior will get worse before it gets better. Because ignoring the problem is part of differential reinforcement, students will actually increase the behavior before it extinguishes. This increase is called an *extinction burst*. As noted above, if a teacher provides attention during an extinction burst, the behavior will get even worse. Second, when selecting an alternative or incompatible behavior, it is important to select a behavior that is relevant and functional. For instance, teaching students to sit and wait as an incompatible behavior to wandering is nonfunctional. Instead students should be taught a behavior that will support their growth and learning. For example, rather than sit and wait, the incompatible behavior could be for students to sit at their desk and turn over a sign (or give some other signal) indicating that they need to ask a question while they continue working at their desk. Lastly, differential reinforcement procedures take time to be effective. If a behavior is particularly disruptive or dangerous, differential reinforcement is not an appropriate intervention.

Response Cost

A response-cost system is one in which students lose a point or token from a behavior management system that is in place as a result of misbehavior. If a teacher is currently using a token economy system, response-cost procedures can be put into place to discourage student misbehavior. However, it is important to ensure that strategies for responding to appropriate behavior are in place before establishing a response-cost system, as this is a punitive strategy that is fairly intrusive. If the teacher is already using a response-cost system or would like to institute such a system, the following are important principles to ensure its success. First, expectations for earning and losing points and rewards must be clear and precise (see section above on establishing a token economy system). Second, the reward that students can earn should they gain the correct number of points/tokens must be truly reinforcing. One of the main reasons that token economies with response cost do not work effectively is because the students do not care if they earn the reward. Third, a system for informing the student or students when they have lost a point needs to be devised to avoid confusion or backlash. For instance, tell students that when they forget to raise their hand before answering, the teacher will simply say, "Please remember to raise your hand—that's

TABLE 8.3. Differential Reinforcement Strategies

Differential reinforcement of …	Example
Other behavior (DRO)	
The teacher ignores the problem behavior while reinforcing any appropriate replacement behavior within a defined period of time.	Teacher gives each student a point if they display zero disruptive behaviors during a series of short intervals (e.g., 2 minutes over a 20-minute period). All students who earn a predetermined number of points (e.g., 8) can exchange them for a small prize.
Alternative behavior (DRA)	
The teacher ignores the problem behavior while reinforcing an alternative appropriate behavior.	The teacher introduces raising a quiet hand as an alternative to shouting out answers during instruction. Then, during instruction, the teacher gives attention to and praises students who raise their hands while ignoring shout-outs.
Incompatible behavior (DRI)	
The teacher ignores the problem behavior while reinforcing an appropriate behavior that actually interferes, either physically or functionally, with the problem behavior.	In a classroom in which students often wander around the room during independent work, the teacher informs them that students who remain seated in their chair doing their assigned work for the 30-minute class period will receive 2 extra credit points.
Low rates of behavior (DRL)	
The teacher reinforces the student only after the target behavior occurs at a predetermined low rate.	In a classroom in which negative comments (i.e., name calling, teasing) occur 10 times within a 30-minute period, the teacher explains to the students that they can earn a group reward if they make five or fewer negative comments during a 30-minute period. The teacher then chooses a 30-minute period, and marks a tally each time a negative comment is heard, without giving it attention. At the end of the 30 minutes, if the students had five or fewer tallies, they earn a reward.
High rates of behavior (DRH)	
The teacher reinforces the students only after the target behavior occurs at a predetermined high rate.	In a classroom in which student participation is low, the teacher explains to the group that if 8 of the 20 students volunteer to answer questions and come to the board to write out problems during math instruction, the group will earn a reward.

1 point." The teacher will then cross off a point on the behavior management chart that is visible to the class.

It is helpful to anticipate possible problems that will occur, such as students trying to explain their behavior or denying that they engaged in the problem behavior. Engaging in lengthy explanations about these issues during instruction interferes with classroom activities and makes it unlikely that the teacher will continue the strategy. To avoid this problem, the teacher can devise a lesson plan to actively teach, model, practice, and reinforce students for behaving appropriately following removal of a point. Fourth, the system should not allow students to go into debt or owe points back. Furthermore, if response cost is used excessively, to the point that students feel that there is no way to earn the reward in a timely manner, then they will give up and stop caring about losing points. In fact, such a situation may increase disruptive behavior because students will view the system as unfair and may retaliate. Given these important considerations, we suggest that response cost be used sparingly in classrooms and only after positive, proactive classroom strategies are solidly in place.

Time Out

The purpose of time out is not to send a student to an aversive setting; rather, it is to remove a misbehaving student from an opportunity to earn positive reinforcement. The overall goal is to communicate to the student that if he or she is disruptive to the class, then the student does not get to participate in the interesting, productive, and enjoyable classroom activities that will continue without them. One important implication here is that classroom activities do indeed need to be *interesting, productive*, and *enjoyable*. Time out will not be effective when used with students who display disruptive behavior as a means of being removed from an activity that they find to be aversive (e.g., Melissa slams her book on her desk because she is frustrated by the lesson). Time out has been used across elementary and secondary settings. Although it has many different names, depending on the setting ("the thinking chair," "quiet space"), the underlying principles are the same, if it is to be effective. Here we present two strategies that can be implemented effectively in school.

TIME OUT IN CLASS

To set up this strategy in the classroom, work with the teacher to identify a low-traffic area. It can be as simple as a chair or desk set off to the side of the room. Next, develop a plan for how the teacher will explain the use of time out in the classroom. Include in the plan the rationale for time out, how long the student will be expected to remain in it, and what will happen following time out. A successful time out is one in which the student goes quietly to the area, completes the time out without further disruption, and rejoins the class with no additional consequences. It can be helpful to have younger children practice going to time out during a time when they are not misbehaving. Older students may find the idea of time out to be too childish for them. The teacher may want to use a sports example to show how adults use time out. For instance, during hockey games players who break the rules are sent to a *penalty box*. In other sports, coaches use time outs to help players regroup, calm down, and come up with a new plan. When teaching students about time out, it is important to explain to them what will happen (i.e., send them out of the classroom and write up a disciplinary referral) if they continue to be disruptive or refuse to go to the time-out location.

> **Time out is not effective with students who display disruptive behavior as a means of being removed from an activity that they find to be aversive.**

TIME OUT IN ANOTHER CLASS

Teachers may report that in their classroom some students are likely to misbehave during time out (e.g., get other students' attention and make them laugh as they sit in time out). Therefore, a plan for using time out in another class may be useful. The teacher should identify another classroom that is nearby with students who are fairly mature. Then, work as a team with the teacher in this classroom to identify the backup time-out area. This teacher will need to discuss with his or her students that when another student comes into their classroom for time out, they should ignore him or her. The idea behind this procedure is that a student is less likely to show off or misbehave in a class in which he or she is unfamiliar.

RESOURCES

You may find many other resources helpful in expanding your knowledge and repertoire of evidence-based classroom management practices that support teachers with students who exhibit challenging behaviors. Below we list additional resources you may wish to consult.

Crone, D., Hawken, L., & Horner, R. (2010). *Responding to problem behavior in schools: The Behavior Education Program* (2nd ed.). New York: Guilford Press.

Crone, D., & Horner, R. (2003). *Building positive behavior support systems in schools: Functional behavioral assessment.* New York: Guilford Press.

Doll, B., Zucker, S., & Brehm, K. (2004). *Resilient classrooms: Creating healthy environments for learning.* New York: Guilford Press.

Good, T., & Brophy, J. (2003). *Looking in classrooms* (9th ed.). New York: Allyn & Bacon.

Rathvon, N. (2008). *Effective school interventions: Evidence-based strategies for improving student outcomes* (2nd ed.). New York: Guilford Press.

Sprick, R. (2006). *Discipline in the secondary classroom: A positive approach to behavior management* (2nd ed.). Eugene, OR: Pacific Northwest.

Sprick, R. (2008). *CHAMPS: A proactive and positive approach to classroom management* (2nd ed.). Eugene, OR: Pacific Northwest.

Sprick, R., Booher, M., & Garrison, M. (2009). *Behavioral response to intervention: Creating a continuum of problem-solving and support.* Eugene, OR: Pacific Northwest.

Sprick, R., & Garrison, M. (2008). *Interventions: Evidence-based behavioral strategies for individual students* (2nd ed.). Eugene, OR: Pacific Northwest.

Sprick, R., Knight, J., Reinke, W., Skyles, T., & Barnes, L. (2010). *Coaching classroom management: Strategies and tools for administrators and coaches.* Eugene, OR: Pacific Northwest.

Webster-Stratton, C. (1999). *How to promote children's social and emotional competence.* Los Angeles: Sage.

SUMMARY

This chapter provides an overview of evidence-based classroom management strategies that cross the critical features of classroom management. Effective classroom teachers use a continuum of strategies across each domain. Moreover, classrooms with positive teacher–student relationships and a solid foundation in positive proactive classroom management strategies will produce the greatest benefit to students. As the consultant, you will guide the process by using your knowledge of theory and research to ensure that critical components of interventions are not removed as strategies are tailored to the specific needs of classrooms. The process should be collaborative with an emphasis on positive, preventive, feasible, and socially valid interventions that target changing the classroom environment to support student behavior while producing observable, measureable outcomes.

Selecting the intervention is only the beginning. To effectively support teachers in integrating new practices, you as the consultant need to determine if the intervention is implemented with a high level of integrity. If the intervention is not implemented well, then one would not expect change in the classroom. Thus, monitoring implementation and providing feedback to teachers on their level of implementation, brainstorming problems with implementation, and celebrating high levels of implementation integrity are vital. Additionally, ongoing data collection and monitoring will help to determine the effectiveness of the intervention, when new interventions can be implemented, and when the current intervention needs to be modified because it is either not working well or not working at all.

CHAPTER 9

Other Applications
and Future Directions

We have described the CCU as a classwide model for promoting effective classroom management practices. In this chapter we consider other applications of the model. The CCU framework is flexible enough to allow consultants to adapt it to other skill development areas and school consultation activities. The guiding principles of the CCU (e.g., foundational consultant skills, MI, and performance feedback) can be used to improve consultation practices across many domains. The CCU forms and handouts can easily be tailored for these new purposes. Below we describe modifications of the CCU as examples.

ADOPTING SPECIFIC
EVIDENCE-BASED PROGRAMS OR CURRICULUM

In recent years there has been increasing emphasis on school accountability, including the implementation of evidence-based practices across school settings. Likewise, researchers and policymakers have become interested in methods that increase teacher (and clinician) fidelity to the implementation of interventions in the context of rigorous evaluations of these interventions. As noted in Chapter 3, educators, researchers, and policymakers now view consultation models as essential to helping teachers learn new practices and implement them as intended. The CCU framework is consistent with these efforts to support school personnel in adopting and successfully implementing best practices across a variety of academic domains.

> Researchers are now beginning to use methods such as the CCU to help teachers implement *specific programs.*

Note that the CCU, as described in this book, is intended to support teacher skills in *global practices* known to promote effective classrooms (e.g., increase specific praise and opportunities to respond, giving clear expectations). Researchers are now beginning to use methods such as the CCU to help teachers implement *specific programs*. Encouraging teachers to make use of particular programs or curricula creates unique challenges that are not inherent in the original CCU model. For instance, on the surface, guiding a teacher to adopt a specific curriculum or program seems incongruent with the MI spirit and with the collaborative planning process that is so essential to effective consultation. As Dr. Miller noted in his review of effective brief interventions (see Chapter 5), people are more likely to adopt new behaviors if they believe they have a menu of options for accomplishing that change. Getting teachers to adopt a specific program would seem to run counter to these notions.

On the other hand, there may be ways to use the CCU model to promote the use of specific programs that is still consistent with these guiding principles. The problem is not unlike one encountered in health care consultations where a physician wants a patient to start or become more adherent to a particular medication regimen. The health provider envisions a particular outcome and guides the patient toward adopting a specific intervention plan (e.g., getting a family to start a child diagnosed with ADHD on a psychostimulant, getting a patient with diabetes to monitor and manage his or her insulin more consistently). In such circumstances, the key is to continue to provide a menu of options for supporting the adoption of any specific behavior change (e.g., choices about when to start, who will help, frequency of appointments, and additional supportive elements needed to make the behavior happen). As always, it is critical for consultants to be forthright about their intentions ("As a health care provider, I think it would be a good idea for you to start taking this medication."), while acknowledging that the ultimate decision rests with the consultee/patient ("At the end of the day, its completely up to you what to do with this information.").

Over the past 2 years, we have been collaborating with the Center for Prevention and Early Intervention (led by Dr. Nick Ialongo) at Johns Hopkins School of Public Health to work through these very issues in the context of helping teachers adopt particular evidence-based programs and practices. In one study, we are attempting to determine if the CCU can bolster implementation fidelity for teachers using the PAX game (the Good Behavior Game) and the PATHS social–emotional curriculum.

Thus far, our efforts have focused on creating a tailored CCU that maps onto these interventions. We have had to revise the interview, observation, and feedback tools to include language consistent with these two programs. In the interview, we simply ask more focused questions related to the socioemotional climate of the classroom (e.g., "Tell me, how do you promote the socioemotional development of children in your class?"). Below is an example of an interview about social emotional climate with a kindergarten teacher being asked to implement the PATHS to PAX curriculum.

Interview	Comments
CONSULTANT: What do you do to support socioemotional learning in your classroom?	Open-ended question
TEACHER: I always use a behavior chart. I use a stop sign with green, red, and yellow to teach students to be aware of their feelings.	

CONSULTANT: What about other things, like making friends or managing feelings?	Probing question for more details
TEACHER: I really don't have a system for managing feelings. So it's good that it is in the PATHS curriculum. With so many things going on, it's easy to forget to do that, so it's nice that it is part of this new curriculum.	
CONSULTANT: That's great. So one reason you are looking forward to using PATHS is that it gives a focus to student feelings.	Affirmation Reflecting change talk
TEACHER: Yes, that is so important and so often gets glossed over these days.	
CONSULTANT: And with your concern about how much pressure is on these young kids to get them ready for first grade, you like the idea of making this a priority.	Reflecting prior content connecting to core values
TEACHER: Exactly.	
CONSULTANT: How important do you think it is to teach students social–emotional skills?	New open-ended question
TEACHER: Very important. They really need to know how to work in a group and get along with others whether they like them or not.	
CONSULTANT: You really see these as important life skills that go beyond the classroom.	Reflecting change talk

The revised Classroom Check-Up Feedback Form tailored to PATHS to PAX (see Figure 9.1) includes ratings of key features of the intervention, including whether or not the teacher played the PAX game and taught the PATHS lessons; how well the teacher counted disruptive behaviors (spleems); whether the teacher identified a Kid of the Day and delivered the group reward; and how engaged students were in the lessons. We elected to retain several core domains that are in the original CCU (praise ratios, quality of interactions, level of disruptive behavior), because these are critical management skills that cut across all classroom interventions.

During the action planning phase, we needed to reconceptualize the menu of options and include choices that matched with the game or curriculum. As before, the model focuses on giving feedback about what the teacher is doing well and any areas in need of attention. These areas in need of attention are then translated into options for where to start ("Which area would you like to focus on first?") and methods for improving teachers' skills in the chosen area (e.g., ongoing feedback, visual prompts/reminders, modeling and role plays). Our experience in making this modification and piloting it in Baltimore City schools gives reason for optimism in creating similar adaptations for other curricula.

In fact, we are working with several other colleagues who are tailoring the CCU model to support effective practices with teachers across a variety of domains. For instance, a group of colleagues, led by Dr. Catherine Bradshaw at Johns Hopkins School of Public

Teacher: _____   Date: _____

PATHS to PAX Game Components

Playing the Game	
PAX Quiet	
Spleem Counting	
Responding to Spleems	
Prize Delivery	
Quality of Prize	
Other:	

Area of Strength ▬▬▬▬▬▬▬▬▬▬▬▬ Needs Attention

PATHS to PAX Lessons

Teaching the Lessons	
Lesson Pacing	
Student Understanding	
Student Engagement	
Kid of the Day	
Other:	

Area of Strength ▬▬▬▬▬▬▬▬▬▬▬▬ Needs Attention

Classroom Climate

Energy Level	
Overall Spleem Count	
Ratio of Interaction	
Type of Praise	
Interactions with Students	
Other:	

Area of Strength ▬▬▬▬▬▬▬▬▬▬▬▬ Needs Attention

FIGURE 9.1. Feedback form tailored to PATHS to PAX.

Health, plan to adapt the CCU to include more attention to cultural variables in the classroom, including culturally informed instruction and infused curriculum. The ultimate goal of the proposed project is to develop a program that reduces the disproportionate representation of culturally and linguistically diverse students in special education and disciplinary settings in order to improve educational outcomes for all students.

THE CLASSROOM AND BEYOND

We know from years of research and practical experience that widespread application of models such as the CCU requires support beyond individual teachers. School- and district-level administrators play a critical role in determining whether consultation models are successfully implemented on a large scale. As school leaders become more likely to view consultation models as essential to helping teachers learn new practices and implement them in the classroom setting, consultation/coaching programs are becoming more common. You can play an important role as a leader of change by consulting with administrators and school leaders to create school-level changes. For instance, you might consider using the CCU model at the schoolwide level to evaluate and determine areas of strength and those in need of attention for schoolwide practices, including current consultation supports to teachers and schoolwide behavior supports for students. The skills used with the CCU model in working with teachers can be effective at different levels of a system as well as impacting broader behaviors than classroom management.

> The skills used with the CCU model can be effective at different levels of a system as well as impacting broader behaviors than classroom management.

Steps to tailoring the CCU model for such purposes include the following:

1. Identify the key features of the intervention or practice that you, your school, or your district want to implement.
2. Determine how to operationalize the key features into specific, clear, and measureable terms.
3. Determine how to best assess the classroom, school, or district on these key features.
4. Tailor the feedback form to include the key features identified.
5. Tailor the menu of options to include practices that will increase the use of the new intervention or practice.

It would be good practice to pilot the tailored CCU tools before large-scale implementation. Finally, remember to monitor, review, and revise your tailored CCU model to ensure that the positive outcomes intended by the model are, in fact, occurring.

CONCLUDING THOUGHTS

There is now a large and growing literature base about classroom attributes that are needed to make school environments positive and health-promoting places for the children and adults who spend so much time in them. In recent years, there has also been growing awareness about a serious gap in helping schools and teachers create these types of places. We all know that it is not enough to simply tell people what to do or describe the changes that are needed for them to happen, yet oddly, that is often what researchers have expected to happen. It has become apparent that our research base, until recently, was missing a key translation piece: how to take that large body of knowledge and put it into practice in real-world classrooms. The equivalent to this critical missing step would be if the world did not have engineers to help bring the vision of the architect into the practical terms of a home builder. In this way, the classroom consultant is much like an engineer who takes a body of knowledge and a plan and makes it fit in the real world. Fortunately, our science is now able to help guide the consultant to be a more effective classroom engineer. The CCU provides a road map for classroom engineers. Happy travels!

> **The classroom consultant is much like an engineer who takes a body of knowledge and a plan and makes it fit in the real world.**

Motivational Interviewing Form

Decisional Balance

Current Practice: _____

Benefits

Good things about _____ :

Barriers

Bad things about _____ :

New Practice: _____

If you were to try it, what might be some benefits:

If you were to try it, what might be some challenges:

APPENDIX B

Classroom Check-Up Interview
and Observation Forms

APPENDIX B.1

Classroom Check-Up Teacher Interview

Teacher: _____   Date: _____   Interviewer: _____

I. *Preparation Dialogue with Teacher*

"I wanted to take just a bit of your time to ask you a few questions that will allow me to get to know you better and provide me with an idea about your classroom management style. Additionally, I plan to ask you some questions about your past consultation experiences, if any, and provide you with an opportunity to share any classroom difficulties in which you would like support."

II. *Teacher Experience*

1. How long have you been a teacher? Have you always taught this grade level?

2. What do you think it was that made you want to become a teacher?

3. What is the best thing about being a teacher? What excited you about teaching?

4. What do you think is the most difficult or hardest thing about being a teacher?

Before moving forward you might provide a brief summary of the conversation thus far. Connect personally with the teacher by giving examples of shared experiences (if appropriate) and normalizing difficulties.

(cont.)

III. *Classroom Management Style*

"The next few questions will be about how you manage behavior in your classroom."

1. What are some of the strategies that you use in your classroom to help with classroom management? What are some things that you feel you need to work on in this area?

If teacher does not provide examples of rules or reward systems, use the following prompts:

Do you have a set of classroom rules? If so, what are those rules?

Do you use a reward system in your classroom? If so, what does that system look like?

2. How do you handle misbehavior in your classroom?

3. What strategies have you found to be most effective?

4. What strategies have you found to be ineffective?

This may be a good place to provide a brief summary of the discussion. Connecting personally and normalizing challenges can be helpful in developing rapport.

(cont.)

V. *The Ideal Classroom*

"We have been discussing many aspects of your classroom. In this next section I would like you to picture your ideal classroom."

1. What would this classroom look like?

2. What are some of the important qualities that you want children to take home from your classroom?

3. What do you hope the students from your classroom remember about you as their teacher at the end of the year? What about in the future?

Briefly summarize before moving into the next section.

VI. *Past Consultation/Coaching Experiences and Description of CCU Model*

1. What has been your past experience with consultation? What did you find helpful/not helpful?

Describe the CCU Model:

"I want to briefly describe what we will be doing together. My role is to support you in implementing effective classroom management strategies in your classroom. The first thing I will do is visit your classroom a few times to observe. During these visits I will be gathering some specific information. For instance, I will be taking a count of the number of disruptions, your use of praise and reprimands, your use of questions during instruction, and how engaged students are during lessons. After I gather all this information I will set up a meeting with you to go over it. We will look at it together to see if there are any areas that you want to improve or perhaps try out a new strategy in your classroom. I will then make regular visits to see how things are going and to brainstorm other ideas if things are not going well.

(cont.)

Do you have any questions or concerns?"

Set up the first observation:

"Okay. Let's find a time that I can come to your classroom to observe. What is a time that you find can be challenging with regard to managing student behavior?"

Mark down the date and time. Provide the teacher with a card that has your name, number, and date of the first observation to help remind him or her of the visit.

"When I come to your classroom, I won't talk to the students or you. However, if I can do so without disrupting, I will check in with you at the end to see how you felt it went."

VII. Specific *Areas of Support*

1. When I come to observe, is there anything in particular that you would like me to notice?

2. Do you have any behavioral challenges in your classroom for which you would like support?

"Excellent, I will see you on [date of first observation]."

Classroom Ecology Checklist—Consultant Version

Please check the box that represents the best answer for each question based on the observation of classroom practices.

A. Classroom Structure				
1. The traffic patterns in the classroom are clearly defined and allow movement without disrupting others.	No ☐	Somewhat ☐	Yes ☐	
2. The desks and furniture in the classroom are arranged so that students can be seen at all times and the teacher has easy access to all areas of the classroom.	No ☐	Somewhat ☐	Yes ☐	
3. The materials in the classroom are clearly labeled, easily accessible, and organized to minimize clutter.	No ☐	Somewhat ☐	Yes ☐	
4. There is a system in place for students to turn in completed work and to retrieve graded materials.	No ☐	Somewhat ☐	Yes ☐	
B. Behavioral Expectations				
1. Classroom routines and expectations are clearly defined, stated in the positive, and visible.	No ☐	Somewhat ☐	Yes ☐	
2. It is easy to figure out the classroom expectations when observing the class.	No ☐	Somewhat ☐	Yes ☐	
3. *Ask the teacher if not directly observed*: The teacher actively teaches classroom rules and expectations several times throughout the year.	No ☐	Only once per year ☐	Yes ☐	
4. When the teacher uses an attention-getting signal, over 85% of the students respond within a few seconds.	Never responded or within 5 minutes ☐	Within a few minutes ☐	Yes ☐	Not observed ☐
5. Transitions between activities occur smoothly, without interruption caused by behavior problems.	No ☐	Somewhat ☐	Yes ☐	
C. Instructional Management				
1. The teacher gains the attention of all students at the beginning of a lesson or transition.	No ☐	Somewhat ☐	Yes ☐	
2. Based on review of the classroom schedule and observation, it appears that 70% or more of class time is allocated to academic instruction.	Less than 50% ☐	50–69% ☐	70% or more ☐	
3. A high percentage of students is observed as being engaged during classroom instruction.	Less than 60% are engaged ☐	61–89% are engaged ☐	90% or more are engaged ☐	

(cont.)

4. The teacher provides an appropriate pace with an optimal number of opportunities to respond while adjusting for complex content (four to six opportunities per minute for new material; nine to twelve per minute for drill and practice).	No ☐	Sometimes ☐	Yes ☐	
5. The teacher solicits both group and individual responses to questions with an effort to provide the majority of students with individual opportunities to respond (not targeting the same students for every question).	No ☐	Somewhat ☐	Yes ☐	
6. The students generally answer questions with a high rate of accuracy during teacher-led instruction.	Less than 60% ☐	61–84% ☐	85% or more ☐	
7. The teacher uses effective error corrections, such as telling, showing, or demonstrating the correct answer, rather than saying "no" or "wrong."	No ☐	Sometimes ☐	Yes ☐	Not observed ☐
D. Interacting Positively				
1. The teacher provides noncontingent attention to every student in the classroom (e.g., greeting them at the door, taking an interest in what they do outside of school).	Not observed ☐	Sometimes ☐	Yes ☐	
2. The teacher acknowledges expected student behaviors more frequently than misbehaviors (positive to negative ratio).	Less than 2:1 ☐	Less than 3:1 ☐	3:1 or higher ☐	
E. Responding to Appropriate Behavior				
1. There is a system for documenting and rewarding appropriate student behavior (classwide and individual students).	No ☐	Somewhat/ Informally ☐	Yes ☐	
2. The teacher uses behavior-specific/descriptive praise to encourage appropriate behavior.	No ☐	Sometimes ☐	Most of the time ☐	
F. Responding to Inappropriate Behavior				
1. The number of problem behaviors/disruptions in the classroom is generally minimal.	No ☐	Sometimes ☐	Yes ☐	
2. The teacher uses a continuum of consequences to discourage rule violations (e.g., ignore, praising others, proximity, explicit reprimand).	No ☐	Somewhat ☐	Yes ☐	
3. There is a documentation system for managing specific behavioral violations.	No ☐	Somewhat/ Informally ☐	Yes ☐	
4. The teacher is consistent when reprimanding/ correcting misbehavior.	No ☐	Sometimes ☐	Yes ☐	
5. The teacher is calm, clear, and brief when providing reprimands/corrections.	No ☐	Sometimes ☐	Yes ☐	

188

Classroom Ecology Checklist—Teacher Version

Please check the box that represents the best answer for each question based on your current classroom practices.

A. Classroom Structure			
1. Are the traffic patterns in your classroom clearly defined, and do they allow for movement without disrupting others?	No ☐	Somewhat ☐	Yes ☐
2. Are the desks and furniture in the classroom arranged so that students can be seen at all times and so that you have easy access to all areas of the classroom?	No ☐	Somewhat ☐	Yes ☐
3. Are the materials in the classroom clearly labeled, easily accessible, and organized to minimize clutter?	No ☐	Somewhat ☐	Yes ☐
4. Do you have a system in place for students to turn in completed work and to retrieve graded materials?	No ☐	Somewhat ☐	Yes ☐
B. Behavioral Expectations			
1. Are classroom routines and expectations clearly defined, stated in the positive, and visible?	No ☐	Somewhat ☐	Yes ☐
2. Do you directly teach and practice classroom routines and expectations regularly?	No ☐	Somewhat ☐	Yes ☐
3. Do you use an attention-getting signal that you have directly taught, practiced, and positively reinforced?	No ☐	Somewhat ☐	Yes ☐
4. Do transitions between activities occur smoothly, without interruption caused by behavior problems?	No ☐	Somewhat ☐	Yes ☐
C. Instructional Management			
1. Do you gain the attention of all students at the beginning of a lesson or transition?	No ☐	Somewhat ☐	Yes ☐
2. How much class time is allocated to academic instruction?	Less than 50% ☐	50–69% ☐	70% or more ☐
3. What percentage of your students would you estimate is engaged during classroom instruction?	Less than 60% are engaged ☐	61–89% are engaged ☐	90% or more are engaged ☐
4. Do you pace your instruction to provide an optimal number of opportunities to respond while adjusting for complex content (four to six opportunities per minute for new material; nine to twelve per minute for drill and practice)?	No ☐	Sometimes ☐	Yes ☐
5. Do you solicit both group and individual responses to questions, with an effort to provide the majority of students with individual opportunities to respond (not targeting the same students for every question)?	No ☐	Somewhat ☐	Yes ☐

(cont.)

6. Do students generally answer questions correctly when you provide instruction? What percentage of the time are they correct?	Less than 60% ☐	61–84% ☐	85% or more ☐
7. Do you use effective error corrections, such as telling, showing, or demonstrating the correct answer, rather than saying "no" or "wrong"?	No ☐	Sometimes ☐	Yes ☐
D. Interacting Positively			
1. Do you provide noncontingent attention to every student in your classroom (e.g., greeting each student at the door, taking an interest in what students do outside of school)?	No ☐	Sometimes ☐	Yes ☐
2. How often do you acknowledge expected student behaviors versus misbehaviors (positive-to-negative ratio)?	Less than 2:1 ☐	Less than 3:1 ☐	3:1 or higher ☐
E. Responding to Appropriate Behavior			
1. Do you have a system for documenting and rewarding appropriate student behavior (classwide and individual students)?	No ☐	Somewhat/ Informally ☐	Yes ☐
2. Do you use behavior-specific/descriptive praise to encourage appropriate behavior?	No ☐	Sometimes ☐	Most of the time ☐
F. Responding to Inappropriate Behavior			
1. Are the number of problem behaviors/disruptions in your classroom generally minimal?	No ☐	Sometimes ☐	Yes ☐
2. Do you use a continuum of consequences to discourage rule violations (e.g., ignore, praising others, proximity, explicit reprimand)?	No ☐	Somewhat ☐	Yes ☐
3. Do you have a documentation system for managing specific behavioral violations?	No ☐	Somewhat/ Informally ☐	Yes ☐
4. Are you consistent when reprimanding/correcting misbehavior?	No ☐	Sometimes ☐	Yes ☐
5. Are you calm, clear, and brief when providing reprimands/ corrections for misbehavior?	No ☐	Sometimes ☐	Yes ☐

Classroom Check-Up 10-Minute Classroom Observation Form

Teacher:	Date:	Topic:
Observer:	Start time:	Activity:

Type of Instruction (circle):   **New Material**   **Drill and Practice**

During the 10-minute observation period, mark a tally for each time the following behaviors are observed in the classroom. Then calculate total, # per minute (rate), % correct academic responding, and ratio of interactions (positive : negative).

10-Minute Frequency Count	Total #	Rate: #/total minutes	% correct = CAR/OTR × 100
Opportunity to Respond (OTR)			( )%
Correct Academic Response (CAR)			
Disruptive Behavior			Ratio pos. to neg. = total rep/total praise = 1 : ( )
Praise Behavior SPECIFIC			Specific + General =
Praise GENERAL			Total: ( )
Reprimand Explicit/Fluent			Explicit + Critical =
Reprimand Critical/Harsh/Emotional			Total: ( )

Comments:

_____

_____

_____

_____

_____

_____

_____

Classroom Check-Up 5-Minute Academic Engagement Observation Form

Teacher:	Date:	Topic:
Observer:	Start time:	Activity:

For the next 5 minutes, every 5 seconds you will indicate if a student is on task or off task. Each box indicates two things: (1) the number of seconds into the observation that you will look up at the student to determine on task (+) or off task (0) at that moment, and (2) the interval number. Continue observing students (repeating students as necessary) until the 5-minute period is complete, for a total of 60 intervals. Then calculate the % of time the students in the classroom were engaged.

+ indicates on task (engaged)
0 indicates off task (not engaged)

5 sec	10 sec	15 sec	20 sec	25 sec	30 sec	35 sec	40 sec	45 sec	50 sec
1	2	3	4	5	6	7	8	9	10
55 sec	1 min	1:05 sec	1:10 sec	1:15 sec	1:20 sec	1:25 sec	1:30 sec	1:35 sec	1:40 sec
11	12	13	14	15	16	17	18	19	20
1:45 sec	1:50 sec	1:55 sec	2 min	2:05 sec	2:10 sec	2:15 sec	2:20 sec	2:25 sec	2:30 sec
21	22	23	24	25	26	27	28	29	30
2:35 sec	2:40 sec	2:45 sec	2:50 sec	2:55 sec	3 min	3:05 sec	3:10 sec	3:15 sec	3:20 sec
31	32	33	34	35	36	37	38	39	40
3:25 sec	3:30 sec	3:35 sec	3:40 sec	3:45 sec	3:50 sec	3:55 sec	4 min	4:05 sec	4:10 sec
41	42	43	44	45	46	47	48	49	50
4:15 sec	4:20 sec	4:25 sec	4:30 sec	4:35 sec	4:40 sec	4:45 sec	4:50 sec	4:55 sec	5 min
51	52	53	54	55	56	57	58	59	60

% on task = # interval + / total number of intervals coded × 100%

1. Total # intervals coded (+) = (_____)

2. Total # intervals coded (+) + (0) = (_____)

3. 1/2 × 100% = (_____)%

Comments:

_____

_____

_____

Classroom Check-Up Overall Classroom Rating Form

Teacher:	Date:	Observer:

Upon completion of an observation visit, rate the classroom on the following items on a scale from 1 to 5, with 5 being excellent compared to other classrooms you have observed, 3 being average, and 1 being poor. For items you rate below average (1 or 2) write down reasons for the lower rating in the comment section provided. For items you rate above average, write your reasons for doing so as well.

Please circle the most appropriate rating for each item using the following scale:
5 = excellent; 4 = above average; 3 = average; 2 = below average; 1 = poor; NO = not observed

Item	Rating	Comments
Use of Active Supervision	5 4 3 2 1 NO	
Use of Attention Signal	5 4 3 2 1 NO	
Followed the Schedule	5 4 3 2 1 NO	
Reinforcement Was Contingent	5 4 3 2 1 NO	
Variety of Reinforcement Used	5 4 3 2 1 NO	
Reviewed Academic Expectations	5 4 3 2 1 NO	
Reviewed Social/ Behavioral Expectations	5 4 3 2 1 NO	
Transitions Were Smooth	5 4 3 2 1 NO	
Overall Climate Was Positive	5 4 3 2 1	
Overall Rating	5 4 3 2 1	

Additional Comments:

_____

_____

_____

_____

_____

APPENDIX C

Classroom Check-Up Feedback and Action Planning Forms

Compiling the Classroom Check-Up Indicators

Indicator and Resource	How to Calculate:
Percent Correct Academic Responding Definition: The percent of opportunities to respond that the students accurately answer. Measure: CCU 10-Minute Observation Form	Step 1: In the right column of each observation calculate the % correct. To do so, divide the total number of CAR by total OTR and multiply by 100. Step 2: Add the % correct number from each observation together. Step 3: Divide the total from Step 2 by the number of observations. Step 4: The resulting number is the mean % correct academic responding across observations. Use this number for determining feedback based on the CCU feedback guidelines in Table 7.1.
Percent Time on Task (Academic Engagement) Definition: The percent of intervals students were coded as engaged. Measure: CCU 5-Minute Academic Engagement Observation Form	Step 1: At the bottom of each observation calculate the % on task. To do so, divide the total number of intervals marked on task (+) by the total number of intervals (i.e., 60) and multiply by 100. Step 2: Add the % on-task number from each observation together. Step 3: Divide the total from Step 2 by the number of observations. Step 4: The resulting number is the mean % time on task across observations. Use this number for determining feedback based on the CCU feedback guidelines in Table 7.1.
Rate of Opportunities to Respond Definition: The number of opportunities to respond divided by the total number of minutes. Measure: CCU 10-Minute Observation Form	Step 1: Add together the total OTRs from each observation conducted. Step 2: Divide the total from Step 1 by the total number of minutes observed. If three full observations were conducted, this number would be 30. Step 3: This number is the rate or number of OTRs per minute. Use this number for determining feedback based on the CCU feedback guidelines in Table 7.1.
Ratio of Interactions Definition: The ratio of praise statements to reprimands combined and across each observation. Measure: CCU 10-Minute Observation Form	Step 1: In the right column of the observation form calculate the overall total number of praise statements for each observation. To do so, add together the total number of behavior-specific praise statements and the total number of general praise statements. Step 2: Add together the total overall praise for each observation calculated in Step 1 for the total number of praise statements across observations. Step 3: In the right column of the observation form calculate the overall total reprimands for each observation. To do so, add together the total number of explicit/fluent and the total number of harsh/critical reprimands.

(cont.)

Indicator and Resource	How to Calculate:
	Step 4: Add together the total overall reprimands for each observation calculated in Step 3, for the total number of reprimands across observations.
	Step 5: Divide the overall total reprimands from Step 4 by the overall total praise statements from Step 2. This number is the number of negatives to positives (e.g., 20 reprimands/10 praise = 2 reprimands for every praise; therefore ratio 1:2).
	Step 6: Calculate the ratio of interaction in the right column for each observation separately. This provides information about consistency.
	Step 7: Use this ratio of interactions calculated in Step 5 and those calculated in Step 6 for determining feedback based on the CCU feedback guidelines in Table 7.1.
	Note: If praise is so low across observations that the total number of praise statements divided by the total number of minutes observed is below one per minute, place feedback in the red.
Behavior-Specific versus General Praise Definition: The total number of behavior-specific praise statements compared to the total number of general praise statements. Measure: CCU 10-Minute Observation Form	Step 1: Add together the total number of behavior-specific praise statements for each observation. Step 2: Add together the total number of general praise statements for each observation. Step 3: Determine which number (behavior-specific vs. general) is higher. Use this number for determining feedback based on the CCU feedback guidelines in Table 7.1. If no praise statements are recorded across any observation, the feedback will automatically be red.
Quality of Interactions Definition: Review of the number of harsh/critical/ emotional reprimands and positive climate ratings. Measures: CCU 10-Minute Observation Form; CCU Overall Classroom Rating Form	Step 1: Mark down the total number of harsh/critical reprimands for each observation. If there are three observations, you will have three numbers. Step 2: Mark down the largest total from Step 1. Use this number for determining feedback based on the CCU feedback guidelines in Table 7.1. Step 3: Review CCU Overall Classroom Rating Form for positive climate ratings. If any rating is below 3, review comments and utilize this information during feedback.
Rate of Disruptions Definition: The total number of disruptive behaviors divided by the total number of minutes observed. Measure: CCU-10 Minute Observation Form	Step 1: Add together the total disruptions from each observation conducted. Step 2: Divide the total from Step 1 by the total number of minutes observed. If three full observations were conducted, this number would be 30. Step 3: This number is the rate or number of disruptions per minute. Use this number for determining feedback based on the CCU feedback guidelines in Table 7.1.

Classroom Check-Up Feedback Form Sources and Guidelines

CCU Feedback Domain	Source of Information	General Guidelines for Classrooms Considered Green
Physical Layout	Observation and CEC	Traffic patterns are clear; desks are arranged to maximize instruction; the teacher has access to all areas of room; students can be seen at all times; classroom materials are organized and easily accessible.
Classroom Rules	Observation and CEC	There are five or fewer classroom rules; the rules are clear, observable, positively stated, and prominently posted.
Classroom Routines	Observation and CEC	Expectations for behavioral routines are clear, posted, and positively stated.
Smooth Transitions	Observation, CEC, CCU Overall Rating Form	Transitions occur quickly, with few disruptions; teacher uses an attention signal to gain attention of all students prior to transitions.
Schedule Posted and Followed	Observations, CEC, CCU Overall Rating Form	A schedule for the day is posted and during observations the teacher kept to the schedule; any change to the schedule was preceded by the teacher clarifying the change; the schedule allots the majority of the day to instructional activities.
Academic Objectives Clear	Observation, CEC, CCU Overall Rating Form	Prior to an academic task, the teacher provided clear expectations to the students; students were clear about the assignments and asked few clarifying questions.
Pacing	CCU 10-Minute Observation Form, CCU Feedback Guidelines (Table 7.1), CEC	The teacher provided four or more opportunities to respond to the students per minute; the teacher asked questions of the group and individual students; most of the students in the class were asked at least one question during instruction.
Student Accuracy	CCU 10-Minute Observation Form, CCU Feedback Guidelines (Table 7.1)	When provided an opportunity to respond, the students were able to answer correctly 80% of the time for new material and 90% of the time for review material; the material did not appear to be too easy for the students.
Student Engagement	CCU 5-Minute Academic Engagement Observation Form, CCU Feedback Guidelines (Table 7.1)	90% or more of students were engaged during instruction.

(cont.)

CCU Feedback Domain	Source of Information	General Guidelines for Classrooms Considered Green
Behavioral Expectations Clear	Observation, CEC, CCU Overall Rating Form	During observation of classroom students appear to generally understand the expected behaviors; You observed or teacher reported actively teaching behavioral expectations, including classroom rules and routines.
Active Supervision	Observation, CCU Overall Rating Form	The teacher moves throughout the classroom, scans with eyes and ears, and interacts with students; The teacher used proximity to prevent problem behavior.
Use of Praise	CCU 10-Minute Observation Form, CCU Feedback Guidelines (Table 7.1), CCU Overall Rating Form	The teacher used more behavior-specific praise than general praise; praise was contingent on expected behavior.
Use of Reprimands	CCU 10-Minute Observation Form, CCU Feedback Guidelines (Table 7.1), CCU Overall Rating Form	The teacher provided explicit reprimands that informed the student of what to do instead; reprimands were brief, consistent, and calm.
Positive-to-Negative Ratio	CCU 10-Minute Observation Form, CCU Feedback Guidelines (Table 7.1), CEC	The teacher provided three or more praise statements for every reprimand.
Used Variety of Reinforcement	Observation, CCU Overall Rating Form, CEC	The teacher used other forms of reinforcement than verbal praise; a system is in place to reward appropriate behavior for individual students or the entire class, and students are aware of the system.
Use of Noncontingent Attention	Observation, CCU Overall Rating Form, CEC	Teacher is observed greeting the students at the door and seems genuinely interested in the students as individuals.
Interactions with Students	CCU 10-Minute Observation Form, CCU Feedback Guidelines (Table 7.1)	The teacher is more positive than negative when interacting with students; the teacher's tone is positive without a negative tone or sarcasm; the teacher provides calm, consistent, and concise reprimands when necessary; no harsh or critical interactions with students were observed.
Level of Disruptive Behavior	CCU 10-Minute Observation Form, CCU Feedback Guidelines (Table 7.1)	The level of disruptions in the classroom was minimal, with less than five during a ten-minute observation.

Classroom Check-Up Feedback Form

Teacher: _____ Date: _____

Classroom Structure

Physical Layout	
Classroom Rules	
Classroom Routines	
Smooth Transitions	
Other:	

Area of Strength ▬▬▬▬▬▬▬▬▬▬▬▬▬▬▬ Needs Attention

Instructional Management

Schedule Posted and Followed	
Academic Objectives Clear	
Pacing	
Student Accuracy	
Student Engagement	
Other:	

Area of Strength ▬▬▬▬▬▬▬▬▬▬▬▬▬▬▬ Needs Attention

Behavior Management

Behavioral Expectations Clear	
Active Supervision	
Use of Praise	
Use of Reprimands	
Positive to Negative Ratio	
Used Variety of Reinforcement	
Other:	

Area of Strength ▬▬▬▬▬▬▬▬▬▬▬▬▬▬▬ Needs Attention

Classroom Climate

Use of Noncontingent Attention	
Interactions with Students	
Level of Disruptive Behavior	
Other:	

Area of Strength ▬▬▬▬▬▬▬▬▬▬▬▬▬▬▬ Needs Attention

Classroom Check-Up Menu of Options

Teacher: _____   Date: _____

| Target Areas for Improvement: |
| Based on the feedback, on what areas would you, as the classroom teacher, like to focus? |
| 1. |
| 2. |
| 3. |

Menu of Options to Increase Effective Classroom Management Strategies:

Collaborative Ideas	Strategy Starters	Ongoing Supports
	To improve positive to negative ratio (goal = 3:1) identify strategies to increase praise and reduce reprimands.	Conduct weekly check-in.
	To improve classroom climate: Increase noncontingent positive reinforcement.	Model strategies in classroom.
	To improve pacing of lessons: Identify strategies to break down complex into smaller chunks and ideas for providing more questions to more students.	Observe and provide performance feedback.
	To improve use of reprimands: Identify strategies for knowing when to use reprimands and when not, as well as ideas for making the reprimands concise and fluent.	Schedule a visit to observe another teacher using strategies.
	To improve correct academic responding: Review lesson material to determine if above or below current level of students. Teach to mastery.	Videotape and review together.
	Identify behaviors of concern and develop a hierarchy of consequences to increase consistency.	Books:
	Develop a lesson plan for teaching classroom expectations. Teach the expectations regularly.	Resources:
	Other:	Other:

NEXT STEP: Identify from the menu one or more strategies to put into place. Complete the Action Planning Form to identify the specific goal (e.g., increase use of behavior-specific praise from 5 to 10 per lesson).

Classroom Check-Up Action Planning Form

Teacher: _____ Grade: _____ Date: _____

Those things going well in my classroom:	Areas I would like to focus on improving in my classroom:

Specifically, my goal is to:

What actions will I take to meet this goal?

Task: What needs to be done?	Description of Plan	Resources: What is needed to get it done?	Timeline

(cont.)

Classroom Check-Up Action Planning Form (*page 2 of 2*)

How **important** is it for you to meet this goal in your classroom?

0   1   2   3   4   5   6   7   8   9   10

Not Important
at All

Very
Important

The **most** important reasons for making this change and meeting this goal is:

How **confident** are you that you will meet this goal in your classroom?

0   1   2   3   4   5   6   7   8   9   10

Not Confident
at All

Very
Confident

Some reasons that **I am confident**:

Is there anything that could get in the way of meeting this goal?

What can I do to help make sure this doesn't get in the way?

Teacher Self-Monitoring Form

1. Write in the date for each day this week.
2. Write in the strategies to be used.
3. Check off those strategies that you use each day.
4. Provide comments about any challenges encountered.

Strategy:	Date:	Date:	Date:	Date:	Date:
	☐	☐	☐	☐	☐
	☐	☐	☐	☐	☐
	☐	☐	☐	☐	☐
	☐	☐	☐	☐	☐
	☐	☐	☐	☐	☐
Comments:					

Strategies for Addressing Common Motivational Barriers

Common Problem	MI Strategies	Personalized Feedback
Teacher who uses harsh and punitive discipline practices	• Use the decisional balance. • Ask the teacher about the pros and cons of harsh practices and of alternative practice (e.g., time out). • Then ask who benefits from the pros and cons of each practice. • Highlight that the benefits of harsh practices are mostly for adults, and that students are mostly impacted by the adverse aspects.	• Collect data that highlight the correlation between harsh responses and frequency of disruptive behavior or some desired outcome. • The goal is to show how the harsh practices actually make the desired outcomes less likely.
Teacher who is disengaged or burned out	• Search for the hidden gem. • What are the values and positive intentions of the teacher? • Focus on the student perspective. • Ask the teacher to reflect on one thing that could make work life better (more enjoyable, meaningful) and see if you can help make it happen.	• Ask the teacher to track daily mood/energy level and see how mood relates to observable changes in the classroom, and vice versa. • Highlight the fact that positive mood/energy begets positive energy from both the teacher and students.
Teacher who avoids the consultant	• Use lots of responsibility language ("It's completely up to you if you want to work with me."). • Focus on building a trusting, nonevaluative relationship.	• Identify targeted student change that the teacher finds meaningful. • Collect systematic data on the effect of the change on the teacher and any factors related to fluctuations in the outcome.
Teacher who has decided that the only reasonable intervention is to place a student in special education	• Emphasize the student's perspective, including what other students in the classroom will learn from that consequence. • Responsibility language is helpful as well ("We can spend a lot of time coming up with a plan, but ultimately it's up to you if you think this is worthwhile.").	• Ask teacher to self-monitor negative versus coping beliefs about the student/situation. • Connect fluctuations of these patterns to teacher's mood and positive changes in student behavior. • Collect data on a target behavior of the student and monitor change over time.

(cont.)

Strategies for Addressing Common Motivational Barriers *(page 2 of 2)*

Common Problem	MI Strategies	Personalized Feedback
	• Give the teacher an out, so that if the student can be successful in class, it doesn't appear that he or she was wrong (e.g., "It's common for students' behavior to fluctuate and to get back on track once we have a comprehensive plan in place"). • Involve the family and build connections between the teacher and caregivers. • Ask the teacher to reflect on his or her perceptions of the student. Provide common examples and ask the teacher if he or she has had any of them (e.g., "Many teachers who have worked really hard to help kids with challenging behaviors end up feeling frustrated and at wit's end. It is common for teachers in this situation to develop negative perceptions about the student or the likelihood of success."). • Common teacher perceptions of challenging students include: "He's really beyond help," "She's just doing this to aggravate me," "I don't like him," and "This is hopeless." • The goal is to help the teacher become aware of these perceptions and their impact on his or her relationship with the child, and ultimately to help the teacher find more adaptive coping beliefs to replace any existing negative beliefs.	• Gather data from other students in the classroom to determine if or how different the behavior of the target student is from his or her peers.
Teacher who uses inconsistent or infrequent consequences and structure	• Highlight value discrepancies (unstructured, inconsistent environments undermine student learning). • Build self-efficacy to implement practices through modeling and by helping with lesson planning. • See extended example with a teacher reluctant to discipline (see page 131).	• Collect data showing how small changes in structure can produce desired outcomes (reduced disruptions, more on-task behaviors, more time for instruction). • Given explicit, ongoing feedback about praise–reprimand ratios. • Give feedback about explicitness and fluency of reprimands.

APPENDIX D

Intervention Planning Forms

Teaching Classroom Rules

Rule

Teach
Provide a verbal description of the rule and why it's important:

Model
Provide a positive example by showing the students the behavior:
Provide a negative example by exhibiting the incorrect behavior:

Practice
Have a student or students demonstrate the rule:

Praise/Reinforce
Provide specific praise to the student or students who demonstrated the rule:
Devise a plan for reinforcing students who follow the rule:

Teaching Behavioral Routines

Routine

Teach
Provide a verbal description of the routine and why it's important:

Model
Provide a positive example by showing the students the behavior:
Provide a negative example by exhibiting the incorrect behavior:

Practice
Have a student or students demonstrate the routine correctly:

(cont.)

Praise/Reinforce
Provide specific praise to the student or students who demonstrated the routine correctly: Devise a plan for reinforcing students for demonstrating the routine correctly:

Precorrection Planning Form

Step 1: Identify a behavioral routine for which students are likely to have difficulty meeting expectations without a reminder.

Step 2: Write the specific precorrection and behavior-specific praise statements that will be used.

Step 3: Determine if the precorrection procedure was effective.

Behavior Routine:	
Precorrection Plan	
Behavior-Specific Praise for Group	
Behavior-Specific Praise for Individuals	
Did 85% of students meet expectations? YES NO	
If no, develop a plan to explicitly teach the behavior routine to the class.	

Catch Students Being Good Form

Step 1: Identify a time of day to "catch" students being good. A time when disruptive behavior is fairly high can be a good target.

Step 2: Write down the common disruptive behaviors that occur during this time.

Step 3: Write down the behavior you would like to see more of.

Step 4: Write down a list of behavior-specific praise statements to use when you "catch" the students displaying the behavior you would like to see more of.

Remember that behavior-specific praise is praise that tells students exactly what they are doing correctly (e.g., "Thank you for raising your hand.").

Time to "Catch" Students:

Problem Behavior	Behavior to "Catch" *This is the behavior you want to see more of. It is often the opposite of the problem behavior.*	Behavior-Specific Praise
Sample: Talking Out	Raising hand and waiting to be called on.	"Thank you for raising your hand and waiting patiently."

Incentive Selection Form

Identify several potential incentives from each of the domains listed below.

Work to add to the number and variety of reinforcements in each column to increase positive student behavior in your classroom.

Social Reinforcer	Activity Reinforcer	Material Reinforcer

Discipline Planning Form

Step 1: Develop a list of misbehaviors that occur in the classroom, beginning with the behaviors that are the *least* disruptive or concerning, and ending with the *most* disruptive or concerning. Be sure that behaviors are specific and observable.

Step 2: Identify a response to each misbehavior.

Misbehavior	Response to Misbehavior

References

Abramowitz, A. J., O'Leary, S. G., & Futtersak, M.W. (1988). The relative impact of long and short reprimands on children's off-task behavior in the classroom. *Behavior Therapy, 19*(2), 243–247.

Allday, A., & Pakurar, K. (2007). Effects of teacher greeting on students' on-task behavior. *Journal of Applied Behavior Analysis, 40,* 317–320.

Amrhein, P. C., Miller, W. R., Yahne, C. E., Knupsky, A., & Hochstein, D. (2004). Strength of client commitment language improves with therapist training in motivational interviewing. *Alcoholism: Clinical and Experimental Research,73,* 99–106.

Amrhein, P. C., Miller, W. R., Yahne, C. E., Palmer, M., & Fulcher, L. (2003). Client commitment language during motivational interviewing predicts drug use outcomes. *Journal of Consulting and Clinical Psychology, 71*(5),862–878.

Anderson, L. M., Evertson, C. M., & Brophy, J. E. (1979). An experimental study of effective teaching in first-grade reading groups. *Elementary School Journal, 79*(4), 193–223.

Bandura, A. (1977). Self-efficacy: Toward a unifying theory of behavioral change. *Psychological Review, 84*(2), 191–215.

Barrett, E. R., & Davis, S. (1995). Perceptions of beginning teachers' needs in classroom management. *Teacher Education and Practice, 11,* 22–27.

Barrish, H. H., Saunders, M., & Wof, M. M. (1969). Good behavior game: Effects of individual contingencies for group consequences on disruptive behavior in a classroom. *Journal of Applied Behavior Analysis, 2*(2), 119–124.

Barton, L. E., Brulle, A.R., & Repp, A. C. (1987). Effects of differential scheduling of timeout to reduce maladaptive responding. *Exceptional Children, 53*(4), 351–356.

Becker, W. C., Madsen, C. H., Arnold, C. R., & Thomas, D. R. (1967). The contingent use of teacher attention and praise in reducing classroom behavior problems. *Journal of Special Education, 1*(3), 287–307.

Brophy, J. E. (1981). On praising effectively. *Elementary School Journal, 81,* 268–278.

Brophy, J. E. (1983). Classroom organization and management. *Elementary School Journal, 83*(4), 265–285.

Brophy, J. E. (1996). *Teaching problem students.* New York: Guilford Press.

Brophy, J. E., & Evertson, C. M. (1976). *Learning from teaching: A developmental perspective.* Boston: Allyn & Bacon.

Burden, P. (2006). *Classroom management: Creating a successful K–12 learning community.* Hoboken, NJ: Wiley.

Cameron, J., & Pierce, W. (1994). Reinforcement, reward, and intrinsic motivation: A meta-analysis. *Review of Educational Research, 64*(3), 363–423.

Carnine, D. W. (1976). Effects of two teacher-presentation rates on off-task behavior, answering correctly, and participation. *Journal of Applied Behavior Analysis, 9*(2), 199–206.

Chaskin, R. J., & Rauner, D. M. (1995). Youth and caring: An introduction. *Phi Delta Kappan, 76*(9), 667–674.

Coalition for Psychology in Schools and Education. (2006, August). *Report on the Teacher Needs Survey.* Washington, DC: Center for Psychology in the Schools and Education.

Coladarci, T., & Gage, N. L. (1984). Effects of minimal intervention on teacher behavior and student achievement. *American Education Research Journal, 1*, 236–248.

Colvin, G., Sugai, G., & Patching, B. (1993). Precorrection: An instructional approach for managing predictable problem behaviors. *Intervention in School and Clinic, 28*(3), 143–150, 164.

Comer, J. P. (1993). *School power: Implications for an intervention project.* New York: Free Press.

Connell, J., & Wellborn, J. (1991). Competence, autonomy, and relatedness: A motivational analysis of self-system process. In M. Gunnar & A. Sroufe (Eds.), *Minnesota symposium on child psychology* (Vol. 22, pp. 43–77). Hillsdale, NJ: Erlbaum.

Conners, D. A. (1983). The school environment: A link to understanding stress. *Theory Into Practice, 22*(1), 15–20.

Conroy, M., Sutherland, K. S., Haydon, T., Stormont, M., & Harmon, J. (2009). Preventing and ameliorating young children's chronic problem behaviors: An ecological classroom-based approach. *Psychology in the Schools, 46*(1), 3–17.

Council for Exceptional Children. (1987). *Academy for effective instruction: Working with mildly handicapped students.* Reston, VA: Author.

Crone, D., & Horner, R. (2003). *Building positive behavior support systems in schools: Functional behavioral assessment.* New York: Guilford Press.

Crone, D., Hawken, L., & Horner, R. (2010). *Responding to problem behavior in schools: The behavior education program* (2nd ed.). New York: Guilford Press.

Delquadri, J., Greenwood, C., Stretton, K., & Hall, R. (1983). The peer tutoring spelling game: A classroom procedure for increasing opportunity to respond and spelling performance. *Education and Treatment of Children, 6*, 225–239.

De Pry, R. L., & Sugai, G. (2002). The effect of active supervision and precorrection on minor behavioral incidents in a sixth-grade general education classroom. *Journal of Behavioral Education, 11*, 255–267.

Didden, R., de Moor, J., & Bruyns, W. (1997). Effectiveness of DRO tokens in decreasing disruptive behavior in the classroom with five multiply handicapped children. *Behavioral Interventions, 12*(2), 65–75.

Dishion, T. J., & Kavanagh, K. (2003). *Intervening in adolescent problem behavior: A family-centered approach.* New York: Guilford Press.

Doll, B., Zucker, S., & Brehm, K. (2004). *Resilient classrooms: Creating healthy environments for learning.* New York: Guilford Press.

Domitrovich, C. E., & Greenberg, M. T. (2000). The study of implementation: Current findings from effective programs that prevent mental disorders in school-aged children. *Journal of Educational and Psychological Consultation, 11*(2), 193–221.

Drabman, R. S., Spitalnik, R., & O'Leary, K. D. (1973). Teaching self-control to disruptive children. *Journal of Abnormal Psychology, 82*(1), 10–16.

Embry, D. (2002). The Good Behavior Game: A best practice candidate as a universal behavioral vaccine. *Clinical Child and Family Psychology Review, 5*, 273–297.

Emmer, E. T., Evertson, C., & Anderson, L. (1980). Effective classroom management at the beginning of the school year. *Elementary School Journal, 80*(5), 219–231.

Engelman, S., & Carnine, D. (1982). *Theory of instruction: Principles and applications.* New York: Irvington.

Espin, C., & Yell, M. (1994). Critical indicator of effective teaching for preservice teachers: Relationships between teaching behaviors and ratings of effectiveness. *Teacher Education and Special Education, 17*, 154–169.

Evertson, C. M., Anderson, C. W., Anderson, L. M., & Brophy, J. E. (1980). Relationships between classroom behaviors and student outcomes in junior high mathematics and English classes. *American Educational Research Journal, 17*(1), 43–60.

Evertson, C. M., & Emmer, E. (1982). Effective management at the beginning of the year in junior high classes. *Journal of Educational Psychology, 74*, 485–498.

Evertson, C. M.., & Weinstein, C. S. (2006). Classroom management as a field of inquiry. In C. M. Evertson & C. S. Weinstein (Eds.), *Handbook of classroom management: Research, practice, and contemporary issues* (pp. 3–15). Mahwah, NJ: Erlbaum.

Feldman, S. (2003). The place for praise. *Teaching PreK–8, 5*, 6.

Fixen, D., Naoom, S., Blase, K., Friedman, R., & Wallace, F. (2005). *Implementation research: A synthesis of the literature* (FMHI Publication No. 231). Tampa, FL, University of South Florida, Louis de la Parte Florida Mental Health Institute, National Implementation Research Network.

Forman, S. G. (1980). A comparison of cognitive training and response cost procedures in modifying aggressive behavior of elementary school children. *Behavior Therapy, 11*(4), 594–600.

Fuchs, D., Fuchs, L.S., & Burish, P. (2000). Peer assisted learning strategies: An evidence based practice to promote reading achievement. *Learning Disabilities Research and Practice, 15*(2), 85–91.

Gable, R. A., Hester, P. H., Rock, M. L., & Hughes, K.

G. (2009). Back to basics: Rules, praise, ignoring, and reprimands revisited. *Intervention in School and Clinic, 44*, 195–205.

Good, C. E., Eller, B. F., Spangler, R. S., & Stone, J. E. (1981). The effect of an operant intervention program on attending and other academic behavior with emotionally disturbed children. *Journal of Instructional Psychology, 9*(1), 25–33.

Good, T., & Brophy, J. (2003). *Looking in classrooms* (9th ed.). New York: Allyn & Bacon.

Greenwood, C. R., Terry, B., Marquis, J., & Walker, D. (1994). Confirming a performance-based instructional model. *School Psychology Review, 23*(4), 652–668.

Grossman, H. (2004). *Classroom behavior management for diverse and inclusive schools*. New York: Rowman & Littlefield.

Gunter, P. L., Hummel, J. H., & Conroy, M. A. (1998). Increasing incorrect academic responding: An effective intervention strategy to decrease behavior problems. *Effective School Practices, 17*, 55–62.

Hall, R., Lund, D., & Jackson, D. (1968). Effects of teacher attention on study behavior. *Journal of Applied Behavior Analysis, 1*(1), 1–12.

Han, S. S., & Weiss, B. (2005). Sustainability of teacher implementation of school-based mental health programs. *Journal of Abnormal Child Psychology, 33*(6), 665–679.

Hawkins, J. D., Catalano, R. F., Kosterman, R., Abbott, R., & Hill, K. G. (1999). Preventing adolescent health-risk behaviors by strengthening protection during childhood. *Archives of Pediatrics and Adolescent Medicine, 153*, 226–234.

Henley, M. (2006). *Classroom management: A proactive approach*. Upper Saddle River, NJ: Pearson Education.

Houston, W. R., & Williamson, J. L. (1992). Perceptions of their preparation by 42 Texas elementary school teachers compared with their responses as student teachers. *Teacher Education and Practice, 8*, 27–42.

Huston-Stein, A., Friedrich-Cofer, L., & Sussman, E. (1977). The relation of classroom structure to social behavior, imaginative play, and self-regulation of economically disadvantaged children. *Child Development, 48*(3), 908–916.

Ialongo, N., Poduska, J., Werthamer, J., & Kellam, S. (2001). The distal impact of two first-grade preventive interventions on conduct problems and disorder in early adolescence. *Journal of Emotional and Behavioral Disorders, 9*(3), 146–160.

Ingersoll, R. M. (2002, August 15). High turnover plagues schools. *USA Today*, p. 13A.

Jerome, A., & Barbetta, P.M. (2005). The effect of active student responding during computer-assisted instruction on social studies learning by students with learning disabilities. *Journal of Special Education Technology, 20*, 13–23.

Johnson, S., & White, G. (1971). Self-observations as an agent of behavioral change. *Behavior Therapy, 2*, 488–497.

Jones, R. T., & Kazdin, A. E. (1975). Programming response maintenance after withdrawing token reinforcement. *Behavior Therapy, 6*, 153–164.

Jones, V. F., & Jones, L. S. (2004). *Comprehensive classroom management: Creating communities of support and solving problems*. Boston: Allyn & Bacon.

Kalis, T. M., Vannest, K. J., & Parker, R. (2007). Praise counts: Using self-monitoring to increase effective teaching practices. *Preventing School Failure, 51*(3), 20–27.

Kellam, S. G., Ling, X., Merisca, R., Brown, C. H., & Ialongo, N. (1998). The effect of the level of aggression in the first grade classroom on the course and malleability of aggressive behavior into middle school. *Development and Psychopathology, 10*(2), 165–185.

Kelley, M. L., & Stokes, T.F. (1984). Student–teacher contracting with goal setting for maintenance. *Behavior Modification, 8*(2), 223–244.

Kunter, M., Baumert, J., & Köller, O. (2007). Effective classroom management and the development of subject-related interest. *Learning and Instruction, 17*(5), 494–509.

Lazarus, B. D. (1993). Guided notes: Effects with secondary and post-secondary students with mild disabilities. *Education and Treatment of Children, 16*(3), 272–289.

Lewis, R. J., & Sugai, G. (1999). Effective behavior support: A systems approach to proactive schoolwide management. *Focus on Exceptional Children 31*, 1–24.

Maag, J. W. (2001). Rewarded by punishment: Reflections on the disuse of positive reinforcement in schools. *Exceptional Children, 67*(2), 173–186.

Madsen, C. H., Becker, W. C., & Thomas, D. R. (1968). Rules, praise, and ignoring: Elements of elementary classroom control. *Journal of Applied Behavior Analysis, 1*(2), 139–150.

Mayer, G. (1995). Preventing antisocial behavior in the schools. *Journal of Applied Behavior Analysis, 28*(4), 467–478.

McAllister, L. W., Stachowiak, J. G., Baer, D., & Conderman, L. (1969). The application of operant conditioning techniques in a secondary school classroom. *Journal of Applied Behavior Analysis, 2*(4), 277–285.

McCormick, L. K., Steckler, A., & McLeroy, K. R. (1994). Diffusion of innovation in schools: A study of adoption and implementation of school-based tobacco prevention curricula. *American Journal of Health Promotion, 9,* 210–219.

McGill, P., Teer, K., Rye, L., & Hughes, D. (2003). Staff reports of setting events associated with challenging behavior. *Behavior Modification, 27*(2), 265–282.

McNeely, C.A., Nonnemaker, J.M., & Blum, R. W. (2002). Promoting student connectedness to school: Evidence from the National Longitudinal Study of Adolescent Health. *Journal of School Health, 72*(4), 138–146.

Mesa, J., Lewis-Palmer, T., & Reinke, W.M. (2005). Providing teachers with performance feedback on praise to reduce student problem behavior. *Beyond Behavior, 15,* 3–7.

Miller, W. R., Benefield, R., & Tonigan, J. S. (1993). Enhancing motivation for change in problem drinking: A controlled comparison of two therapist styles. *Journal of Consulting and Clinical Psychology, 61*(3), 455–461.

Miller, W. R., & Rollnick, S. (2002). *Motivational interviewing: Preparing people for change* (2nd ed.). New York: Guilford Press.

Miller, W. R., Yahne, C. E., Moyers, T. B., Martinez, J., & Pirritano, M. (2004). A randomized trial of methods to help clinicians learn motivational interviewing. *Journal of Counseling and Clinical Psychology, 72,* 1050–1062.

National Research Council. (2002). *Minority students in special and gifted education: Committee on Minority Representation in Special Education.* Washington, DC: National Academy Press.

Nevin, A., Johnson, D. W., & Johnson, R. (1982). Effects of group and individual contingencies on academic performance and social relations of special needs students. *Journal of Social Psychology, 116*(1), 41–59.

Noell, G. H., Witt, J. C., LaFleur, L. H., Mortenson, B. P., Ranier, D. D., & LaVelle, J. (2000). Increasing intervention implementation in general education following consultation: A comparison of two follow-up strategies. *Journal of Applied Behavior Analysis, 33,* 271–284.

O'Leary, K., & Becker, W. (1968). The effects of the intensity of a teacher's reprimands on children's behavior. *Journal of School Psychology, 7,* 8–11.

Patterson, G. R., & Forgatch, M. S. (1985). Therapist behavior as a determinant for client noncompliance: A paradox for the behavior modifier. *Journal of Consulting and Clinical Psychology, 53*(6), 846–851.

Peterson, R. (1992). *Life in a crowded place: Making a learning community.* Portsmouth, NH: Heinemann.

Phelan, P., Yu, H. C., & Davidson, A. L. (1994). Navigating the psychosocial pressures of adolescence: The voices and experiences of high school youth. *American Educational Research Journal, 31*(2), 415–447.

Pianta, R. (1999). *Enhancing relationships between children and teachers.* Washington, DC: American Psychological Association.

Rao, S. (1998). *The short-term impact of the Family Check-Up: A brief motivational intervention for at-risk families.* Unpublished dissertation, University of Oregon, Eugene.

Rathvon, N. (2008). *Effective school interventions: Evidence-based strategies for improving student outcomes* (2nd ed.). New York: Guilford Press.

Reider, B. (2005). *Teach more and discipline less: Preventing problem behaviors in the K–6 classroom.* Thousand Oaks, CA: Corwin Press.

Reinke, W. M., & Herman, K. C. (2002). Creating school environments that deter antisocial behaviors in youth. *Psychology in the Schools, 39*(5), 549–560.

Reinke, W. M., Lewis-Palmer, T., & Martin, E. (2007). The effect of visual performance feedback on teacher use of behavior-specific praise. *Behavior Modification, 31*(3), 247–263.

Reinke, W. M., Lewis-Palmer, T., & Merrell, K. (2008). The Classroom Check-Up: A classwide teacher consultation model for increasing praise and decreasing disruptive behavior. *School Psychology Review, 37*(3), 315–332.

Reinke, W. M., Stormont, M., Herman, K. C., Puri, R., & Goel, N. (2011). Supporting children's mental health in schools: Teacher perceptions of needs, roles, and barriers. *School Psychology Quarterly, 26,* 1–13.

Ringeisen, H., Henderson, K., & Hoagwood, K. (2003). Context matters: Schools and the "research to practice gap" in children's mental health. *School Psychology Review, 32*(2), 153–168.

Rollnick, S., Miller, W.R., & Butler, C. C. (2008). *Motivational interviewing in health care: Helping patients change behavior.* New York: Guilford Press.

Rose, L. C., & Gallup, A. M. (2002). The 34th annual Phi Delta Kappa/Gallup Poll of the public's attitudes toward the public schools. *Phi Delta Kappan, 84*(1), 41–46.

Rose, L. C., & Gallup, A. M. (2006). The 38th annual Phi Delta Kappa Gallup Poll of the public's attitudes toward the public schools. *Phi Delta Kappan, 88,* 41–56.

Scheuermann, B. K., & Hall, J. A. (2008). *Positive behavioral supports for the classroom.* Upper Saddle River, NJ: Pearson/Merrill Prentice Hall.

Schuldheisz, J. M., & van der Mars, H. (2001). Active supervision and students' physical activity in middle school physical education. *Journal of Teaching in Physical Education, 21*, 75–90.

Sheridan, S., Welch, M., & Orme, S. (1996). Is consultation effective?: A review of outcome research. *Remedial and Special Education, 17*, 341–354.

Shores, R. E., Cegelka, P., & Nelson, C. (1973). Competency-based special education teacher training. *Exceptional Children, 40*, 192–197.

Shores, R. E., Gunter, P. L., & Jack, S. L. (1993). Classroom management strategies: Are they setting events for coercion? *Behavioral Disorders, 18*(2), 92–102.

Silver-Pacuilla, H., & Fleischman, S. (2006). Technology to help struggling students. *Educational Leadership, 63*(5), 84–85.

Simonsen, B., Fairbanks, S., Briesch, A., Myers, D., & Sugai, G. (2008). Evidence-based practices in classroom management: Considerations for research to practice. *Education and Treatment of Children, 31*(3), 351–380.

Skinner, C. H., Belfiore, P. J., Mace, H. W., Williams-Wilson, S., & Johns, G. A. (1997). Altering response topography to increase response efficiency and learning rates. *School Psychology Quarterly, 12*, 54–64.

Skinner, C. H., Smith, E. S., & McLean, J. E. (1994). The effects of intertrial interval duration on sight-word learning rates in children with behavioral disorders. *Behavioral Disorders, 19*, 98–107.

Sprick, R. (2006). *Discipline in the secondary classroom: A positive approach to behavior management.* (2nd ed.). Eugene, OR: Pacific Northwest.

Sprick, R. (2008). *CHAMPS: A proactive and positive approach to classroom management* (2nd ed.). Eugene, OR: Pacific Northwest Publishing.

Sprick, R., Booher, M., & Garrison, M. (2009). *Behavioral response to intervention: Creating a continuum of problem-solving and support.* Eugene, OR: Pacific Northwest.

Sprick, R., & Garrison, M. (2008). *Interventions: Evidence-based behavioral strategies for individual students.* (2nd ed.). Eugene, OR: Pacific Northwest.

Sprick, R., Knight, J., Reinke, W., Skyles, T., & Barnes, L. (2010). *Coaching classroom management: Strategies and tools for administrators and coaches.* Eugene, OR: Pacific Northwest.

Stevenson, R., & Ellsworth, J. (1993). Dropouts and the silencing of critical voices. In L. Weis & M. Fine (Eds.), *Beyond silenced voices* (pp. 259–271). Albany: State University of New York Press.

Stormont, M., Covington, S., & Lewis, T. J. (2006). Using data to inform systems: Assessing teacher implementation of key features of positive behavior support. *Beyond Behavior, 15*(3), 10–14.

Stormshack, E., & Dishion, T. J. (2002). An ecological approach in child and family clinical and counseling psychology. *Clinical Child and Family Psychology Review, 5*, 197–215.

Strein, W., Hoagwood, K., & Cohn, A. (2003). School psychology: A public health perspective. *Journal of School Psychology, 41*, 83–90.

Sutherland, K. S., Alder, N., & Gunter, P. L. (2003). The effect of varying rates of opportunities to respond to academic requests on the classroom behavior of students with EBD. *Journal of Emotional and Behavioral Disorders, 11*(4), 239–248.

Sutherland, K. S., & Wehby, J.H. (2001). Exploring the relationship between increased opportunities to respond to academic requests and the academic behavioral outcomes of students with EBD: A review. *Remedial and Special Education, 22*(2), 113–121.

Sutherland, K. S., Wehby, J., & Copeland, S. (2000). Effect on varying rates of behavior-specific praise on the on-task behavior of students with EBD. *Journal of Emotional and Behavioral Disorders, 8*, 2–8.

Sutherland, K. S., Wehby, J. H., & Yoder, P. (2002). Examination of the relationship between teacher praise and opportunities for students with EBD to respond to academic requests. *Journal of Emotional and Behavioral Disorders, 10*(1), 5–13.

Thevos, A., Fred, A., Kaona, A., Siajunza, M., & Quick, R. (2000). Adoption of safe water behaviors in Zambia: Comparing educational and motivational approaches. *Education for Health, 13*(3), 366–376.

Trussell, R. (2008). Classroom universals for prevention of problem behaviors. *Interventions in School and Clinic, 43*, 179–186.

Van Acker, R., Grant, S. H., & Henry, D. (1996). Teacher and student behavior as a function of risk for aggression. *Education and Treatment of Children, 19*(3), 316–334.

Walker, H. M., Colvin, G., & Ramsey, E. (1995). *Antisocial behavior in school: Strategies and best practices.* Belmont, CA: Thomson Brooks/Cole.

Watson, T. S., & Robinson, S. L. (1996). Direct behavioral consultation: An alternative approach to didactic consultation. *School Psychology Quarterly, 11*, 267–278.

Webster-Stratton, C. (1999). *How to promote children's social and emotional competence.* Los Angeles: Sage.

Webster-Stratton, C., Reid, M., & Hammond, M.

(2004). Treating children with early-onset conduct problems: Intervention outcomes for parent, child, and teacher training. *Journal of Clinical Child and Adolescent Psychology, 33*(1), 105–124.

Weinstein, C. S. (1977). Modifying student behavior in an open classroom through changes in the physical design. *American Educational Research Journal, 14*(3), 249–262.

Weinstein, C. S. (2007). *Middle and secondary classroom management: Lessons from research and practice* (3rd ed.). New York: McGraw-Hill.

White-Blackburn, G., Semb, S., & Semb, G. (1977). The effects of a good-behavior contract on the classroom behaviors of sixth-grade students. *Journal of Applied Behavior Analysis, 10*(2), 312.

Williams, R. L., & Anandam, K. (1973). The effect of behavior contracting on grades. *Journal of Educational Research, 66*(5), 230–236.

Witt, J. C., Noell, G. H., LaFleur, L. H., & Mortenson, B. P. (1997). Teacher use of intervention in general education settings: Measurement and analysis of the independent variable. *Journal of Applied Behavior Analysis, 30*, 693–696.

Witt, J. C., VanDerHeyden, A. M., & Gilbertson, D. (2004). Troubleshooting behavioral interventions: A systematic process for finding and eliminating problems. *School Psychology Review, 33*(3), 363–383.

Yarbrough, J. L., Skinner, C. H., Lee, Y. J., & Lemmons, C. (2004). Decreasing transition times in a second grade classroom: Scientific support for the timely transitions game. *Journal of Applied School Psychology, 20*(2), 85–107.

Zwald, L., & Gresham, F. M. (1982). Behavioral consultation in a secondary class: Using DRL to decrease negative verbal interactions. *School Psychology Review, 11*(4), 428–432.

Index

An *f* following a page number indicates a figure; a *t* following a page number indicates a table.